The Gender of Crime

THE GENDER LENS SERIES
Series Editors
Judith A. Howard, University of Washington
Barbara Risman, University of Illinois, Chicago
Joey Sprague, University of Kansas

The Gender Lens series has been conceptualized as a way of encouraging the development of a sociological understanding of gender. A "gender lens" means working to make gender visible in social phenomena; asking if, how, and why social processes, standards, and opportunities differ systematically for women and men. It also means recognizing that gender inequality is inextricably braided with other systems of inequality. The Gender Lens series is committed to social change directed toward eradicating these inequalities. Originally published by Sage Publications and Pine Forge Press, all Gender Lens books are now available from The Rowman & Littlefield Publishing Group.

BOOKS IN THE SERIES

Judith A. Howard and Jocelyn A. Hollander, *Gendered Situations, Gendered Selves: A Gender Lens on Social Psychology*

Michael A. Messner, *Politics of Masculinities: Men in Movements*

Judith Lorber, *Gender and the Social Construction of Illness*

Scott Coltrane, *Gender and Families*

Myra Marx Ferree, Judith Lorber, and Beth B. Hess, editors, *Revisioning Gender*

Pepper Schwartz and Virginia Rutter, *The Gender of Sexuality: Exploring Sexual Possibilities*

Francesca M. Cancian and Stacey J. Oliker, *Caring and Gender*

M. Bahati Kuumba, *Gender and Social Movements*

Toni M. Calasanti and Kathleen F. Slevin, *Gender, Social Inequities, and Aging*

Judith Lorber and Lisa Jean Moore, *Gender and the Social Construction of Illness, Second Edition*

Shirley A. Hill, *Black Intimacies: A Gender Perspective on Families and Relationships*

Lisa D. Brush, *Gender and Governance*

Dorothy E. Smith, *Institutional Ethnography: A Sociology for People*

Joey Sprague, *Feminist Methodologies for Critical Researchers: Bridging Differences*

Joan Acker, *Class Questions: Feminist Answers*

Oriel Sullivan, *Changing Gender Relations, Changing Families: Tracing the Pace of Change over Time*

Sara L. Crawley, Lara J. Foley, and Constance L. Shehan, *Gendering Bodies*

Yen Le Espiritu, *Asian American Women and Men: Labor, Laws, and Love*

Scott Coltrane and Michele Adams, *Gender and Families, Second Edition*

Manisha Desai, *Gender and the Politics of Possibilities*

Jocelyn A. Hollander, Daniel G. Renfrow, and Judith Howard, *Gendered Situations, Gendered Selves: A Gender Lens on Social Psychology, Second Edition*

Dana M. Britton, *The Gender of Crime*

The Gender of Crime

Dana M. Britton

ROWMAN & LITTLEFIELD PUBLISHERS, INC.
Lanham • Boulder • New York • Toronto • Plymouth, UK

Published by Rowman & Littlefield Publishers, Inc.
A wholly owned subsidiary of The Rowman & Littlefield Publishing Group, Inc.
4501 Forbes Boulevard, Suite 200, Lanham, Maryland 20706
http://www.rowmanlittlefield.com

Estover Road, Plymouth PL6 7PY, United Kingdom

British Library Cataloguing in Publication Information Available

Library of Congress Cataloging-in-Publication Data

Britton, Dana M.
  The gender of crime / Dana M. Britton.
    p.   cm. — (The gender lens series)
  Includes bibliographical references and index.
  ISBN 978-1-4422-0969-5 (cloth : alk. paper) — ISBN 978-1-4422-0970-1 (pbk. :
alk. paper) — ISBN 978-1-4422-0971-8 (electronic)
  1. Female offenders. 2. Criminals. 3. Sex role—Social aspects. I. Title.
  HV6046.B825 2011
  364.3—dc22
                                                                    2010047437

Printed in the United States of America

5/12

Contents

Acknowledgments

This project has been many years in development—my first conversations about it took place in the fall of 2002 with Mitch Allen, then an editor at AltaMira, and Judy Howard, Barbara Risman, and Joey Sprague, editors of the Gender Lens series. I was at that time a newly tenured associate professor who had, more or less by accident, found myself teaching criminology courses. I am by training and inclination a sociologist of gender, with a specific research interest in gender and work. My dissertation research, and then my first book (*At Work in the Iron Cage: The Prison as Gendered Organization*, NYU Press, 2003), had focused on a not particularly typical work environment, however—the prison. I chose prisons not because of any particular interest in criminology or corrections, but because men's and women's prisons offered a unique occupational case—a set of at least nominally parallel occupations in which one (work in men's prisons) had historically been dominated by men, and the other (work in women's prisons) had historically been dominated by women.

My research on work in prisons led me to a position teaching criminology (among other courses) and ultimately to think and write more broadly about gender and social control. As I spent more time at this disciplinary intersection, I found myself alternately frustrated with mainstream criminology, which—though presumably studying one of the most gender-differentiated of all social phenomena—often seemed to be oblivious to gender; and with the sociology of gender, which—though purportedly interested in the intersections of race, gender, and class—often ignored the lives of women and men who became casualties in America's escalating war on crime. Hence when the opportunity to turn a "gender lens" on criminology came along, I was eager for the chance to write a book that would inform both disciplines, a book that would teach those interested in criminology something about the importance of gender, and one that would encourage those interested in gender to bring their skills to understanding crime, victimization, and social control.

This project has proceeded by fits and starts over the past ten years, delayed by other projects, administrative responsibilities, and life. In that time I have accumulated a number of intellectual debts. First and foremost, I am grateful to the feminist criminologists whose own work has made this book possible. Many of them are cited in the following chapters. Given the page limitations I faced, I have not even attempted anything approaching a comprehensive review of their work; I apologize in advance for errors of omission. Instead I have chosen to highlight particular studies that I see as demonstrating the importance and value of viewing crime, punishment, victimization, or work in the system through a lens shaped by the intersections of gender, race, class, and sexuality. It is my hope that readers will use these examples as starting points for their own further reading and research. There is now a vibrant body of research that falls under the rubric of feminist criminology.

I am also grateful to my editor on this project, Judy Howard. Judy has been patient (obviously!) and always encouraging; her fine editorial sense has helped shape this project from its outset. Thanks also to Christine Williams, who invited me to write the review article that started the conversation about this book in the first place. At the other end of the process, I am grateful to my editor at Rowman & Littlefield, Sarah Stanton, and her editorial assistant, Jin Yu, who helped shepherd the book through the final stages. Over the years, a number of my graduate students have provided comments on drafts or gathered literature and references. For this and for many conversations about the topics discussed in this book, I thank Andrea Button, Jessica Dickson, Sarah Donley, Sarah Jones, Laura Logan, and Cindy Whitney. Among my extended colleagues, Jody Miller and Jill McCorkel read early chapter drafts, and Susan L. Miller read a near-final draft of the entire book and pointed me to many useful resources. Any errors that remain are, of course, my own.

1

A Gender Lens on Criminology

Consider the following timeline:

February 2, 1996, Moses Lake, Washington: Two students and one teacher killed when fourteen-year-old Barry Loukaitis opens fire in his algebra class.

February 19, 1997, Bethel, Alaska: One student and one principal killed by Evan Ramsey, sixteen.

October 1, 1997, Pearl, Mississippi: Two students killed by Luke Wood-ham, sixteen.

December 1, 1997, West Paducah, Kentucky: Three students killed by Michael Carneal, fourteen.

March 24, 1998, Jonesboro, Arkansas: Four students and one teacher killed by Mitchell Johnson, thirteen, and Andrew Golden, eleven.

May 21, 1998, Springfield, Oregon: Two students killed by Kip Kinkel, fifteen, who also killed his parents.

April 20, 1999, Littleton, Colorado: Twelve students and one teacher killed by Eric Harris, eighteen, and Dylan Klebold, seventeen. The shooters also killed themselves.

March 5, 2001, Santee, California: Two students killed by Charles Andrew Williams, fifteen.

September 24, 2003, Cold Spring, Minnesota: Two students shot and killed by John Jason McLaughlin, fifteen.

March 21, 2005, Red Lake, Minnesota: One teacher, one security guard, and five students killed by Jeff Weise, sixteen, who also murdered his grandfather and his grandfather's girlfriend. The shooter killed himself.

October 6, 2006, Nickel Mines, Pennsylvania: Five girls killed and six
   other girls injured by Charles Carl Roberts, thirty-two, who also killed
   himself. The girls ranged in age from six to thirteen.
April 16, 2007, Blacksburg, Virginia: Thirty-two students and faculty
   killed by Seung-Hui Cho, twenty-three, who also killed himself.
February 14, 2008, DeKalb, Illinois: Six students killed by Steven
   Kazmierczak, twenty-seven, who also killed himself.

You will undoubtedly recognize this as a list of some of the most notorious school shootings of the past two decades. Many of us remember the
news reports, the talk shows, and the magazine articles that appeared after
these incidents. Headlines screamed about the seemingly new American
phenomenon of homicidal "troubled kids" (Gibbs et al. 1999). Experts
seeking to explain the apparent epidemic pointed to the availability of
guns, the proliferation of video games, a crisis in the family, or adolescent
growing pains. In a brochure on youth violence entitled "Warning Signs,"
the American Psychological Association cautioned: "Often people who act
violently have trouble controlling their feelings. They may have been hurt
by others. Some think that making people fear them through violence or
threats of violence will solve their problems or earn them respect" (American Psychological Association 1999). But while the array of experts focused
correctly on one of the things these shootings had in common—the age of
the offenders—they missed other obvious points. Every one of the perpetrators on this list is a boy or young man (with the exception of Charles
Roberts, who was thirty-two), and all but one of them (Seung-Hui Cho, a
South Korean citizen) are white. Yet no headlines questioned the trouble
with white boys, and few experts sought to understand why girls are so
much less likely to be "people" who have "trouble controlling their feelings" and resort to violence to "solve their problems" (for exceptions, see
Danner and Carmondy 2001; Katz and Jhally 1999; Kimmel 1999). Still
fewer noted that the majority of victims—often the sole victims—in most
of these cases were girls.
   To notice that the shooters in all of these cases were boys and young men
and to explore the connections between masculinity and violence is to employ a *gender lens* on crime, that is, to ask how gender shapes the patterns of
offending and victimization we observe in our society. Such a perspective,
though it highlights gender, also draws attention to social characteristics
such as race, class, and sexuality. Almost no one has asked about the relationship between whiteness and the school shootings—or mass and serial
killings in general—though nearly all such offenders are white. All of the
schools in which these shootings took place were attended by middle- and
working-class students—none was in a poverty-stricken area—yet again we
have had little debate about what might be going wrong in middle-class

families. In Jonesboro, Arkansas, one of the killers was reportedly motivated by a breakup with a girlfriend and told his friends, "No one's going
to break up with me." And in Littleton, Colorado, the shooters, excluded
as social outcasts, were taunted by popular, athletic classmates who labeled
them "wimps" and "gay." However, few commentators have drawn attention to norms around the construction of heterosexuality and heterosexual
masculinity that might have provided the context for these seemingly random acts of violence.

This book will turn a gender lens on criminology. Later chapters examine
the connections between gender, race, class, sexuality, and criminal offending, the crime processing system, victimization, and work in the system.
The necessity of bringing this kind of understanding to the study of crime
is obvious; few social issues so clearly illustrate the fault lines of social
stratification. According to official statistics collected by the Federal Bureau
of Investigation (FBI), in 2009, more than thirteen million people were arrested. Of these, 75 percent were men, and 25 percent were women. For the
violent crimes tracked by the FBI (murder, rape, robbery, and aggravated
assault), men were 81 percent of those arrested. In 2009, whites were 69
percent of those arrested for all crimes, 59 percent for violent crimes. African Americans make up about 13 percent of the American population but
are *overrepresented* among arrestees, accounting for 28 percent of the total,
39 percent for violent crimes (Federal Bureau of Investigation 2010).[1] The
FBI publishes no data on arrests by race *and* sex, but we know from other
sources that African American men and women are overrepresented relative
to whites.

Neither the police nor any other agency collects data on the income or
social class of individuals who are arrested. Surveys of prison populations
tell us, however, that those who end up in the nation's prisons are among
the poorest of our citizens. In 2004 (the most recent date for which such
data are currently available), while 73 percent of male state prison inmates
and 58 percent of female inmates reported holding a job prior to arrest,
their incomes were extremely low; 49 percent of men and 65 percent of
women reported making less than fifteen thousand dollars per year (author
calculation from Bureau of Justice Statistics 2007).

We have no systematic information, official or otherwise, on the sexual
orientation of those arrested. Sexuality is embedded in the law and implicated in patterns of criminal offending, however. In 2009, 76,864 people
were arrested for rape and "other" sexual offenses (a category that includes
sexual battery, statutory rape, sodomy, "lewd and lascivious behavior,"
etc.); 93 percent of these were men. Prostitution is one of the only offense
categories for which arrests of women consistently outnumber those of
men—women accounted for 70 percent of all such arrests. Women are, in
fact, more likely than men to work as prostitutes, but the preponderance

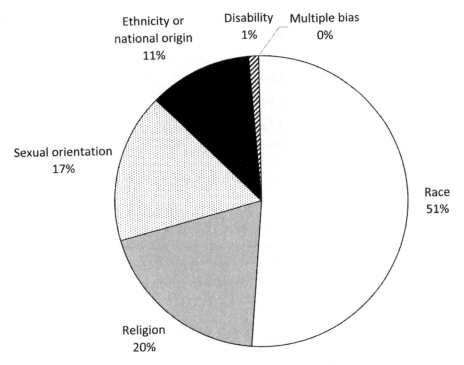

Figure 1.1. Distribution of Reported Bias Crime Incidents, 2008

Source: Federal Bureau of Investigation 2009.

of women in this category also reflects law enforcement practices that have focused more attention on prostitutes than on their clients, who are mostly men—regardless of the sex of the prostitute whose services they purchase. And of course there are many more clients of prostitutes than prostitutes themselves. Only since 1992 has the FBI collected statistics on crimes motivated by bias, and substantial numbers of lesbians and gay men are victims of hate crimes each year. Figure 1.1 depicts the distribution of bias crime incidents reported in 2008. Of the total 7,783 offenses, 1,297 (17 percent) were motivated by bias against the sexual orientation of the victim.

This graph also underlines the role of race, religion, and other group characteristics in shaping the chances of victimization, however. The most common hate crimes are those based on race—there were 3,992 such incidents in 2008. Whites are the most common offenders in these incidents, blacks, the most likely victims. Among crimes motivated by religious bias, anti-Semitism is the most common root, accounting for 1,013 of the 1,519 such incidents in 2008. The incidence of bias crimes often rises and falls in the aftermath of politically significant events; for example, crimes motivated by anti-Islamic sentiment rose sharply in the years after the terrorist attacks of September 11, 2001, from 28 incidents in 2000 to a total of 481 in 2001 (there were 105 such incidents in 2008).[2]

A gender lens on crime draws attention to the way that gender and a range of other dimensions of social inequality, such as race, class, and sexuality, shape one's chances of committing crimes or becoming victims of crime. In later chapters in this book, I address what we know about these topics in much greater detail. Before we can proceed, however, we need to start by defining some basic terms. In the discussion to this point, I have written as if we understand what crime is. This issue is not nearly as straightforward as it might seem. Some behaviors, such as the selling of sexual services, are much more likely to be defined as criminal than others, like the buying of such services. Defining crime is fundamentally a *social* process, with power relations based in gender, race, class, and sexuality all influencing the definitions that emerge. We thus need to begin our discussion by exploring what is meant by crime. I will then set the stage for the chapters that follow by discussing what is meant by gender and what it means to argue, as I do here, that offending, victimization, and other aspects of criminology are gendered.

WHAT IS CRIME?

Case 1: In 1998, twenty-one people were killed and one hundred injured when they consumed Ball Park franks contaminated with the listerium bacteria. A report in the *Detroit Free Press* alleged that the company that makes Ball Park franks, Sara Lee, stopped performing tests for bacteria in the factory from which the contaminated product came after recording too many positives. The company disputed this charge, and the U.S. attorney who prosecuted the case asserted that there was not enough evidence to prove that the company knew about the presence of listeria in its hot dogs, and hence to substantiate a felony charge. Sara Lee recalled thirty-five million pounds of meat products, and the case was ultimately settled after the company pled guilty to two misdemeanor counts and paid a $200,000 fine.

Case 2: In 2002, research began to demonstrate that hormone replacement therapy (HRT), routinely recommended for many decades for menopausal women, led to an increased risk of invasive breast cancer, heart disease, stroke, and dementia. Yet from 1998 to 2005, the drug company Wyeth played a major role in producing academic articles supporting the use of HRT. The articles were ghostwritten for Wyeth by private medical communications companies, which then sought prominent physicians to sign their names as authors and publish the articles in leading medical journals. Wyeth's sales of its HRT drugs topped $2 billion in 2001. The company has defended the practice as "routine."

Case 3: In 2000, Kenneth Payne, twenty-nine, was convicted of felony theft. Payne had been caught with a stolen Snickers candy bar, valued at one dollar. Because he had ten previous convictions for petty thefts (including one for stealing a bag of Oreo cookies), Payne was classified as a habitual offender and the case tried as a felony. The jury recommended he spend sixteen years in prison.

Which of the above cases is a crime? Only one, case 3, fits our conventional sense of what crime is and who criminals are. Kenneth Payne is a habitual offender and has been charged with and convicted of a felony. For most people, this is the kind of person who comes to mind when they think of the typical criminal. In cases 1 and 2, though society has clearly been harmed, from the perspective of the law no serious offense has been committed. While case 3 is not representative—most candy bar thieves are not sentenced to serve sixteen years in prison—the combination of these scenarios helps illuminate some of the very difficult issues in the debates over the definition of crime.

The Legalistic Definition

In the criminological literature, definitions of crime range from a relatively narrow, legalistic view to more critical, philosophical positions. Perhaps the most straightforward definition sees crime simply as a violation of law, more specifically, criminal law. Criminal law is a body of statutes that covers property, violent, and other less serious offenses, and in which punishment is pursued on behalf of the state. Crimes may be acts of commission (such as shoplifting) or omission (such as failing to pay taxes) and carry punishments that range from the minor—fines—to, in thirty-five states and the federal court system, the death penalty. Criminal law is usually differentiated from civil law, which regulates private matters, and regulatory law, which governs the actions of businesses and other agencies. In civil cases, punishments are defined in terms of damages awarded to injured parties; in regulatory cases, companies might be served with warnings by the government or fined for illegal or harmful business practices.

Though we think of crime in unambiguous terms—acts either are or are not criminal—criminal law is the outcome of a process of *social* construction. Many acts that are crimes today were not defined as such in the past. The use of substances such as marijuana, cocaine, and heroin, the current focus of a concentrated "war on drugs," was made illegal only during the first half of the twentieth century, with cocaine and heroin regulated by the federal government in 1914, marijuana in 1937. During the eighteenth century, such substances were widely available, with opium (of which heroin is a derivative) among the most common ingredients in over-the-counter pain medications and patent medicine "tonics." The pharmaceutical company

Parke-Davis provided cocaine to consumers in varied forms for sniffing, smoking, and injecting, and advertised the drug as a substance that "can supply the place of food, make the coward brave, the silent eloquent and . . . render the sufferer insensitive to pain" (quoted in Musto 1991, 40). Conversely, acts that were once defined as criminal, such as obtaining an abortion, are now legal (though there is a vigorous political movement seeking—with some success—to restrict the exercise of this right). Until the 1973 Supreme Court decision in *Roe v. Wade* (410 U.S. 113, 1973), those who provided abortions were subject to criminal prosecution, a situation which meant that women risked, and sometimes lost, their lives undergoing abortion procedures performed by minimally trained practitioners working outside of hospital systems.

In both instances, changes in the law were brought about at least partly through the actions of individuals and groups who worked as "moral entrepreneurs" to change the public's view of behaviors or laws that they saw as problematic. In doing so, they drew on widely held notions about gender, race, and class. Those who opposed legal access to drugs such as cocaine, heroin, and marijuana evoked racist stereotypes to support their claims. For example, advocates for the regulation of cocaine asserted that drug-crazed black men were essentially impervious to bullets and posed an extreme danger to law enforcement officers (Lusane 1991). Conversely, those who favored a woman's right to choose an abortion utilized liberal feminist ideals to argue that women, as well as men, were entitled to the right to privacy and to control over their bodies. Definitions of crime are not a body of rules encoding a sort of natural or absolute moral code, but rather are shaped by interest groups and governments that draw on and respond to changing assumptions, values, and power relations.

Critical Definitions of Crime

The cases that open this section illustrate some of the problems with defining crime strictly as the universe of acts that violate criminal law. In case 1, the Sara Lee Corporation's products were implicated in the deaths of twenty-one people. The company was charged in federal court and ultimately pled guilty to misdemeanor offenses defined by regulatory law. If an individual were involved in the deaths of multiple victims, he or she might be charged with murder (if it could be proved that the intent was to kill) or perhaps manslaughter (if evidence of intent were lacking or not provable in court). Those they killed would be labeled as legitimate victims of crime by the system. Yet no one was charged with murder or manslaughter in this case; rather, the company was charged with selling adulterated meat. Those who died do not appear in any official count of murder victims. Case 2 does not qualify as a crime under any existing legal definition.

Wyeth (and other drug manufacturers) continue to contract with private firms to ghostwrite medical journal articles favorable to their products. The intention, of course, is to induce physicians to prescribe a company's drugs rather than other, competing therapies (or perhaps no drug at all). Yet to the extent that HRT has been clearly linked to heart disease, stroke, cancer, and dementia, the company's products are implicated in thousands of illnesses—and in fact they continue to be prescribed. Wyeth now faces more than 8,400 lawsuits from women who claim their illnesses were caused by HRT. The company has never been held criminally liable, nor have the physicians who signed their names to articles written by private companies on behalf of Wyeth.

These cases and dozens like them every year underline the fact that the legalistic definition of crime is biased toward acts committed by those at the bottom of the socioeconomic ladder—"street" criminals—rather than by those at the top (sometimes called "suite" criminals). Yet there is little question that the acts of corporate executives and political figures, a group still predominantly white, financially well off, and male, cause more social harm to Americans than do those of street criminals, a population that is predominantly poor, male, and white (though disproportionately made up of members of racial and ethnic minority groups). Every year, many more people die from unsafe working conditions, dangerous products, toxic waste, and other corporate actions than die from murder.

The recent Deepwater Horizon/British Petroleum oil spill is a compelling example of the wide ranging and devastating effects of corporate crime and of the unwillingness of regulators to prevent corporate crime or to hold corporations meaningfully responsible for their criminal actions. The Deepwater Horizon drilling rig exploded on April 20, 2010, killing eleven platform workers and injuring seventeen others. The explosion resulted in a spill, the largest in the history of the petroleum industry, which is estimated to have released about five million barrels of oil into the Gulf of Mexico. Oil from the spill subsequently contaminated ocean water, beaches, and wildlife habitats; remediating the damage is expected to take decades. Yet the spill was far from a random accident. Rig workers reported that they had serious concerns about safety before the explosion and that many key components—including parts of the blowout preventer ultimately responsible for the spill—had not been inspected since 2000 (though such inspections are required by law every three to five years). Many workers feared raising these issues due to the possibility of reprisal by management—as one worker put it: "The company is always using fear tactics" (quoted in Urbina 2010). A survivor of the disaster said that four weeks before the explosion the blowout preventer had been damaged in an accident—a fact that was never reported by rig supervisors, who were under pressure to keep costs low and finish the drilling project quickly (CBS News 2010).

Both British Petroleum (BP), which owned the rig, and Transocean, the company that operated it, have long histories of safety violations. In two separate incidents prior to this explosion, thirty BP workers were killed and more than two hundred were seriously injured. In the five years between 2005 and 2010, BP admitted to breaking U.S. environmental and safety laws and paid $373 million in fines to avoid prosecution. In this regard, BP's record was far worse than its competitors—over the three years from 2007 to 2010, BP refineries in Ohio and Texas accounted for 97 percent of the violations for "egregious and willful" practices imposed by the Occupational Safety and Health Administration (Thomas et al. 2010). Transocean's record was no better. Nearly 75 percent of incidents that triggered federal investigations into conditions on deepwater drilling rigs in the Gulf of Mexico since 2008 occurred on rigs operated by Transocean (Transocean operated 58 percent of oil rigs in the gulf during this time) (Casselman 2010). By any definition, these companies are repeat offenders, responsible for deaths, injuries, and financial losses by individuals and communities. Yet no one from either company has ever been criminally prosecuted for these actions.

Similarly, acts such as fraud, false advertising, and price fixing cost society exponentially more than do all conventional property crimes combined (Reiman and Leighton 2009). In just one widespread corporate scandal, the savings and loan (S&L) crisis of the 1980s, more money was lost to fraud and outright theft, $1.4 trillion, than all street criminals put together will steal in more than two thousand years. Between 1987 and 1992, however, 75 percent of all S&L fraud cases referred to the Justice Department for prosecution were dropped. Those found guilty were sentenced to an average of two years—this compares to an average sentence of eight years for bank robbery (Simon 2002). Similarly, in 2007, British Petroleum agreed to pay $303 million to avoid prosecution on civil charges that it cornered the propane market and inflated heating costs for more than seven million Americans, mostly living in rural areas. As part of the scheme, BP purchased large quantities of propane—enough to allow the company to control the market—and then drove up prices by more than 50 percent by keeping fuel off the market (Mufson 2007). The estimated cost to consumers was $53 million. Four traders were indicted by the government on criminal fraud after they were caught on tape conspiring to manipulate the market. These charges were dismissed in 2009 (Sachdev 2009). The $303 million fine the company ultimately paid in this case represented slightly more than 2 percent of its $14 billion in profits in 2009 (Thomas et al. 2010).

Some argue that corporations cannot commit crime in the legalistic sense of the word. Richard Parker, a professor at George Mason University Law School, argues that "Crime exists only in the mind of an individual. Since a corporation has no mind, it can commit no crime" (quoted in

Mokhiber 2005). Criminologists critical of the legalistic definition of crime have proposed a number of alternatives, however.[3] Jeffrey Reiman (2006), for example, argues that we should define crimes as those acts that cause harm to society, and that punishment should be calibrated according to the amount of harm inflicted. Under this definition, acts such as burglary and larceny would still be criminal, but so, too, would corporate executives be prosecuted for murder or assault when the actions of their companies lead to deaths or injuries (Reiman 2006).[4] Herman and Julia Schwendinger (1975) argue for a more expansive view, suggesting that crime be defined in terms of actions that violate basic human rights. These include those essential to life, such as food, shelter, and health, and those "essential to a dignified human existence" such as education, freedom of movement, and bodily integrity (Beirne and Messerschmidt 2000). Again, this definition would criminalize the current range of street crimes but also acts of corporations and governments that take life, perpetuate poverty, and deny health care and opportunities to live a decent life.[5]

It is hard to imagine how these definitions of crime might be enforced. Images of armed police beating down the gates guarding corporate leaders' mansions or hauling government officials away in handcuffs leap to mind—certainly a very different picture than on "reality" television offerings such as *COPS*. In truth, it seems unlikely that lawmakers will ever turn to one of these more critical definitions to reshape the criminal code or that the focus of law enforcement efforts will shift from the lower to the upper classes. I offer these definitions and case examples by way of an exercise in critical thinking, a method to encourage readers to expand their thinking beyond the narrow range of commonsense notions of what crime is. Beginning from these different standpoints demonstrates that definitions of crime do not exist in a vacuum; rather, they are fundamentally shaped by power relations. The actions of those who hold the dominant positions in the social order are simply less likely to be criminalized than are those at the bottom.

Race, Sex, Sexuality, and Legal History

The United States has a long history of laws encoding discrimination. After the Civil War, for example, many Southern states adopted "black codes" that controlled the movements of newly freed slaves. These codes relied in part on vagrancy statutes to reinstitute plantation labor. Blacks who were unemployed (an extremely common condition among freed slaves) or who were judged to have no visible means of support (generally broadly interpreted in favor of the law) were arrested by the hundreds and literally auctioned off to plantation owners for the price of their fines. One of the most notorious of these codes, in Mississippi, specified that blacks were required annually to provide written evidence of employment for the year.

This was usually a contract for plantation labor (Colvin 1997, 218). Blacks who failed to do so were subject to arrest for vagrancy and available to be auctioned to plantation owners willing to pay their fines.

Beginning in 1868, many Southern states (among them Mississippi, Georgia, Alabama, Arkansas, Louisiana, Tennessee, Texas, Florida, and the Carolinas) adopted a system of "convict leasing" in which prisoners—again almost exclusively black—were leased to private contractors to work on plantations, in lumber camps and mines, and in other back-breaking, labor-intensive enterprises. Leasing contracts were extremely valuable to the state, and lawmakers created statutes explicitly aimed at increasing prison populations. In Mississippi, Texas, and other states, legislatures passed "pig laws," which defined grand larceny as the theft of a farm animal or any property worth more than ten dollars. Such laws were enforced almost exclusively against blacks, who then became bodies available to be leased. These laws, along with vagrancy statutes, were useful tools for states interested in maximizing revenues—in one instance in Florida, a new leasing contract led to an 800 percent increase in arrests in a single county.[6] Though convict leasing gave way to prison farms in the South after the turn of the century (a topic I discuss in more detail in chapter 3), race continued to be encoded in law in the North and the South, with Jim Crow statutes mandating segregation in a wide variety of public accommodations, from schools, to railroad cars, to water fountains.

From the earliest establishment of the American colonies, laws have regulated the rights and privileges of men and women. Many of these distinctions survived well into the twentieth century, and some persist even now. Until as late as the 1980s, rape laws in many states were explicitly written such that only women could be legally considered victims of rape (though this certainly did not guarantee that even women victims would be taken seriously). One important early case that tested the right of the state to discriminate between men and women was *Craig v. Boren* (429 U.S. 190, 1976). This case presented a challenge to an Oklahoma law allowing the sale of 3.2 percent beer to women over the age of eighteen but setting the legal age for men at twenty-one. The state based its decision on statistics showing that men between the ages of eighteen and twenty-one were far more likely to be involved in drunk driving offenses than were women. The plaintiffs challenged this statutory discrimination, drawing on the Fourteenth Amendment guarantee of equal protection. The court ultimately ruled in favor of the plaintiffs, overturning Oklahoma's law. Importantly, however, the court did not invalidate the right of the government to discriminate between men and women, holding only that such discrimination must be substantially related to a legitimate government objective.[7] This rationale continues to be used to justify legalized discrimination, such as the exclusion of women in the military from direct combat positions.

Laws that explicitly discriminate on the basis of race and sex are now generally prohibited. Even so, critics argue that race and sex discrimination are pervasive in the enforcement of law, a topic I consider in more detail in chapter 3. It is still legal, however, to discriminate on the basis of sexual orientation. Outside of the few municipalities and states with explicit anti-discrimination ordinances, today it is perfectly legal to deny employment, housing, or other services on the basis of someone's sexual orientation. Though there is a proposed federal statute to prohibit sexual orientation discrimination in employment (the Employment Non-Discrimination Act, or ENDA), Congress has as yet failed to enact it into law.[8]

WHAT IS GENDER?

It is my aim in this book to turn a "gender lens" on criminology. Most of us think we know what gender means—these days, it seems that someone is always asking us to check a response on a survey form for which the question looks something like this: "What is your gender?" _____ Male _____ Female. Though the question seems straightforward to most, it is an incorrect usage of the term *gender*. In sociology, we differentiate gender from sex and use the term *sex* to represent the presence of certain bodily secondary sex characteristics, such as a vagina, or breasts, or a penis. Someone who has breasts and a vagina is female, while someone who lacks these traits is male—though even this is not as simple as it seems. The term *gender*, on the other hand, typically refers to the social and psychological attributes and behaviors that individuals, social institutions, and society expect from those who are labeled female or male, and we refer to this set of traits as femininity or masculinity. When most people answer the survey question above, they understand it as a question about the type of body they inhabit, hence, the better phrasing of the item would be "What is your sex?"

In this section, I will provide some definitions that will orient the discussion of gender to follow in the rest of this book. First, I explain why defining sex and gender is more complex than the brief discussion above suggests and why the difference between the two is more than a matter of terminology. Second, I define some other terms that I use throughout the book, such as sexuality, race, and class. Finally, I offer a brief discussion of what it means to argue, as I will throughout, that institutions, or practices, or interactions are gendered.

Sex versus Gender: What's the Difference and What Difference Does It Make?

Mostly, we live in a world in which people believe they may safely take sex for granted. Individuals are either male or female, and there is no in between. This is one of the bedrock assumptions underlying our social interactions. Most of us have at one time encountered someone whom we could not instantly recognize as male or female, and we have usually experienced some discomfort until we could categorize the person. The fact that we often cannot even interact with someone unless we "know" their sex provides some clues about how important such designations are at a subconscious level, even if we consciously believe that we do not treat people differently based on such designations. Most of the time, people are easily categorized. In cases, like those of babies, where sex is ambiguous, parents or others often provide helpful cues through clothing or other devices. My niece, who was born with very little hair, actually came home from the hospital with a pink bow stuck to the top of her head with syrup! My nephew was fortunately spared this fate.

The problem with this core belief in only two sexes is that in a fairly substantial minority of cases it simply does not hold true. About one in one hundred babies are born with ambiguous genitalia, that is, with genitalia that do not identify them clearly as male or female. Historically, such individuals sometimes chose their own gender identities, and in some cultures they held important social and religious roles. In the contemporary United States, science has intervened. Currently, gender "correction" surgery is performed in about one or two of every one thousand births—in 2009, that would have totaled between four thousand and eight thousand babies in the United States. In the past, such surgeries were often done without parents' consent or knowledge. Even now, those who undergo these procedures are rarely old enough to give their consent to surgeries that can have lasting ill effects, including extensive scar tissue and lifelong sexual dysfunction (Fausto-Sterling 2000). For these individuals biological sex is not innate, it is constructed, literally carved out by the physician's scalpel. The notion that there are two, and only two, sexes is in fact the result of an active process in which difference is purposefully erased.

Even beyond these cases, the assignment of sex in everyday interaction is the outcome of a social process. While individuals move about the world making routine decisions about whether people are male or female, they must usually do this without positive proof that they are correct (Kessler and McKenna 1978). We look for markers, like bodily features or clothing (or stuck-on bows), that allow us to assign people to the "proper" categories. For this reason, some sociologists have argued that rather than sex, the term *sex category* more accurately describes how most people perceive maleness and femaleness in the course of daily interactions (West and Zimmerman 1987; West and Fenstermaker 1995). If we learn that our assignments to categories are not "correct," we are usually just embarrassed. In extreme cases, however, such misidentifications have served as the basis for hate crimes, such as in the murder of Brandon Teena. In 1993, Teena, a Nebraska teen, was raped and killed by two of his girlfriend's male friends, who were enraged to find that though he "passed" as male, he was biologi-cally female.[9]

That one may be male and pass as female, or vice versa, helps to under-line the difference between sex and gender. Gender consists of attributes and behaviors that are organized in relationship to sex category (Connell 2002). Attached to maleness and femaleness are sets of behaviors, modes of dress and bodily movement, and ways of thinking and behaving that have been socially defined as masculine or feminine. In any society, there is a range of masculinities and femininities; for example, the rational, capi-talist masculinity of Bill Gates (founder of Microsoft) is not the same as the aggressive, athletic masculine performance of Arnold Schwarzenegger (action film star and California governor), nor do Hillary Clinton (U.S. senator from New York and secretary of state) and Sheryl Swoopes (WNBA star) represent femininity in the same way. It thus makes sense to speak of multiple masculinities and femininities, though the range of culturally acceptable forms is not infinite, as the disdain that accrues to "deviants" such as women body builders illustrates. Gender is not innate, but rather is accomplished through performance and display of masculine and feminine traits and behaviors—one "does" gender (West and Zimmerman 1987).

This performative aspect of gender—the fact that it is what one does, rather than what one is—is what makes it possible to pass; one may be female but act masculine. Sometimes, as in the case of drag shows or Hal-loween parties, this is only about performance. In other cases, one may enact the gender that one feels is most authentic, that which corresponds to one's internal gender identity. Usually, sex, gender, and gender identity cor-respond. One is biologically female, performs socially acceptable feminin-ity, and feels both female and feminine. For some people, however, these things do not go together seamlessly. Those whose gender identities do not conform to their biological sex are transgender. Some might pursue medi-cal interventions like surgeries or hormones, others live as members of the opposite sex, and still others may eschew both of these options and work to carve out broader, more flexible definitions of masculinity and femininity or to blur the lines between the two.

Gender identity is more than a matter of individual expression, however. Gender attributions also signal and reinforce privilege. In the workplace, for example, masculinity generally accrues economic and status benefits that femininity does not. In a fascinating series of studies, Kristen Schilt (2006, 2010) has shown how transmen, biological women who transition into living as men, benefit from moving from one side of the gender divide to the other. In one such case,

Thomas, an attorney, relate[d] an episode in which an attorney who worked for an associated law firm commended his boss for firing Susan [his female name], because she was incompetent—adding that the "new guy" [i.e., Thomas] was "just delightful." The attorney did not realize that Susan and "the new guy" were the same person with the same abilities, education, and experience. (2006, 476)

Schilt's work also demonstrates an economic advantage for many trans-men, who find that their salaries increase along with their privilege. Certainly not all transmen benefit, however. Race matters—masculinity does not carry the same privileges for black men as it does for white men. As "Keith," another of Schilt's respondents who transitioned at work put it: "I went from being an obnoxious black woman to a scary black man" (2006, 485).

Blurring the lines between sex and gender comes with enormous consequences as well. The law has historically regulated the lines between sex and gender and has shown little tolerance for divergence between the two. Transgender individuals, like Brandon Teena, are disproportionately victims of hate crimes such as murder and assault, yet as of this writing only nine states and the District of Columbia have passed hate crimes laws that include victims targeted on the basis of gender identity.[10] Fifteen states and the District of Columbia (California, Colorado, Connecticut, Hawaii, Illinois, Iowa, Maine, Maryland, Minnesota, New Jersey, New Mexico, Oregon, Rhode Island, Vermont, and Washington) have laws prohibiting discrimination on the basis of gender expression or identity. In the remaining states, transgender individuals may be fired, be refused public accommodations, or face other bias, and no penalty will accrue to individual or organizational discriminators. Though gender identity, gender, and sex can diverge, the fact that those who act masculine are also usually categorized as male speaks to the conflation of sex and gender (and gender identity) in our daily experience. People expect that sex and gender will correspond, for example, that those who are male will act masculine. In fact, some argue that gender is simply a reflection of sex, that we are compelled to behave in masculine or feminine ways by our biology. At the other end of the spectrum are those who contend that gender has no connection at all to biology, that it is a complex of learned behaviors and expectations and can thus be unlearned. Though I will not attempt to resolve this debate, the fact that there is considerable variation across time, contexts, and cultures in the behaviors identified as masculine and feminine suggests that cultural and social factors play important roles in shaping gender.

This is what makes the distinction between sex and gender much more than a matter of terminology. Outside of the realm of medical intervention, sex can generally not be changed (though sex category can be manipulated, of course). Because it exists (in whatever portion) at the level of personality, social structure, and society, gender is both more variable and more subject to change. This distinction is what makes the study of gender possible. If gender is not isomorphic with sex, we can ask questions like why certain gender markers, for example, red tights on men's legs, denote superhero masculinity in one context and ballet dancer masculinity in another. We can also examine how gender is manifested in some situations versus others, as Jody Miller (1998) has done in a study of men and women street robbers (which I discuss in more detail in chapter 2). This distinction also enables us to talk about change. If gender were inextricably linked to sex, then efforts to change society's ideas about gender-appropriate traits and behaviors would be extremely difficult, if not pointless.

Intersecting Categories: Sexuality, Race, and Class

While a "gender lens" prioritizes gender in analyzing social phenomena such as crime and the law, gender never exists alone. Gender is shaped by and in turn influences beliefs about sexuality, race, class, and myriad other social statuses. For example, nineteenth-century medical experts believed that white middle-class women who engaged in vigorous physical or intellectual activities would suffer severe damage to their reproductive capabilities. Slave women and poor immigrant women, on the other hand, they believed, were naturally suited to hard labor and dangerously overfertile (Ehrenreich and English 1989). In these experts' pronouncements, notions about sexuality, and race, and class combine to produce very different ideas about gender for people who occupy the same sex category. Similarly, ideas about all of these traits have shaped and continue to influence the development of laws and government policies and the enforcement practices of the police and the criminal justice system. This is a topic I treat in detail in the chapters that follow.

Sexuality

Sexuality is a set of practices and behaviors oriented with relationship to desire (Connell 2002). In conventional terms, people are usually further categorized in terms of their sexual "object," for example, heterosexual if one engages in sexuality exclusively with members of the opposite sex, or homosexual (or gay or lesbian) if one has sex with members of the same sex. As in the debate over the links between sex and gender, there is a similar controversy around the relationship between biology and sexual orientation. Some take an essentialist position, arguing that one's choice of sexual object is largely hardwired at birth. Others argue that sexual orientation is a matter of choice or is shaped and influenced by social factors, such as the institutional privileging of heterosexuality and the repression of alternatives.

Though it does not necessarily resolve the debate, evidence from studies of sexual practice tells us that designations such as heterosexual, homosexual, and bisexual are often arbitrary and that the link between labels and sexual behaviors is not always clear. During World War I, for example, the U.S. Navy launched an investigation of homosexuality at its Newport, Rhode Island, Naval Training Station. During the investigation, "decoys" employed by the navy testified to engaging in homosexual acts with the defendants in order to gather evidence to rid the Navy of "queers." That these men did not see themselves (and to some degree were not seen by others) as "queer" attests to the malleable nature of the lines between sexual identity and sexual behavior (Chauncey 1985). As this study and many others like it have amply demonstrated, many heterosexuals have had sexual experiences or experienced sexual desire for members of the same sex, and the contrary is true for gays and lesbians. Bisexuals may express desire or sexuality within a broad range of partners, from mostly opposite sex to mostly same sex. Further, one may engage in a significant amount of same-sex activity but still define oneself as heterosexual, as did the men in Laud Humphreys' study of impersonal sex in "tearooms" (Humphreys 1975).

The law has imposed clear lines between legally acceptable and unacceptable sexual conduct, however. Some of these laws, like those establishing a legal age of consent for sexual activity or criminalizing incest or other forms of nonconsensual sex now seem relatively uncontroversial, though in many cases their adoption and evolution were the objects of concerted struggles by moral entrepreneurs and organized social movements. Still other statutes regulate sexual behavior between consenting adults and in so doing efface the complexity of individual sexual practice. Under statutes governing sodomy, states criminalize those who engage in consensual sex with same-sex partners. In some states, a conviction for sodomy carries a felony charge. The state has also regulated consensual heterosexual practice under these statutes. In the state of Kansas, for example, "sodomy" is defined as "oral contact or oral penetration of the female genitalia or oral contact of the male genitalia; anal penetration, however slight, of a male or female by any body part or object; or oral or anal copulation or sexual intercourse between a person and an animal" (Kansas Statute 21-3501). Aside from the last part of this statute, which prohibits bestiality, the rest of the language criminalizes conduct (oral or anal sex) in which the overwhelming majority of heterosexual couples report having engaged at one time or another. I leave aside for the moment the prohibition on bestiality but note that Kansas is not alone among states that regulate "sodomy" between humans and sex with animals in the same statute.[11] Such statutes are rarely enforced—at least those pertaining to humans—but they remain on the books in a substantial minority of states.

While we may separate them analytically, in everyday practice, sex, gender, and sexuality are often conflated. Men are expected to act in a masculine way and seek women as sexual partners; for women, the opposite is true. Gay men are sometimes stereotyped as effeminate, lesbians as hypermasculine. These patterns demonstrate the social mapping of gender onto desire; those who seek women as sexual partners must be masculine in some ways, regardless of their sex or their own sense of identity.

Race

As gender is the set of social meanings that attach to sex, race is the set of meanings associated with visible physical characteristics such as skin color, facial structure, or other bodily markers. Defining races and deciding who "counts" as a member of a particular race is very much a social process that varies across time and space. Such distinctions are always arbitrary—skin color is a crucial marker, but not eye color, for example—we never speak of the "blue" versus the "hazel" race. In fact, because race is a social rather than a biological category whose boundaries are established by dominant groups, some have suggested the use of the word *racialization* instead of race. By this logic, there are no such things as racial groups, only *racialized* groups.

The boundaries of racialized categories have also changed over time. During the eighteenth and nineteenth centuries in the United States, many white immigrant groups were racialized. The Irish, for example, were regarded as a group apart by the European American native-born population, its members identifiable through physical and behavioral characteristics, such as red hair, a ruddy complexion, a love of alcohol, and a hot temper. Over time, Irish immigrants assimilated into the European American mainstream and became "white" (Ignatiev 1995). Similarly, the racialization of the Jews was a primary objective of Nazi propaganda in Germany, and images of Jews as fundamentally socially and physically different (and deviant) persist to this day in white supremacist literature (Daniels 1997).

Other societies have counted and divided people in different ways. In Brazil, there is a wide spectrum of racial designations based largely on the actual color of one's skin, a set of categories ranging from *bem-branca* (very white) to *baiano* (ebony). In South Africa, those who were "colored" (mixed race) made up a separate racial group during the rule of the apartheid regime. In the United States, on the other hand, the rule of hypodescent applies; if one's racial ancestry mixes European heritage with any other racial group, one is not considered white, but rather a member of the lower-status group. This assumption has been encoded in law as the "one drop" rule or the "traceable amount" rule. This statute, which first appeared in the legal codes of the antebellum South, was originally intended to reserve the property of white slave owners for the children of their white wives but has since become a commonsense principle of racial categorization in the United States (Davis 1991; Haney-López 1996). Those with a racial heritage that mixes European and other ancestry are almost never considered "white."

The state remains fundamentally involved in the process of shaping racial categories. In the United States, governmental and other organizations usually identify people in terms of a multicategory scheme; one is white, black, Asian, Hispanic/Latino, Native American, or "other." This tells us quite a lot about the distinctions the government does and does not find salient. Such categories are arbitrary, however, and reflect the presumptions of the dominant racial group. The category "Asian," for example, includes a large number of groups from all over the world, such as Koreans, Vietnamese, Malaysians, Japanese, and those from India. The histories of these diverse peoples and their experiences in the United States have been very different, and it is understandable that they might not feel a commonality with others labeled "Asian." Yet for the federal government, as for most white Americans, such distinctions and experiences are simply erased by the use of a generic category.

In the case of agencies that collect most of the official data available to criminologists, racial categories are often even more restrictive. In its annual report of arrest and crime statistics, the FBI until very recently presented data for "whites," "blacks," and "others" (there are now categories for "American Indian or Alaska Native" and "Asian or Pacific Islander"). Though this is arguably not the intention, this method of reporting has helped to shape research and public discourse about crime in terms of distinctions between blacks and whites. We have no similar data on Hispanic Americans, now the largest minority group in the United States, and are thus quite limited in what we can say about their rates of involvement with the criminal justice system. As the FBI also provides no data on arrest rates by race *and* sex, we can draw conclusions about the arrest rates of whites, or blacks, or men, or women, but not about white *men* versus black *women*, for example. Other sources of data allow some inferences, and I will discuss these in more detail in chapter 2. The fact remains however, that the most widely used official source for these statistics defines racial categories in a way that draws attention to only one racial distinction.

Class

Social class refers to one's location in the economic stratification system of society; in the narrowest sense, social class is defined in terms of the economic resources we possess or to which we have access. Sociologists and economists divide the population in different ways and into various numbers of categories. We might speak, for example, of the upper, middle, working, and lower classes or use even finer distinctions, splitting the lower class into the working poor and the poor or adding a category for the upper middle class. Regardless of the scheme we employ, the categories are hierarchical and reflect the fact that the United States is a deeply stratified society. In 2004, the top 20 percent of the population controlled more than 80 percent of all wealth (this includes income and resources such as investments, property, etc.); the bottom 60 percent of the population shared only 5 percent (United States Census Bureau 2010b). As I noted at the outset of this chapter, those we find represented in official criminal justice statistics are disproportionately drawn from the bottom ranks of the latter group.

Class is about more than resources, however. It is also the set of social meanings that accompany our place in the system. We sometimes speak, for example, of "high culture," which is a body of knowledge, tastes, preferences, and experiences said to be common to the upper class and upper middle class. Attending the opera, "coming out" at a debutante ball, enjoying caviar, and knowing which of several forks to use when presented with the fish course in a multicourse meal are all examples of high culture. This does not mean, of course, that anyone cannot learn or enjoy high culture, simply that those with more resources acquire such habits and knowledge in the usual course of their socialization. Because members of the upper and upper-middle classes are disproportionately influential in setting the agendas for governments and educational institutions, high culture is valued over other forms. It is important for poor children to learn about Shakespeare, for example, but the stock of knowledge that some possess about hip hop music, surviving on the street, or living off the land is ignored and devalued by their teachers. Some criminological theorists have argued that this kind of cultural alienation may be at the root of lower-class street crime. While this remains the subject of debate among criminologists, for the moment it is important to note that the dominance of upper-class culture (and the corresponding *lack* of cultural alienation among the wealthy) apparently does little to deter "suite" crime.

Is Gender a Verb? Gendering Individuals, Practices, and Institutions

Throughout this book, I will argue that crime and criminology are "gendered." This use of the term is relatively new; gender has customarily been used to refer to individuals. For example, men and women possess a socially defined gender. As I have noted, however, gender is both social and performative. That is, gender is not only a characteristic but also a practice. We "do" gender when we engage in behavior or display markers that, whether we intend this or not, can be interpreted as masculine or feminine. Hence one can speak of individuals or individual practice as "gendered."

Social phenomena, like crime, may also be gendered. Crime (or victimization, or work in the criminal justice system) is gendered to the extent that it draws on and reproduces existing assumptions about masculinity and femininity. For example, for some men, violent crime can serve as an avenue for proving masculinity. Diana Scully (Scully and Marolla 1985; Scully 1994) found that many of the convicted rapists she interviewed saw raping women as a conquest, the ultimate confirmation of their masculinity. One likened it to successfully riding a mechanical bull. Similarly, the rape of men *by* men is a dramatic demonstration of masculine dominance, understood as such by both perpetrators and victims. Referring to a crime like rape as "gendered" is not at all the same thing as observing that men are the overwhelming majority of rapists. A social practice is not gendered because mostly men or mostly women engage in it; in crude terms, it is "sexed," not "gendered." Rather, a social practice is gendered when it reflects and reinforces and reproduces ideas and assumptions about masculinity and femininity.

We can also speak of social institutions and their policies as gendered. The reformers who established a system of separate prisons for women in the United States argued that women were inherently more domestic than men and should thus be housed in "cottage-style" institutions in which they could live in family groups. These institutions trained women in "the secret of starch [and] ironing" (Freedman 1981) and paroled them to positions as domestic workers in the homes of middle-class women (Rafter 1990). Even today these assumptions persist; women's prisons are still more likely than men's to employ women in domestic chores or to offer classes in cosmetology, secretarial work, and parenting. Men's prisons developed along equally gendered lines, utilizing regimes of silence, hard labor, and military-style discipline in an effort to reconstitute appropriate masculinity (Britton 2003).

Inequality is deeply embedded in assumptions about gender and practices of gendering. Masculinity and femininity are not just different, they also represent different relationships to power and resources. Jobs that draw on socially defined feminine attributes such as nurturing or interpersonal skills, for example, pay less than jobs that require purportedly masculine traits, such as mechanical aptitude. This is true regardless of whether workers in the job are male or female.[12] In the same way, gendered practices are also linked to the perpetuation of inequality. Male rapists' enactments of masculinity through sexual violence in turn shape and reinforce a subordinate femininity. Women's fears for their safety affect their choices about living and working conditions in ways that most men simply never have to consider.

CHAPTER PREVIEW

In the remainder of this book, I employ a gender lens to examine various aspects of crime, the criminal justice system, victimization, and work in the institutions devoted to controlling it. In chapter 2, I examine what we know about criminal offending, and in particular, about the connections between gender and the contexts in which crime is committed. In chapter 3, I turn my attention to the criminal justice system itself and to its treatment of men and women as criminal offenders. Chapter 4 focuses on victimization and the link between cultures, structures, and violence. Chapter 5 explores the experiences of women and men working as attorneys, police officers, and prison officers. Finally, I close in chapter 6 by evaluating the utility of a gender lens and assessing what this perspective adds to our understanding of criminology.

One final note. Though I use the term *gender lens* in this book to indicate a view of criminology that makes gender central, I do not—as I hope has already become clear—view gender in isolation from other axes of social inequality. As victimization and offending are gendered, so, too, are they raced and classed. The focus of the criminal justice system on street crimes committed largely by the poor along with the system's almost complete neglect of the much more socially harmful actions of corporations (and of the wealthy, mostly white, mostly heterosexual men who control them) is but one indication of the fact that gender is intimately intertwined with race, class, and sexuality in this arena of social life, as it is in all others. So while a focus on gender motivates this project, any understanding of social life is incomplete without an understanding of the intersections between multiple axes of privilege and difference. This emphasis on gender in intersection with race, class, and sexuality, is fundamental to the chapters that follow.

2

Gender and Criminal Offending

We just like dudes to them [male gang members]. We just like dudes, they treat us like that 'cause we act so much like dudes they can't do nothing. They respect us as females though, but we just so much like dudes that they just don't trip off of it. ("Latisha," African American gang member, quoted in Miller 2002b, 446)

Sex and gender are both implicated in the study of crime; men and women can be criminals, and criminality structures opportunities for the expression of varieties of masculinity and femininity. The quote from this gang member underlines the need for a gendered analysis of criminal offending. Girls in gangs may "act like dudes"—possessing female bodies but performing masculinity. This tells us that biological sex is only part of the story. Girls can "do" masculinity and boys can perform femininity. Latisha's story and those of other gang girls (Miller 2002b) also illustrate the limits of performance. Though girls may engage in masculinity, they are still females who are "just like" men, occupying an honorific but unstable position. At any moment their performance can be discredited, the actors exposed as not really masculine.

In this chapter, I explore the ways that men and women do gender while also engaging in crime, as well as the mechanisms through which a gendered social structure presumes and shapes particular masculinities and femininities expressed or interpreted through crime. After a long period in which the discipline essentially ignored gender, during the past two decades criminological studies have begun to dramatically expand our understanding of the connections between gender and criminal offending. This research reveals gender similarity as well as difference and the resiliency of a gendered social structure that shapes men's and women's opportunities in the criminal economy just as it does in the legitimate workforce.

THE OFFICIAL DATA AND THE STORY THEY TELL

In absolute terms, we have no idea how much crime actually occurs in the United States. Reports of the crime rate or of race and sex differences in criminal offending are the products of data collection procedures in which the rules and assumptions guiding the process also dictate what we can know about crime. As I note in chapter 1, prevailing definitions of crime already narrow the field of potential behaviors to acts committed primarily by the powerless, rather than the powerful, even though the consequences of the latter's actions are much more serious in terms of loss of life and property. Data collection that begins with these definitions can thus tell us only about this preselected universe.

This is certainly the case for the primary source of data on criminal offending, the Uniform Crime Reports (UCR), issued annually by the Federal Bureau of Investigation (FBI). The FBI collects data on two categories of offenses. There are eight part I, or "index," crimes, further subdivided into violent offenses: homicide, forcible rape, aggravated assault and robbery, and property offenses: burglary, larceny-theft, motor vehicle theft, and arson. When public officials or the media speak of the "crime rate" in a generic sense, they are speaking of the incidence rate for these eight offenses. Part II crimes, considered less serious by the FBI, constitute the bulk of all offenses. This category includes property and violent offenses (e.g., fraud and "simple" assault) as well as public order crimes such as drunkenness, disorderly conduct, and drug abuse violations.

The UCR is based on data collected from police departments in all fifty states. To appear in the statistics a given crime must first be reported or otherwise come to the attention of the police; offenses that fit neither of these criteria cannot be counted in the UCR. Even the most conservative estimates suggest that this first step excludes about 60 percent of violent and property crimes. More worrisome is evidence that nonreporting is not randomly distributed. We know, for example, that people are less likely to report violent acts committed against them by family members, meaning that the major source of violence to women is undoubtedly undercounted. We also know that reporting varies by race and class. In many distressed urban settings, African Americans may be reluctant to trust the police due to their experiences with brutality or a perception of racism on the part of the criminal justice system (Cobbina, Miller, and Brunson 2008; Jones 2009; Miller 2008). Members of Hispanic and Asian communities may be less likely to turn to the police for these reasons, but also—if they are undocumented—due to the fear of deportation. This has a particularly chilling effect on reporting of domestic violence by undocumented women, whose batterers commonly use the threat of deportation to keep their victims silent (Loke 1997; Erez, Adelman, and Gregory 2009; Shaw 2009).

Beyond simply being reported, an offense also must be "founded" to be counted in the UCR, which requires that the police must affirm that they have reason to believe that it has actually occurred. This process is also subject to bias. Some victims, particularly those who are poor or otherwise marginal, may have little credibility with the police. Administrative pressures also matter. To artificially inflate their rates of success, police departments are sometimes motivated to "unfound" crimes that are especially difficult to solve. Again, offenses against women, such as sexual assault, are particularly likely to fall into this category (see chapter 4 for a discussion of problems with statistics on women's victimization).

Information on race and sex differences in criminal offending is the product of yet another layer of assumptions and procedures. These data consist of counts of arrests (rather than reported offenses) for part I and part II offenses provided to the FBI by police departments. According to the UCR (Federal Bureau of Investigation 2010), the probability of arrest for any given offense is relatively low, around 20 percent.[1] Further, as I will discuss in more detail in chapter 3, the likelihood of arrest is much higher for some groups than for others. This means that information on arrests is skewed in a way that overrepresents those with the least social power. Interestingly enough, however, self-reports and other surveys tell us that official data are a relatively accurate representation of the sex difference in criminal offending; when asked directly in surveys whether they have committed acts defined as criminal, the proportions of men and women who say "yes" are relatively close to those in official data on arrests. So while the data overrepresent the less powerful, they appear to give us a relatively accurate picture of sex differences in rates of criminal behavior.

Sex Differences in Arrests—A Story of Sameness and Difference

At first glance, UCR data on arrests by sex reveal a high level of similarity in men's and women's criminal behavior. Simply put, men and women tend to be arrested for the same things. As table 2.1 indicates, the top nine crimes for women appear in a slightly different order on the list for men, a pattern that has been relatively constant over time. Larceny-theft, a category that encompasses thefts without force and includes shoplifting, invariably tops the list for women. Simple assaults, defined as those in which a weapon is not used and life is not endangered, rank second for women and third for men, and substance-related crimes taken together (drug abuse violations, driving under the influence, drunkenness and liquor law violations) make

Table 2.1. Top Offenses by Sex, UCR 2009

Women	% of Arrests	Men	% of Arrests
Larceny-theft	17.1	Drug abuse violations	13.2
Simple assault	9.9	Driving under influence	10.7
Driving under influence	9.3	Simple assault	9.6
Drug abuse violations	8.9	Larceny-theft	7.4
Disorderly conduct	5.1	Drunkenness	4.9
Liquor laws	4.7	Disorderly conduct	4.7
Drunkenness	2.9	Liquor laws	4.0
Aggravated assault	2.7	Aggravated assault	3.2
Fraud	2.6	Burglary	2.5
Runaways	1.5	Vandalism	2.2
Prostitution	1.5	Weapons offenses	1.5
Vandalism	1.4	Fraud	1.2
TOTAL ARRESTS	2,714,361	TOTAL ARRESTS	8,026,796

Source: Author calculation from Federal Bureau of Investigation 2010.

up about one-third of men's arrests and one-quarter of women's. Contrary to stereotypes about women's offending, prostitution arrests are relatively rare, accounting for less than 2 percent of the total for women.

As total number of arrests indicates, however, many more men are arrested each year than women, with almost three times as many men as women arrested in 2009. This difference is also captured by calculations of arrest rates, in which the total number of arrests for a particular group is divided by the total population in that group (and then multiplied by 100,000 to produce numbers that are easier to comprehend). In 2009 the total arrest rate for men was 6,830 (per 100,000 men in the population); for women, the rate was 2,219. Again we see that men were three times more likely to be arrested than women. Differences in arrest rates are particularly stark for serious offenses, as table 2.2 indicates.

Table 2.2. Index Arrest Rates by Sex, 2009

	Women	Men
Murder	1	7
Forcible rape	0	14
Robbery	10	76
Aggravated assault	60	220
Burglary	29	170
Larceny-theft	379	508
Motor vehicle theft	9	45
Arson	1	7

Source: Author calculation from Federal Bureau of Investigation 2010.

Gaps by sex are particularly wide for the part I violent offenses, forcible rape, murder, robbery, and aggravated assault (defined as the taking or attempted taking of property by force or fear). There are also substantial gaps for violent part II crimes, with the largest for "other" sex offenses (excluding forcible rape of adult women and prostitution) and weapons offenses. The smallest sex gaps in offending are for relatively less serious property crimes such as larceny-theft, fraud (a category that includes welfare fraud), and forgery (including writing fraudulent checks). The only categories in which arrests of women consistently outnumber those of men are prostitution and runaways (a juvenile offense), both crimes for which women and girls are about 60 percent of those arrested. Data on juvenile arrests (of those under eighteen) largely replicate these patterns. Boys and girls are involved in the same kinds of offenses, with larceny-theft and simple assault topping the list for both, yet boys are about two and one-half times more likely to be arrested overall, and they heavily predominate in the most violent categories. Overall, boys are almost five times as likely to be arrested for violent index crimes as are girls. These data demonstrate the influence of gender on criminal offending; as the connection between the construction of masculinity and aggression would suggest, men dominate the relatively serious violent crimes. Traditional femininity is certainly less compatible with crime, and the data indeed show that women rarely account for the majority of arrests in any category; where their rates approach those of men, these are for pettier, nonviolent property crimes. Arrest data also indicate dramatic differences by race, as table 2.3 shows.

There are two issues of note here. First, in raw numbers, whites are the overwhelming majority arrested for each kind of crime. Drug abuse violations are the single largest category of arrests tracked by the UCR

Table 2.3. Total Arrests and Arrest Rates by Race, 2009

	Number of Arrests			Arrest Rate	
	Violent Index Offenses	Property Index Offenses	Drug Abuse Violations	Violent Index Offenses	Property Index Offenses
White	268,346	922,139	845,974	140	48
Black	177,766	406,382	473,623	575	1,3
American					
		17,599	8,588	234	
			44	48	

million in 2009, or more than one in ten arrests) and include both possession (82 percent of arrests) and sale (18 percent of arrests) of illegal drugs.
In this category about twice as many whites are arrested as blacks; the same
is true for property and violent crimes. However, since blacks account for
only about 12 percent of the U.S. population, their arrest *rates* are significantly higher. African Americans are three times more likely to be arrested
for drug and property crimes as whites, four times more likely to be arrested
for violent offenses. The FBI also reports arrests for two other racial categories, "American Indian or Alaska Native" and "Asian or Pacific Islander."
These categories include considerable ethnic and regional diversity, so saying anything meaningful about them is difficult. Both groups have far lower
numbers of arrests than whites, and their rates of arrest are generally lower
(with the exception of the property and violent offenses for American In-
dians and Alaska Natives). Importantly, the FBI does not report arrest data
in the UCR for Hispanics because the category "Hispanic" is considered by
he U.S. government to be an ethnicity rather than a race. This means that
spanics can appear in any racial category but are likely found in these
largely among whites.

note in chapter 1, the FBI publishes no information on arrests by race
This means that we can talk about differences between men and
between whites and blacks, but we can say nothing at all about
es of white versus black women (or men). The limited data
come from studies of unpublished FBI data and research
rts, show that African American women have higher rates
le, aggravated assault, and other index offenses than do
on and Ellis 1995). For some offenses, for example,
plifting), arrest rates for African American women
for white men (Simpson and Ellis 1995; Som-
ton and Datesman 1987). This suggests that
making blanket comparisons between men
re likely to conceal considerable variation
es. The same holds true, of course, for
veen races.

ender?

dom holds that gender an
hear, long ago
ent and
e on

Drug Abuse
Violations
442
1,414

358

734   86

166

Gaps by sex are particularly wide for the part I violent offenses, forcible rape, murder, robbery, and aggravated assault (defined as the taking or attempted taking of property by force or fear). There are also substantial gaps for violent part II crimes, with the largest for "other" sex offenses (excluding forcible rape of adult women and prostitution) and weapons offenses. The smallest sex gaps in offending are for relatively less serious property crimes such as larceny-theft, fraud (a category that includes welfare fraud), and forgery (including writing fraudulent checks). The only categories in which arrests of women consistently outnumber those of men are prostitution and runaways (a juvenile offense), both crimes for which women and girls are about 60 percent of those arrested. Data on juvenile arrests (of those under eighteen) largely replicate these patterns. Boys and girls are involved in the same kinds of offenses, with larceny-theft and simple assault topping the list for both, yet boys are about two and one-half times more likely to be arrested overall, and they heavily predominate in the most violent categories. Overall, boys are almost five times as likely to be arrested for violent index crimes as are girls. These data demonstrate the influence of gender on criminal offending; as the connection between the construction of masculinity and aggression would suggest, men dominate the relatively serious violent crimes. Traditional femininity is certainly less compatible with crime, and the data indeed show that women rarely account for the majority of arrests in any category; where their rates approach those of men, these are for pettier, nonviolent property crimes. Arrest data also indicate dramatic differences by race, as table 2.3 shows.

There are two issues of note here. First, in raw numbers, whites are the overwhelming majority arrested for each kind of crime. Drug abuse violations are the single largest category of arrests tracked by the UCR (1.3

Table 2.3. Total Arrests and Arrest Rates by Race, 2009

	Number of Arrests			Arrest Rate		
	Violent Index Offenses	Property Index Offenses	Drug Abuse Violations	Violent Index Offenses	Property Index Offenses	Drug Abuse Violations
White	268,346	922,139	845,974	140	482	442
Black	177,766	406,382	473,623	575	1,313	1,414
American Indian or Alaska Native	5,608	17,599	8,588	234	734	358
Asian or Pacific Islander	5,245	18,289	9,444	48	166	86

Source: Author calculation from Federal Bureau of Investigation 2010.

million in 2009, or more than one in ten arrests) and include both possession (82 percent of arrests) and sale (18 percent of arrests) of illegal drugs.
In this category about twice as many whites are arrested as blacks; the same
is true for property and violent crimes. However, since blacks account for
only about 12 percent of the U.S. population, their arrest *rates* are significantly higher. African Americans are three times more likely to be arrested
for drug and property crimes as whites, four times more likely to be arrested
for violent offenses. The FBI also reports arrests for two other racial categories, "American Indian or Alaska Native" and "Asian or Pacific Islander."
These categories include considerable ethnic and regional diversity, so saying anything meaningful about them is difficult. Both groups have far lower
numbers of arrests than whites, and their rates of arrest are generally lower
(with the exception of the property and violent offenses for American In-
dians and Alaska Natives). Importantly, the FBI does not report arrest data
in the UCR for Hispanics because the category "Hispanic" is considered by
the U.S. government to be an ethnicity rather than a race. This means that
Hispanics can appear in any racial category but are likely found in these
data largely among whites.

As I note in chapter 1, the FBI publishes no information on arrests by race
and sex. This means that we can talk about differences between men and
women or between whites and blacks, but we can say nothing at all about
the arrest rates of white versus black women (or men). The limited data
available, which come from studies of unpublished FBI data and research
based on self-reports, show that African American women have higher rates
of arrest for homicide, aggravated assault, and other index offenses than do
white women (Simpson and Ellis 1995). For some offenses, for example,
larceny-theft (usually shoplifting), arrest rates for African American women
most closely match those for white men (Simpson and Ellis 1995; Sommers and Baskin 1992; Chilton and Datesman 1987). This suggests that
we should exercise great care in making blanket comparisons between men
and women as a whole, as these are likely to conceal considerable variation
within these groups across racial lines. The same holds true, of course, for
broad comparisons of differences between races.

Change over Time: A Liberated Female Offender?

We live in an age in which the prevailing wisdom holds that gender and
racial inequality are relics of the past. As we often hear, long ago we had a
women's rights movement and a civil rights movement and solved all that
messy unfairness. Blacks and whites now compete on a level playing field,
and men and women are equal in all aspects of social life. And if this is
true in the legitimate economy, that is, if women can be corporate CEOs
just like men, it must also be the case in the illegitimate economy. Women

are purportedly now just as violent as men, equally likely to be urban "gangstas" and drug kingpins. As a sociologist I take pains to debunk these notions—the average African American or Hispanic family in the United States possesses only one-tenth of the wealth held by the average white family, and women who work full-time still make only about seventy-six cents for every full-time man's dollar (United States Census Bureau 2010a). Nor do the statistics on crime paint a picture of gender or racial equality in the illegitimate, criminal economy.

The modern debate over the existence of a new, more violent, more equal female criminal actually dates back more than thirty years. It began in 1975, a year that saw the publication of Freda Adler's *Sisters in Crime* and Rita James Simon's *Women and Crime*. Written as the second wave of the American women's movement began to gather steam, both books make the same general theoretical argument, which has come to be known as emancipation theory. Adler and Simon contended that women's heretofore lower rates of participation in crime could be explained by their confinement to the household and to discrimination (Daly and Chesney-Lind 1988). They suggested that women who thought of themselves primarily as homemakers and spent their time performing domestic duties did not have the opportunity to commit crimes in significant numbers nor were they able to conceive of themselves as violent criminals. With the advent of the women's movement the situation could be expected to change, however:

> If one assumes that the changes in women's roles, in their perceptions of self, and in their desire for expanded horizons that began in the latter part of the sixties will not be abated . . . then we would expect that one of the major by-products of the women's movement will be a higher proportion of women who pursue careers in crime. (Simon 1975, 1)

Adler believed that women would inevitably become more violent as they began to take on men's social and political roles. Simon argued that opportunities created by women's higher levels of labor market activity would lead to higher arrest rates for property and occupational crimes, such as fraud, larceny, and embezzlement. Adler did consider the influence of race, noting black women's historically higher rates of work outside the home and inferring a correspondingly higher level of emancipation. For her this explained black women's higher rates of participation in crime: "If one looks at where Black women are as criminals today, one can appreciate where white women are headed as liberated criminals in the coming years" (154). According to emancipation theory, the women's movement would make men and women equal in both the suites and the streets.

Though their findings were decried by feminists at the time (and since), Adler's and Simon's books actually began a very important conversation about the relationship between *gender* and crime. To the extent that criminologists had thought about sex differences in criminal offending previously, they tended to explain women's lower levels of participation as a function of sex, not gender. Cesare Lombroso, one of the founders of modern criminology, wrote

> That women less often are engaged in highway robbery, murder, homicide, and assault is due to the very nature of the feminine constitution. To conceive an assassination, to make ready for it, to put it into execution demands, in a great number of cases, not only physical force, but a certain energy and combination of intellectual functions. In this sort of development women almost always fall short of men. (Lombroso 1911, 185)

Paradoxically, Lombroso here sees men's criminality as a result of their inherent superiority—men are simply stronger and smarter than women, and hence more able to be successful criminals. Conversely, women conform because they are constitutionally unable to commit crime. In both cases, however, Lombroso attributes differences in offending to sex—to biology.

Adler and Simon, on the other hand, point to gender. Their argument implies that men are more likely than women to offend because of the norms of masculine socialization and men's participation in social and political roles in the public sphere. As women increasingly moved out of the private sphere and took on these roles, they believed, their behaviors would come to emulate those of men. Women's sex would not change, of course, but their roles and ideas about femininity in the larger society would be reshaped in ways that would give women opportunities to be criminal and allow them to engage in behaviors, like violence, previously defined as exclusively masculine. They predicted that the women's movement would change notions about gender and thus allow women to engage in crime as never before.

Emancipation theory's legacy extends to the present day, a moment in which evidence that women are now equally as violent as men seems to be everywhere (Chesney-Lind and Jones 2010). In the popular media, fictional portrayals of hyperviolent women are now commonplace. Xena, the Warrior Princess (on television from 1995 to 2001) regularly wiped out entire armies of men with only the assistance of her trusty female sidekick Gabrielle. In Quentin Tarantino's 2003 film, *Kill Bill* (and in its 2004 sequel—and in dozens of other films since), female characters stabbed, sliced, and decapitated their way through the film. Parodying a slogan of the women's movement, one critic writing about the film put it this way: "The message from Hollywood is clear: You've come a long way, baby. Now kill someone" (Leland 2003). This message can be heard across the media spectrum. In video games players can become female characters and lay waste to entire planets. Television talk shows frequently feature "gangsta girls," and true crime programs speculate about the prevalence of female serial killers. Popular science outlets have contributed to this trend as well. In November 1999, *Psychology Today*'s cover announced the arrival of a new breed of "Bad Girls," and the author of the accompanying article wondered whether women were now "taking 'women's liberation' a step too far" (Yeoman 1999). A *Newsweek* story in 2005 ominously trumpeted the headline "Bad Girls Go Wild" (Scelfo 2005). It certainly appears that violence, kept in check for decades by the labors of cooking, cleaning, and laundry, has been newly liberated in women. According to these accounts the women's movement has, perhaps unintentionally, emancipated women to be just as criminal as men. The persistence of this belief and the popularity of the stereotype of the new, more violent woman criminal should lead us to consider whether the evidence supports the claims of emancipation theory. Have women indeed become more like men in their criminal behavior? Are women now just as likely to murder, rob, and embark on criminal careers?

The data on arrest rates already presented provide part of the answer. Women simply do not engage in violent crimes at anything close to the rate at which men do (Steffensmeier et al. 2005, 2006). Men's arrest rates for homicide and robbery are seven times greater than women's; the difference for aggravated assault is a factor of four. Overall, men are more than three times as likely to be arrested as are women. On the basis of these data, at least, we can conclusively say that at the present moment men and women are not the same in terms of violent offending or even criminal behavior more generally.

But strictly speaking, emancipation theory hypothesizes change over time—the argument is that women will become more like men as they are increasingly liberated. Adler used data on robbery arrests from 1960 to 1972 to demonstrate that women's rates were *converging* with men's. She observed that women's arrests increased by 277 percent over this period, while men's increased by only 169 percent. If this difference were sustained over a long period, women would indeed eventually catch up to men. So the more appropriate assessment of emancipation theory requires data on change over time to determine whether women are actually becoming more like men in their criminal behavior.

This is relatively easy to do by drawing on information from the UCR. Table 2.4 gives raw numbers of arrests, arrest rates, and the percentage change in rates for each of the violent index crimes, larceny-theft, the property crime index, and drug offenses from 1988 to 2009. Several features of this table are noteworthy. For most offenses both men's and women's arrests are down. In many cases however, men's rates have fallen faster than women's. For forcible rape, for example, men's arrest rate fell by 56 percent from 1988 to 2009, women's by 49 percent (though because women commit very few crimes in this category, this is not a particularly meaningful statistic—more on this below). We see a similar pattern for larceny-theft

Table 2.4. Changes in Men's and Women's Arrests, Selected Offenses, 1988–2009

| | 1988 | | | | 2009 | | | | Percentage Change in Rates | |
| | Total Arrests | | Arrest Rates | | Total Arrests | | Arrest Rates | | | |
	Men	Women	Men	Women	Men	Women	Men	Women	Men	Women
Homicide	11,432	1,663	16	2	8,755	1,020	7	1	-53[a]	-62[a]
Rape	22,410	248	31	0	16,234	208	14	0	-56[b]	-49[b]
Robbery	70,198	6,409	97	9	88,783	11,919	76	10	-22[c]	14[c]
Aggravated Assault	214,181	32,743	297	44	258,467	72,905	220	60	-26[c]	37[c]
Larceny	649,742	287,007	901	383	597,246	463,508	508	379	-44[b]	-1[b]
Prop Index	1,020,304	325,309	1,416	434	858,016	511,642	730	418	-48[b]	-4[b]
Drugs	554,768	104,848	770	140	1,062,777	242,414	904	198	17[c]	42[c]

Source: Author calculation, Federal Bureau of Investigation 1998, 2010.

[a]Divergence (women's rates falling faster than men's)

[b]Men's rates falling faster than women's (both falling)

[c]Women's rates rising faster than men's

and the overall index of property crimes. Assuming current rates of change remain constant, this means that men's and women's rates for these offenses would eventually converge. Contrary to the predictions of emancipation theory however, what is interesting about these offenses is that men's rates *are falling to meet women's*. In crude terms we might say that men are becoming more like women, rather than the reverse.

There are four categories that do not fit this trend. Women's arrest rates for homicide are falling faster than men's and hence diverging, a trend definitely contrary to emancipation theory. For robbery and aggravated assault, women's arrest rates are rising while men's are falling, indeed indicating convergence—though again in the direction of men's rates falling to meet women's (the same is true for simple assault; see Lauritsen, Heimer, and Lynch 2009). Similarly, while arrest rates for both women and men are rising for drug offenses, women's are increasing faster, again denoting rates that are converging over time such that women's rates are rising to meet men's (though assuming current rates of change this would happen almost a century from now, when there would be a total of 50 million arrests for drug offenses—a prospect that seems highly unlikely). At the very least, the evidence offers a mixed bag of results for emancipation theorists.

The best cases for the theory appear to lie in the data for robbery, drug offenses, and aggravated assault. But even in these instances we should be cautious. All of these data demonstrate the problem with relying, as emancipation theorists invariably do, on percentage change as an indicator of similarity. As table 2.4 indicates, women's rates of arrest for most offenses are very low. To take a simple example, consider the statistics for homicide. Women's arrest rate for homicide in 2009 was 1 per 100,000, with 1,020 total arrests. To produce a 100 percent increase, to a rate of 2, it follows that 1,020 more women would have to be arrested. Men's arrest rate for homicide in 2009 was 7; 8,755 men were arrested. To produce a 100 percent increase, to a rate of 16, 8,755 additional men would need to be arrested. Exactly the same percentage increase in rates requires that almost eight times as many men would have to be arrested as women. This demonstrates a basic mathematical fact about comparing percentage changes for vastly different base numbers: because women's initial arrest rates are so low, a very small increase in numbers produces a very large percentage change. We should thus always be wary of comparisons of the percentage change in men's and women's arrest rates (and, as we shall see in chapter 3, incarceration rates). The magnitude of percentage change over time is invariably misleading. Larger increases in women's rates almost never indicate substantive equality.

The data on aggravated assault and drug offenses also demonstrate this clearly. In 2009 there were about 240,000 women arrested for drug offenses, compared with more than one million men. Similarly, while approximately

259,000 men were arrested for aggravated assault, only 73,000 women faced the same fate. Though the rates for these offenses may be statistically converging in an abstract sense, there is simply no defensible way to claim that the numbers of women committing such crimes makes them "like men" in any real fashion. While we should certainly be concerned with the magnitude of these numbers, the very substantial differences between them are indicative of a continuing, and substantial, sex difference in arrests.

In thinking about the implications of these data, at least three other issues bear mentioning. First, it is worth remembering that while we sometimes speak of sex differences in rates of criminal offending, we usually do this by reference to data on rates of arrest. This is important because while the women's movement has undoubtedly changed women, it has also altered the social context in which their behavior is evaluated. There is in fact some evidence to suggest that police may now be more willing to arrest women than they have been in years past. This means that increases in women's arrest rates over time may be less indicative of changes in their behavior than of changing patterns of policing (Chesney-Lind and Irwin 2008; Schwartz and Rookey 2008; Steffensmeier et al. 2005, 2006). Second, if liberation produces emancipated women criminals, we should expect that those who commit crime would exhibit more liberal attitudes about gender than women in the general population. Studies have consistently shown, however, that women offenders are generally quite conservative in their attitudes about gender and are in fact extremely *un*likely to be feminists (Simpson 1989; Steffensmeier and Allan 1996). Third, these data fail to consider the context of offending. As I will demonstrate in chapter 4, simple counts of incidents like "assault" do not account for the fact that most women's assaults occur in the gendered context of violent relationships; men's assaults are more likely to involve acquaintances or strangers.

The weight of the evidence simply does not support the claims of emancipation theorists. Women are not now just as likely to be as violent as men, machine-gun wielding actresses in movies notwithstanding.[2] Whatever other changes it has wrought, the women's movement has not loosed a new breed of violent female criminals on society (Chesney-Lind and Irwin 2008; Lauritsen, Heimer, and Lynch 2009). So where does that leave gender? Emancipation theory in itself actually offers an account of the demise of gender; Adler and Simon contended that the women's movement would take women beyond the social constraints of femininity, that liberation would make gender irrelevant. Given continuing substantial sex differences in arrests, must we return to biological accounts that link higher rates of criminality to masculine physical superiority? On the contrary. In fact, research demonstrates the enduring importance of gender's role as a key element shaping men's and women' criminal opportunities and participation in crime.

THE INVISIBLE MAN—MASCULINITIES AND CRIME[3]

One of the earliest projects of sociological criminologists was to develop theories that would account for crime in social, rather than biological, terms. In 1938, for example, Robert Merton offered "strain theory," which pointed to an unequal social structure to explain criminal behavior. Instead of viewing crime as the result of biological predisposition, Merton drew attention to society itself, arguing that those without access to legitimate means—such as education or well-paying jobs—to reach the American Dream might turn to illegitimate, criminal methods to succeed (Merton 1938). Still other theorists pointed to different aspects of society. In his theory of differential association, Edwin Sutherland (1947) argued that crime, like all behavior, is learned from others in a social context. If this is so, then anyone could potentially acquire the knowledge and values conducive to crime; those with criminal associates, he suggested, would be most likely to do so. Still other theorists offered rival accounts, singling out factors such as the characteristics of neighborhoods or the strength of the bond between individuals and society; fierce debates among proponents of modern versions of various theoretical schools continue in criminology to the present day.

By drawing attention to the social context in which crime is committed, all of these perspectives represent a fundamental advance over the crude biologism of Lombroso and his followers. Although all begin from disparate assumptions and produce different models of behavior, they share one thing in common. While claiming to account for "crime" generically, each was developed and has been applied primarily to understanding the criminality of men. In fact, until quite recently criminological theory has in effect been an enterprise dedicated to understanding and predicting men's crime. The assumptions and mechanisms that characterize Merton's and Sutherland's purportedly general theories underline this fact. Historically it has been men, more than women, who have faced intense social pressure to reach the American Dream; this was certainly true at the time Merton offered the theory, in 1938. And though Sutherland himself did not offer a gendered account of the learning of crime, the disproportionately greater responsibilities of women for domestic labor and the sex segregation of public spaces have meant that it has been men, too, who have been more likely to have delinquent peers and criminal associates. A similar argument could be made for most of the classic works of criminological theory and would hold for most of their modern descendants as well.

These theories leave us with an interesting paradox. Although they help us to understand the criminality of men, they lack an understanding of masculinity. Most criminological theory can tell us why criminals, who happen to be men, commit crimes, but they give us little insight into the role of masculinity in shaping that motivation. A rare exception among the classics in criminology is the work of Albert Cohen (1955). Cohen applied a modified version of Merton's strain theory to understand the formation of street gangs by working-class boys. He argues that the inability of these boys to achieve appropriate middle-class masculinity, with its trappings of economic and academic success, leads them to form groups in which they can succeed by other means, largely by relying on physical violence and street smarts. He reasons that boys are more likely than girls to feel social pressure to succeed, hence their adaptation to failure is likely to be more extreme and instrumentally oriented to seeking alternate avenues for success.[4] In simple terms, boys are more likely to feel pressure to succeed and thus more likely to turn to crime.

This early insight about the connection between masculinity and crime would lie largely forgotten in criminology over the next two decades. Theorists continued to produce accounts of the causes of crime for criminals, sex and gender unspecified, who were nevertheless overwhelmingly likely to be men. Masculinity was simply not on the agenda for mainstream criminology. The topic would ultimately be reintroduced from outside the discipline in the form of studies of women's victimization sparked by the second wave of the women's movement. Focusing at first on the experiences and anger of women victims themselves, in fairly short order feminists began to make the link between male dominance and the laws and social values that both facilitated crime against women and ensured that it was rarely taken seriously. At the dawn of the second wave of the women's movement, for example, laws in many states required that "legitimate" rape victims be virgins, upheld a "right of consortia" under which married men could have sex with their wives regardless of their consent, and treated the husband as the head of household in all legal, financial, and property matters. Feminists argued that the law reflected and encouraged masculine dominance over women and men's entitlement to women's bodies. In this context the rape and battering of women could be understood not as the actions of a few pathological men but rather as the logical outcome of mainstream norms and values about masculinity and femininity (for early discussions on this theme, see Brownmiller 1975; Dworkin 1979; and Griffin 1981).

Inspired by this observation, studies focusing on men began to demonstrate the links between masculinity and crimes against women. Evidence was not difficult to find. Surveys have fairly consistently shown that about one third of college men say they would commit rape if they were assured that they would not be caught (e.g., Malamuth 1981 and Osland, Fitch, and Willis 1996). Dozens of subsequent studies of "rape myth" acceptance have found that men tend to hold rape victims more culpable for the crimes committed against them than do women, and that both men and women with conservative or traditional ideas about gender tend to attribute greater responsibility to rape victims than do those with more egalitarian ideas (e.g., Brown and Testa 2007; Hockett et al. 2009; Locke and Mahalik 2005; and Schneider et al. 2009).

Diana Scully's (1994; see also Scully and Marolla 1985) landmark work, in which she interviewed 114 convicted rapists serving time in Virginia prisons, dramatically demonstrates the connections between conventional ideas about masculinity and sexual assault. Echoing social norms concerning masculinity and sexuality, Scully found that many of the men she interviewed believed they were simply entitled to sex. When a woman refused his advances, one man seriously physically assaulted and raped his victim, claiming: "I think I was really pissed off at her because it didn't go as planned. I could have been with someone else. She led me on but didn't deliver. . . . I have a male ego that must be fed" (Scully and Marolla 1985, 258). For most, the theme of dominance prevailed:

> Rape gave me the power to do what I wanted without having to please a partner or respond to a partner. I felt in control, dominant. Rape was the ability to have sex without caring about the woman's response. I was totally dominant. (quoted in Scully and Marolla 1985, 259)

Still another man who raped and murdered five women saw sexual assault as the ultimate masculine accomplishment: "It seemed like so much bitterness and tension had built up and this released it. I felt like I had just climbed a mountain and now I could look back" (Scully and Marolla 1985, 261).

The notions of entitlement, dominance, and accomplishment expressed by the men in Scully's study are in fact all key parts of heterosexual masculine socialization in American culture. Young boys learn that to be "real men" they must be dominant, in control. As boys reach adolescence they learn to view heterosexual sex as an accomplishment, with greater numbers of sexual encounters indicative of higher levels of masculine prowess (Pascoe 2007). For young women, the social consequences of multiple sexual experiences are not nearly so positive. The notice that boys garner through male-dominated activities like sports and their observations of the status that grown men hold in the world lead them to expect a certain level of privilege and attention, particularly from women. All of this is common in the everyday process of masculine socialization. Yet it is also these values that lie behind the actions of the rapists interviewed by Scully. By "doing" rape, these men are also doing gender. They are in control, dominant, entitled. Though most men would undoubtedly decry their actions, the sentiments the rapists express are intimately intertwined with mainstream notions about masculinity in American culture.

Researchers who study domestic and relationship violence come to similar conclusions. The norms of heterosexual relationships, at least in their traditional form, dictate that men have exclusive access to women's bodies but also have the right to expect feminine submission and, in marriage or cohabiting heterosexual relationships, domestic labor. When women do not fulfill men's expectations, these men in turn can justify violence as a response. Men's rationalizations for battering often cite behavior from their wives or girlfriends that they see as controlling or insufficiently subservient (Anderson and Umberson 2001; Ptacek 1990) or point to other perceived violations of femininity. As a man sentenced to a batterer's intervention program explained:

> I was upset with my wife. I asked if she could fold the laundry by today . . . and things weren't done yet. She also just threw a steak on the burner and forgot about it and it burnt up. . . . When I sit down to eat, I expect to see a fork, plate, dishes, a drink. But there was nothing ready. I told her to get her head out of her ass and to do it right. (quoted in Schrock and Padavic 2007, 635–36)

The fact that this man, who had been convicted of domestic violence, was sentenced to a diversion program rather than jail or prison time suggests something about the seriousness with which the legal system takes such crimes, a topic I treat further in chapter 3.

Masculine privilege is not equally distributed across race and class. Regardless of social class, black men ordinarily do not enjoy the same level of power and entitlement as white men, and poor men of all races often find it difficult to obtain the resources to become "real men" in accord with the middle-class model. Yet to some degree all boys and men in our society face the challenge of proving their masculinity. This disconnect between social norms and social structure sets up an inherent conflict. As Cohen (1955) noted more than four decades ago, some social groups experience a wide gap between the goal of middle-class masculinity and the legitimate means to achieve it. In recent years theorists have resurrected this early insight, arguing that those who cannot achieve masculinity in other ways may commit criminal acts out of frustration or may use crime to achieve status that is otherwise unavailable to them. James Messerschmidt's (2000) interviews with white working-class boys convicted of sexual and other violent offenses underline this point. One of the most consistent themes among their otherwise diverse accounts is their repeated but failed attempts to prove themselves "real men" among their peers. All report being bullied by higher-status groups of boys at school, feeling unpopular with girls, being labeled as "wimps," and being made fun for their relative poverty. Messerschmidt argues that for these boys crime may be an attractive alternative route for proving themselves as men. As "Sam," a young boy who molested two young girls (ages six and eight) put it:

[When I assaulted girls] I didn't feel like I was small anymore, because . . . with people my own age, I felt like I was a wimp. . . . But when I did this to the girls, I felt like I was big, I was in control of everything.

These themes of control and entitlement differ little from those observed by Scully (1994) in her study of adult male rapists. Yet here they are coupled with an argument grounded in the recognition of an unequal social structure; it is the gap between the goal of acceptable masculinity and the means to achieve this goal that gives rise to criminal offending.

Hegemonic masculinity is about physical power and status, but it is also, as these accounts suggest, about sexuality. To be a real man in American society implies heterosexuality. Among adolescent boys, to be called a "fag" may be the worst of all possible insults (Pascoe 2007). Entwined with masculinity, heterosexuality also shares its instability, with acceptable heterosexuality seemingly requiring unremitting confirmation. Boys and men boast about their heterosexual exploits in school locker rooms and their adult equivalents, and men may be called upon at any time to defend themselves against implications that they are anything other than blatantly and enthusiastically heterosexual. The ubiquitous taunts of the schoolyard provide one means to assert heterosexual masculinity; crimes motivated by hatred of homosexuality provide a more extreme alternative. Gay men are disproportionately the victims of this kind of hate crime, and young white working-class men are the most common perpetrators.

The case of Donald Aldrich presents one such example. Aldrich was petty criminal who in 1994 was part of a group of young men who, whi out on a night of "fag bashing," abducted a gay man, Nicholas West, fro a park in Tyler, Texas. The group took West to a remote location wh they punched, kicked, and pistol-whipped him with a .357 Magnum. T then gathered around and shot him as many as fifteen times. Aldrich h tenth-grade education, had grown up working class, and at the time arrest was in a troubled marriage and lived in a trailer park in a small in Texas. Between times in prison, he had worked in jobs at fast-fo taurants. After the killing, the group rode around town in West's red truck, where police eventually found them and arrested them. Ald plained his actions this way:

I work all the time trying to have something nice and make somethin self. About the best job I can get is working in a restaurant making m wage or just barely over it, and it's like, I get no breaks. From the t a kid it seemed like there was a lot against me, and yet here they something that God totally condemns in the Bible. But look at [gays] have, they've got all this nice stuff. They've got all these goo they've got money. So yeah, I resented that. (Bissinger 1995, 88)

Aldrich received the death penalty for the killing, the first ever handed down for a hate crime in the state of Texas. Like the boys interviewed by Messerschmidt (2000), Aldrich's account of his life is clearly one of frustrated entitlement, coupled with anger that men he perceives as lesser than he, that is, gay men, have unfairly achieved more. Yet it is more than this purely psychological analysis would suggest. Aldrich is in fact a representative of a particular race and class location, one whose members enjoy fewer opportunities than those higher up the social ladder. For these men social norms dictate a model of masculinity that they simply do not possess the resources to achieve. Along the lines of Merton, Cohen, and also Cloward and Ohlin (1960), his story is in fact a classic sociological example of how blocked opportunities to achieve a socially acceptable goal—in this case, successful heterosexual masculinity—can give rise to violence.

To argue that social inequality may lead to criminality is not the same thing as to suggest, as biologically influenced criminologists did, that the poor are predestined to commit crime. Instead sociologists argue that crime, like all human behavior, happens in a social context. In the examples discussed above, this is an environment in which all men face pressure to achieve a particular form of masculinity yet few possess the resources to do so. Failing to succeed in middle-class terms can lead such men and boys to choose alternative avenues for proving masculinity, among which are crime or other kinds of criminal acts.

If the poor are not in fact inherently criminal, this suggests that social forces may also produce criminality among the middle classes or the rich. This is a theoretical possibility that has thus far been little explored in criminology. Criminological theories are best adapted to the criminality of men, and so, too, have criminologists focused almost exclusively on the criminal acts of the poor—and by extension, crimes of men who are poor. Yet as I note in chapter 1, acts of corporate governments cause significantly more harm every year—in financial loss, death, and injury—than the thefts or violence of the poor. And as is the case among street criminals, those who lack power in these institutions are also disproportionately

Sociological theory largely fails us in accounting for wealthy men who serve as heads of corporations and models of successful masculinity. They are in fact its architects. Yet their behavior? There have been very few studies of such men and almost no attempts to frame such men's actions in terms of the prevailing norms of masculinity. One exception is Messerschmidt's study of the Challenger disaster. Challenger exploded on January 25, 1986, killing all seven crew members aboard. A presidential commission later determined that the cause of the crash was a defective O-ring, a rubber gasket intended to seal a gap in the shuttle's solid rocket boosters and prevent the escape and ignition of hot gases during launch. There is abundant documentation to show that the manufacturer of the defective part, Morton-Thiokol Incorporated (MTI), and the National Aeronautics and Space Administration (NASA) had known about problems with the O-ring for many years. MTI managers and engineers initially counseled NASA to abandon the January launch over concerns that the low temperatures would cause the O-ring to become too hard to effectively seal the joint. As the commission's report documents, however, despite the insistence of their own engineers that the O-ring would fail, MTI managers eventually decided that level of risk was acceptable and approved the launch.

Most would not recognize the actions of MTI managers as criminal. Indeed, no one was ever prosecuted for murder, or manslaughter, or fraud. The seven crew members of the *Challenger* were not counted in the FBI's annual report of homicide victims, nor were the MTI managers enumerated in the UCR's statistics on homicide offenders. But these very circumstances underscore the hidden nature of corporate and governmental actions that cause so much social harm—such acts are not counted as crimes, nor are their perpetrators numbered among the criminal. The fact remains, however, that seven people died as a result of the decisions of managers who had well-documented reasons to know better.

Not unlike the more conventional criminals discussed to this point, these men, too, were doing masculinity—though in a very different context. Like the streets, corporations, too, are gendered. When one imagines a successful manager one almost invariably sees a man, and the image evokes the qualities of middle-class masculinity. Managers are rational, goal oriented, and impersonal, they are risk takers focused on maximizing profit. The corporate context in which they operate is also profoundly gendered, explicitly designed to be "lean, mean, aggressive, goal oriented, efficient and competitive" (Acker 1992, 253). As Messerschmidt (1995) notes, the *Challenger* launch decision posed a number of threats to MTI managers. Worried about losing their contract, under severe pressure from NASA flight control, and afraid of appearing indecisive in the face of uncertainty, MTI managers did masculinity by invoking the masculine stereotype of the risk taker, and in so doing reaffirmed their identities as men. As in the BP/Deepwater Horizon oil spill, the gendered social context of the corporation and the norms of appropriate managerial masculinity ultimately led to an act that in the context of the streets would almost certainly be regarded as negligent homicide.

The juxtaposition of these examples of both street crime and suite crime illustrate the key argument of the first generation of sociological criminologists—social context matters. They also demonstrate the power of applying a gender lens to understanding criminal behavior, the contribution that might be made by viewing men *as men*, rather than as generic criminal actors. In both settings, norms about masculinity combine with a gendered social structure to create an environment favorable to crime, and crime in turn serves as a powerful vehicle for doing masculinity. This emphasis on context also illuminates potential avenues for change. Social contexts, unlike biological predispositions, can be altered. Alternative models of masculinity are possible, and indeed such forms already exist. Changing the "culture of cruelty" (Kindlon and Thompson 1999; Messerschmidt 2000) in schools by discouraging bullying and harassment is clearly one mechanism that could encourage the development of less violent, less rigidly hierarchical forms of masculinity (Pascoe 2007). So, too, would changes in family life that deemphasized violence as part of the socialization of boys and in which men and women shared more equally in parenting and other household chores (Messerschmidt 2000). Conversely, increasing opportunities for economic success among those who currently find such routes blocked could make crime seem a less attractive alternative. In the "suites," creating a climate more focused on corporate responsibility to workers and to the public would certainly make extreme risk taking of the kind that precipitated the *Challenger* disaster less likely. Regardless of the direction of change, we are unlikely to be successful in addressing the causes of crime if we fail to understand its intimate relationship with masculinity.

SHEMALE OR DANCING QUEEN? GENDER AND WOMEN'S CRIMINAL OFFENDING

The integration of gender into criminology's understanding of women offenders has taken a stranger and more circuitous route than in the case of men. One reason for this is the sex ratio I discussed in chapter 1. Since statistics on crime have been collected, both in the United States and internationally, it has been clear that crime is a male-dominated domain. This is particularly true for the most serious violent offenses and is consistent with what we already know about gender. It does not take a broad logical leap to connect masculinity with crime. Traditional notions about femininity, on the other hand, would seem to leave little leeway for criminal behavior. Proper women—proper white, middle-class women, at any rate—should be nurturing, passive, and protected. This makes them excellent victims but does not equip them very well for engaging in crime. Criminal women are thus oddities in a way that criminal men are not, and it has been this fact that has lain behind both their virtual neglect in criminological theory and the general tenor of explanations for their behavior.

So seemingly strange are criminal women, and so masculine is crime, that early biological criminologists believed that women who engaged in crime must essentially *be* men. Lombroso argued that criminal women were hermaphrodites who lacked "natural" female instincts:

> This want of maternal feeling becomes comprehensible when we reflect on the one hand upon the union of masculine qualities which prevent the female criminal from being more than half a woman. . . . Her maternal sense is weak because psychologically and anthropologically she belongs more to the male than to the female sex. (Lombroso 1909, 153)

Criminal behavior was synonymous with masculine biology, Lombroso believed, such that women criminals must have evolved in such a way that they had—psychologically if not physically—become partly male. Such women engaged in clearly masculine behavior and exhibited no "natural" feminine feeling or instinct. The clear implication of this argument is that no real woman could ever engage in crime.

Women offenders did not fare much better with early sociological criminologists. Most ignored them entirely—though to be fair they also paid little attention to the masculinity of the male offenders they studied. In the rare case that theorists turned their attention to women, it was largely to dismiss them as serious criminals. Cohen (1955), one of the first to propose a link between masculinity and crime among working-class boys, nevertheless held that women and girls had other priorities:

> For the adolescent girl as well as for the adult woman, relationships with the opposite sex and those personal qualities which affect the ability to establish such relationships are central in importance. . . . Dating, popularity with boys, pulchritude, "charm," clothes and dancing are preoccupations so central and so obvious that it would be useless pedantry to document them. (Cohen 1955, 142–47)

Cohen believed the goals of appropriate femininity—beauty and heterosexual relationships—were simply much more accessible than those of masculinity. By and large women had no need to engage in crime to reach those goals. They might shoplift dresses or cosmetics or perhaps engage in premarital heterosexual sex, but one certainly would not expect instrumental criminal acts or serious violence. Though his approach was novel in that it considered femininity at all, it did so within the bounds of an extremely rigid and narrow conception that was—even at the time it was written—both unaware of the realities of most women's lives and unable to account for the range and diversity of women's criminal offending.

I have argued that feminist scholars contributed in an important way to the focus on the link between masculinity and crime that has emerged during the past twenty-five years, making the first crucial links between women's victimization and social norms and practices that shape entitled, aggressive masculinity. Feminists have in fact made the cause of women victims of men's violence central to both theorizing and practice, an issue I discuss in more depth in chapter 4. Women who commit crime pose a much thornier problem. Feminist theory has been most comfortable with women offenders who are victims, as in the case of the battered woman who, after years of abuse, murders her batterer. Surely such cases are important, and there is no question that these women are often treated unfairly by the court system (see chapter 3). But this scenario does not represent the reality of crime for most women. As the tables earlier in this chapter indicate, most crimes for which women are arrested are mundane—petty property offenses, drug crimes, and simple assaults. Yet theorizing about gender has largely ignored such women.

One complication is that the lines between victimization and offending are not clear. By some accounts, up to 80 percent of women in prison in the United States have experienced physical or sexual abuse, much of it at the hands of intimates. Few of these women directly victimize their abusers, however. And it is these instances—which constitute the great majority of criminal offending among women—that have been the hard cases for feminist theorizing. Daly and Maher (1998) frame the questions that have thus far kept criminal women largely hidden from view:

> How should feminist scholars represent women who abuse, harm, or hurt others? Or women who steal from others? How should the idea of responsibility relate to these acts, or would feminist legal or criminological discourse propose a different definition of "responsibility"? . . . Where does victimization end and responsibility for acts that harm others begin? How do we characterize women when they do things that are wrong? (137–49)

Ignoring criminal women or viewing them only as victims essentially reiterates the arguments of early biological and sociological criminologists. Criminal women are either *not women* and thus safely outside the purview of a discipline focused on studying them, or they are *not criminal* and their apparent offending need not be considered. The challenge for feminism is to integrate even the "bad girls" into our understanding of gender and into our strategies for change. This project is still very much a work in progress. What is required is a more nuanced way of understanding women's involvement in crime, one in which we recognize that many women do indeed engage in acts that harm others. At the same time, however, we must acknowledge that crime, like all behavior, takes place in a gendered social context that shapes and directs both the performance and the rewards of that behavior. The best work on women's criminal offending takes just such a both/and perspective, admitting the reality of women's criminality while at the same time highlighting the power of the gendered social structure in which it takes place.

Jody Miller's (1998; Miller and White 2004) study of women street robbers is a particularly good example. Robbery—defined as the taking of property by force or threat—is one of the most sex-differentiated of all crimes; almost 90 percent of those arrested for this offense in 2009 were men. Robbery is also masculine gender-typed, in that masculinity is a seemingly logical requisite for taking someone's property by force. Miller interviewed fourteen women in St. Louis who admitted engaging in street robbery; she then compared these accounts with interviews of twenty-three male street robbers conducted as part of the same study (Wright and Decker 1997). Her work thus gives us a unique comparative vantage point from which to view the intersections between gender and crime.

Perhaps surprisingly, Miller finds that men and women report engaging in robbery for the same reasons. The primary incentive for both is to acquire resources and luxury items such as jewelry; as "Libbie" puts it: "You can get good things from a robbery" (Miller 1998, 44). Another woman explains: "I be sitting on the porch and we'll get to talking and stuff. See people going around and they be flashing in they fancy cars, walking down the street with that jewelry on, thinking they all bad, and we just go get 'em" (1998, 45). Men similarly describe their motivations for engaging in robbery; as one puts it, "[I rob people] when I'm tired of not having money" (1998, 45). In terms of the reasons for committing robbery, the influence of gender appears to be relatively minimal. Both men and women commit street robbery because they want to acquire money or property.

Miller finds that gender fundamentally shapes the methods and rewards of robbery, however. Very much in line with norms of conventional masculinity, men almost invariably commit their offenses with guns and approach their victims directly. When men do not use guns, they employ strong-arm techniques, relying on sheer physical force to induce victims to part with their property. Women use a range of different tactics. Some combine forces with other women to commit robberies, most often with no weapon at all. One describes a recent robbery that fits this mold:

> I was like with three other girls and we was like all walking around . . . walking around the block trying to find something to do on a Saturday night with really nothing to do and so we started coming up the street, we didn't have no weapons on us at the time. All we did was just start jumping on her and beating her up and took her purse. (1998, 53)

When women do use weapons to commit robbery they tend to use knives instead of guns. Unlike men, women also rarely describe approaching their victims alone and using sheer physical force to accomplish their objectives.

Both men and women choose their targets from the same general pool—victimizing others involved in street life or who live in their neighborhoods. The major difference is that men tend to attack other men while women target women. Miller argues that the men in her study do not see robbing women as a particularly valuable demonstration of masculinity—women are "easy to get," as one puts it. Robbing men on the other hand provides a resource for doing masculinity, it is a "masculine accomplishment in which men compete with other men for money and status" (Miller 1998, 50). In the male-dominated world of the street, dominating the strong is one avenue through which men can appear powerful to themselves and to other men.

For women who commit street robberies, the most common targets are other women. This is because like their male counterparts, women see other women as easier targets, as weaker and less likely to resist. As "Libbie" puts it: "I wouldn't do no men by myself [but women victims] ain't gonna do nothing because they be so scared" (Miller 1998, 52). Street robbery is hence a crime with a pattern of intrasex victimization—men target other men, women prey on women victims. This is a product of a gendered status hierarchy. For men, robbery becomes a vehicle for demonstrating masculinity by dominating other, perhaps stronger, men, and for women the choice of "weaker" targets is one way of doing femininity. This gendered pecking order has implications in terms of the material rewards of crime as well. Though Miller does not collect data on her subjects' earnings from robbery, it is very likely that for women, street robbery is a less lucrative enterprise than it is for men. As one male robber put it, "I rob men [because] they got money" (Miller 1998, 50). Women on the street are less likely to carry substantial cash and hence the rewards of robbing them are not as great.

As a general rule, women acting alone never target men. When women do rob men, they almost always describe working in concert with male accomplices. There is one exception to this rule, however, and it provides an interesting window into the operation of gender on the streets. The most common methods lone women use to rob men revolve around appearing sexually available or playing on men's notions about women's vulnerability. Some of these robberies take place in the context of prostitution; in other situations women might flirt with a man at a nightclub or party and then go with him to a car or a private place, where they confront him with a knife. Other women exploit men's stereotypical expectations about femininity. As "Quick" explains: "They don't suspect that a girl gonna try to get 'em. . . . So it's kind of easier cause they like, she looks innocent, she ain't gonna do this, but that's how I get 'em. They put they guard down to a woman" (Miller 1998, 55). In these situations women deploy men's sexism to their advantage, relying on the fact that men do not see women as particularly threatening or powerful. In both of these cases women actively use gender as a resource that facilitates their criminal activity.

Taken together, these findings demonstrate both gender similarity and difference. Women do not engage in robbery in order to meet different needs or to accomplish different goals. The differences that do emerge, however, reflect practical choices made in the constrained context of a stratified environment (Miller 1998, 61). Men and women robbers act in the gendered milieu of the streets, one in which men are the dominant players. Women do not commit robberies in the same way nor do they participate in robberies on an equal basis with men. Men dominate other men through sheer force; women choose "weaker" targets, are less likely to use guns, and play on ideas about femininity to set up male victims. Gender thus both shapes the context in which robbery occurs—that is, it is a key dimension of power on the streets, and robbery in itself serves as a resource for doing gender (Miller 2008).

This is true of other crimes as well. Lisa Maher's (1997) study of sex and drug markets in a poor neighborhood in Brooklyn demonstrates many of the patterns apparent in Miller's work. In line with the wage gap experienced by women street robbers, Maher finds that women are at the lowest levels of the drug trade, rarely allowed to sell drugs by the men who control the market. When women do sell, they generally occupy riskier locations and are allotted less merchandise, meaning that their incomes are low relative to men who sell drugs. As in the legitimate economy, men and women tend to engage in different kinds of criminal occupations, a phenomenon that sociologists of work have called job stratification by sex. Men dominate the most lucrative illegal activities, like drugs sales and theft. Women more often work as prostitutes, sometimes exchanging sex for drugs or in other instances making as little as two dollars per transaction. The necessarily private and vulnerable conditions under which prostitution occurs mean that women are especially susceptible to victimization, and indeed many tell horrific stories of serious physical assault.

Locked out of the most lucrative venues in the drug market, Maher finds that women innovate, creating economic niches by providing services related to the demand for drugs. Women can make money by "tipping," or directing potential customers—many of who come from outside the neighborhood—to locations where they can buy drugs. "Yolanda" describes how this works:

> They come up to me . . . they ask me what dope is good. They would come to me, they would pay me. They would come "What's good out there?" I would tell them "Where's a dollar?," and that's how I use to make my money. (Maher 1997, 89)

Women also sell or rent the paraphernalia needed to use drugs, the crack pipes used to smoke cocaine, and the "works" necessary to inject heroin. As most states have made the possession of such items a criminal offense, many customers prefer to buy or rent such items on site. Women also make money by "copping" drugs, or buying them for customers who are unwilling to take the risk of buying drugs for themselves. "Rosa" says:

> You would be surprise [*sic*]. They'd be people very important, white people like lawyer, doctors that comes and gets off, you'd be surprised. I got two lawyers . . . they come give me money to go cop. I have been copping for them like over six months already. (1997, 102)

All three of these strategies allow women to make money in a highly gender-stratified environment. As the marginality of these activities makes clear, however, the income from such ventures does not begin to approach that acquired from the direct sale of drugs themselves. One other aspect of these accounts is worth noting. These women exploit yet another niche in the market, the race and class divide between buyers and sellers. Customers from outside the neighborhood, who are likely more race and class privileged than those for whom it is home, are by definition most likely to need or desire these services. This is clearly the case for the white doctors and lawyers for whom Rosa "cops" drugs. Their willingness to serve in these roles is double-edged, however; though it clearly brings them important resources, it also exposes them to considerable risk.

Recent studies of women's role in the production and use of methamphetamines document similarly gendered strategies. Men disproportionately control methamphetamine markets, "cook" the drug, and acquire the most integral components required in its manufacture (Brecht et al. 2004; Jenkot 2008; Lopez, Jurik, and Gilliard-Matthews 2009; Senjo 2005, 2007). Though some women participate in these roles, as in crack markets, they often perform secondary tasks, for example, scraping red phosphorous from matchbook covers or shopping for the pseudoephedrine pills that are essential ingredients in methamphetamine. As "Brandy" explains: "I would shop a lot, you know go get the pills. Truck stops are great for that, plus you get to go on a nice drive!" (Jenkot 2008, 678). Sex work is not as intimately intertwined with methamphetamine markets as it has been with crack cocaine. Even so, women still describe relying on gendered and sexualized strategies to obtain the drug, as in the case of Selena: "I think that it's easier for girls to get drugs. I would just sit there and look pretty and they would just give me drugs. . . . Guys have it and they sell it more than girls do, but girls just get it like that [snaps fingers]. . . ." (Lopez, Jurik, and Gilliard-Matthews 2009, 240–41). As in the legitimate economy, women's roles in the criminal world (as well as men's) are shaped by gendered constraints and expectations that both limit women's participation at the highest levels of criminal enterprises and dictate their behavior in line with norms about what women can and should do.

These studies represent the best of a new generation of feminist criminology that is taking on the women who present "hard cases" for feminism and applying a gender lens to understand their participation in crime. Contrary to traditional accounts of women's behavior in mainstream criminology, this work shows that women who commit crime are neither pseudo-men, acting out a fantasized masculinity, nor are they casual participants in crime, interested only in relationships and shoplifting the latest fashions. Further, and in contradistinction to the arguments of liberation theorists, neither are women liberated female "ganstas," enjoying power and status equal to their male counterparts. Women (and men) instead engage in crime in the gendered context of the street, a world that shapes their opportunities, rewards, and performances of gendered identities.[5]

ENGENDERING THE OUTLAW—VIEWING OFFENDING THROUGH A GENDER LENS

Crime is not committed in a social vacuum by generic individuals. Indeed, one of the most important contributions of sociological criminology has been to foreground the importance of social context in shaping criminal behavior, whether it takes the form of the characteristics of neighborhoods, one's social class position, or one's associates. Applying a gendered analysis takes us yet another step in this process, arguing not only that context is important, but that it is also gendered. We can see this along at least two dimensions. Sociologists who study work and organizations (e.g., Acker 1990; Britton 2003; Martin 2003) in the legitimate economy have noted that these social institutions are gendered in a structural sense—they are built on assumptions and characterized by divisions of labor, policies and practices that tend to benefit men. These sociologists of the mainstream economy rarely turn their attention to crime, and criminologists rarely study work. As Messerschmidt's analysis of the *Challenger* disaster demonstrates, the same gendered structures that these sociologists have documented in corporations and in the state are also conducive to crime. Similarly, criminal offending at the level of the streets is structurally gendered in much the same way as work in the legitimate economy—men dominate the upper levels of the hierarchy, control the most lucrative activities and reap the greatest rewards. Women rarely participate in this world on an equal basis with men, but instead must make choices in an opportunity structure in which only the least lucrative options are available to them. They occupy what we might characterize as the "service sector" of the criminal economy and their returns from criminal activity are comparatively lower.

Criminal offending is also gendered in the sense of performance of identity. Both men and women do gender by engaging in crime. The activities in which men engage on the street reflect assumptions about masculinity. Men are more likely to be involved in violent crimes, and their targets, methods and understandings of their actions also reflect cultural ideals of masculinity. As "Perry," one of the boys interviewed by Messerschmidt (2000) puts it:

> [Being masculine is] Having the courage to do things . . . if you had balls enough to go break into a house or steal a car. . . . And being masculine [is] screwing the most girls, who could fight the best . . . who could hold the most beer, smoke the most weed. (70)

For Perry, and very much in line with mainstream notions of masculinity, being a man entails competition, dominance, and "having the balls" to do things. Crime is simply one avenue, though an illegitimate one, through which masculinity may be expressed.

Women also do gender by engaging in crime. The connection between femininity and criminal offending is less obvious than the link to masculinity, however. Traditional (white, middle-class) femininity is passive, crime is by definition active. Given this, it is hard to imagine what a feminine criminal would look like, a fact that perhaps led Lombroso to conclude that such women were actually hiding male genitalia under their skirts. Women's prostitution is the one crime that has been categorized by criminologists as the feminine crime par excellence, involving as it does the sexual "servicing" of men by women who respond to their requests. But even this view minimizes the role that prostitutes themselves play in selecting their clients, controlling the choices of sexual activities, and negotiating rates of payment (Bernstein 2007). Criminal women are in fact active agents who nonetheless may still enact femininity through their offenses. We see this clearly in the cases of the women in Miller's study (1998) who deploy femininity as a resource in robbing unsuspecting men, or in the strategies of the women Maher (1997) studied who carve out economic niches for themselves in the service sector of the criminal economy. The rewards of doing gender through crime are less for women than for their male counterparts, and in many ways draw on and reproduce notions about femininity that help to rationalize gender inequality.

The fact that gender and sex are not one and the same opens the possibility of a sort of transgendered criminology. Theoretically, we might say that men could do femininity through crime or that women could do masculinity. This latter combination is the subject of some debate in criminology (the former has thus far been unexplored) (see for example the exchange between Miller and Messerschmidt—Miller 2002a, 2002b; Messerschmidt 2002). What do we make, for example, of "Latisha," the girl whose account opens this chapter? Formulating their answers against a legacy of theory in which criminal women have been characterized as virtual hermaphrodites or as liberated pseudo-men, theorists have understandably been cautious in making claims. If we are to take the distinction between sex and gender seriously, however, we must allow for the possibility that women too can perform masculinity—as men can do femininity. As they are for men, however, women's performances of masculinity are always unstable and contingent. Men perform masculinity at continual risk of being exposed as less than "real men." For women the situation is even more complex. As Latisha says: "We just like dudes, they treat us like that. . . . They respect us as females though." Taking Latisha's experiences seriously requires a conception of gender that does not fall into the old dichotomies of masculinity and femininity—that does not see the latter simply as whatever women do—but instead views gender as a dynamic range of forces and identities. Latisha "acts like a dude" but gets "respect as a female." It is ironic indeed that the lives of women so utterly ignored by the mainstream of gender theorizing may in fact be so instrumental in pushing the boundaries of our understandings of gender.

3

Gender and the Criminal Justice System

There's a few things about women inmates I've learned. Women convicts are usually more violent, have been given several more chances. And that's just the way we were raised, as a society was raised. You respect women, you don't take women away from their children. And all these inmates, you go back and start pulling files, have these many chances as far as the law. . . . And, whereas, you look at a guy's record, it might be the second offense and they're doing time. Society's just raised to be more lenient toward women before you lock them up. (male correctional officer, quoted in Britton 2003)

In this chapter I turn to a gendered analysis of the criminal justice system.[1] By criminal justice system (CJS) I mean the body of statutes that makes up the criminal law and describes violations and penalties as well as the network of agencies—the police, the courts, and the prison system—charged with enforcing those statutes. Like the officer quoted here, most Americans believe that women are treated more leniently by the CJS, that they are less likely to be arrested and to receive harsh punishments. This is an idea that criminologists have labeled "chivalry" theory. As I will demonstrate, this notion is largely inaccurate; at the very least the picture is considerably more complicated than this bit of folk wisdom suggests.

For most of our history, laws in the United States have made explicit distinctions between individuals, between men and women, blacks and whites, the rich and the poor, and the CJS has acted to enforce those distinctions. The founding document of the United States, our Constitution, in fact differentiated between "free persons," slaves, and "all other persons" (in actuality, everyone except slaves and free white property-holding men). The law did not recognize those in these last two categories as fully human; each was to be counted as three-fifths of a person for the purposes of apportioning legislative representation (U.S. Constitution, Article 3). Decisions of the U.S. Supreme Court have affirmed laws mandating differential treatment for some groups, for example, upholding the doctrine of "separate but equal" in the segregation of the races (*Plessy v. Ferguson*, 163 U.S. 537, 1896), allowing the forced removal of Asian Americans to internment camps during World War II (*Korematsu v. United States*, 323 U.S. 214, 1944), and affirming the forced sterilization of "feeble minded" women (*Buck v. Bell*, 274 U.S. 200, 1927).[2] Practices of incarceration, like the growth of the reformatory system during the late nineteenth and early twentieth centuries—in which reformers targeted the most "redeemable" (white) inmates (Pisciotta 1994; Freedman 1981; Rafter 1990)—further reflected and perpetuated long-standing patterns of race, class, and gender inequality. For most of U.S. history the CJS has been one of the primary instruments through which systems of inequality have been encoded and maintained.

We now live in an age in which most laws are sex (and race, and class) neutral on their face and in which most of us expect, or at least hope, they will be enforced without prejudice. Examples like *Plessy v. Ferguson* and the other instances described above now serve as markers of how far we have come and are often used to illustrate the excesses and irrationalities of a system now purportedly reformed. Yet from the perspective of most observers, justice in America remains only an ideal. Viewing the criminal justice system from a perspective that highlights gender, race, and class (among other dimensions) is one way to assess our progress toward that ideal.

CURRENT CRIMINAL LAW AND SOCIAL INEQUALITY

There remain very few instances of criminal statutes that explicitly distinguish between classes of people. Perhaps the largest set of such laws make a distinction on the basis of age—it is, for example, illegal to run away from home if you are under the age of eighteen; it is not criminal to do so if you are nineteen or older. Similarly, it is now illegal in all U.S. states for people under the age of twenty-one to buy alcoholic beverages. Crimes like running away, breaking curfew, and underage drinking are known as "status offenses," that is, the behavior is criminal only because of the status (in this case the age) of the offender.

Most other laws that make such distinctions between classes of people apply to family relationships. The law in many states defines sexual relations between adults and related children as incest, for example, and between adults and unrelated children as sexual assault (or perhaps as indecency with a child). As recently as 1976, most laws on rape did not apply to husbands and wives—if a husband had sex with his wife without her consent he could not be prosecuted. Though some form of marital rape is now a crime in all fifty states, vestiges of the old laws remain. In Kansas, for example, though a husband (or a wife) can be charged with rape—defined as sexual intercourse without consent—the statute on sexual battery (essentially, sexual assault without intercourse, and a lesser offense than rape) explicitly excludes spouses:

> Kansas Statute 21-3517. Sexual battery. (a) Sexual battery is the intentional touching of the person of another who is 16 or more years of age, *who is not the spouse of the offender* and who does not consent thereto, with the intent to arouse or satisfy the sexual desires of the offender or another. (Kansas Statutes unannotated, current as of May 2010, emphasis mine)

The Kansas case is not unique; the majority of states retain laws that in some ways shield sexual coercion from punishment when it is committed in the context of a married or cohabiting relationship.

Until very recently, criminal laws in almost all states also discriminated on the basis of sexual orientation, criminalizing sexual behavior (usually oral or anal sex) between members of the same sex that was legal for opposite-sex couples. For example, while Kansas recognized oral and anal sex between heterosexuals as sodomy, it nonetheless did not criminalize such behavior.[3] In *Lawrence v. Texas* (539 U.S. 558, 2003) the Supreme Court declared that such distinctions violate the Constitution's Fourth Amendment guarantee of equal protection—that is, that they single out one group (gay men, lesbians, and bisexuals) for punishment for engaging in the same behavior that is legal among members of another.[4] It is worth noting that civil, family, and administrative law, though not the focus of this chapter, also discriminate on the basis of sexual orientation. As of this writing, gays and lesbians are generally barred from marrying and may be fired or denied housing on the basis of sexual orientation. These restrictions create profound ripple effects; according to a government report (General Accounting Office 1997), there are 1,138 benefits that accrue to married heterosexual couples that are not available to gay and lesbian couples. These include a range of rights, from receiving social security benefits after the death of a spouse, to enjoying lower tax rates by filing joint returns, to the ability to receive unpaid leave to care for an ailing spouse. Discrimination on the basis of sexual orientation may in fact be the most entrenched explicit form of class-based unequal treatment remaining in American law.

Discrimination by Effect

Beyond these instances, most criminal law no longer singles out particular classes of individuals for punishment. The law's purported neutrality does not mean that the law itself—as written—cannot be discriminatory, however. In fact, the most common way that the law now discriminates is *by effect*. For example, a guideline prescribing a high bail for a particular offense is by its nature discriminatory on the basis of class; those with more wealth will be able to afford bail while the poor will remain in jail, where they often face a lengthy wait for their cases to be adjudicated. Sixty-three percent of those in American jails—almost five hundred thousand people—have not been convicted of the offense for which they were arrested; they are awaiting trial and have either been denied bail or are being held in lieu of a bond being paid (Minton and Sabol 2009). A law prescribing a high bail discriminates not in its intention but in its *effect*; though the statute is facially neutral, in application it penalizes one group more than another.

Federal drug sentencing guidelines offer another extremely important example of discrimination by effect. In 1986, Congress enacted a set of mandatory minimum sentences for a specific set of drug offenses. The guidelines specify mandatory five- and ten-year sentences triggered by the amount of a particular substance an offender possesses, either for sale or consumption. Only in exceptional circumstances may judges depart from these guidelines—all offenders with the requisite amount of a drug must receive the minimum sentence regardless of the circumstances of their crime. For LSD, the possession of one gram (an amount approximately equal to one packet of sweetener) requires the imposition of a minimum five-year sentence; ten grams means a ten-year sentence.[5]

The most controversial part of the policy lies in the distinction Congress made between crack cocaine and powder cocaine. Pharmacologically the same drug, crack is a form of powder cocaine that is combined with other substances and cooked into a rock form. It is less pure than powder cocaine and also less expensive, a fact that has made it especially popular among drug users who are poor. Under federal mandatory minimums as of 2009, a sentence of five years is required if an offender possesses five hundred grams (about a pound) of powder cocaine, but only twenty grams (0.7 ounces) of crack cocaine. Ten-year sentences are triggered by five kilograms (about ten pounds) of powder cocaine, but only 150 grams of crack cocaine (slightly more than five ounces). There is thus more than a twenty-five-to-one disparity in the quantity of powder versus crack cocaine that trigger the very same sentences (as of 2010, this disparity has been reduced to eighteen to one).[6] For methamphetamine, a drug that has recently been the subject of considerable public attention, the comparable numbers are five years for five grams (0.175 ounces) of "actual" (pure) methamphetamine and ten years for five hundred grams.[7] These guidelines are not explicitly racist; they apply to all offenders equally, regardless of race or class.

According to statistics from the 2008 National Survey of Drug Use and Health (NSDUH), whites were 65 percent of those who had used crack during the past year, African Americans 23 percent, and Latinos 8 percent (Substance Abuse and Mental Health Services Administration 2009). As African Americans make up about 13 percent of the U.S. population, this means that African Americans are disproportionately likely to be subject to the harsher crack cocaine sentencing guidelines. In specifying higher penalties for a type of cocaine more likely to be used by African Americans, mandatory minimums thus discriminate *by effect*; the law exposes one group to much higher penalties than another for using what is essentially the same substance. It is important to remember, however, that whites—not African Americans, are the majority of crack users.

Discrimination in Practice

If all defendants convicted of crack cocaine offenses were in fact equally subject to sentencing under the guidelines, we would expect that whites would receive about 65 percent of sentences for crack cocaine, African Americans 23 percent, and Latinos 8 percent. Sentencing data indicate a much larger disparity in the enforcement of the law, however. As table 3.1 indicates, in the year 2009, 79 percent of those prosecuted for crack cocaine in federal courts were African American, 10 percent were white, and 10 percent were Hispanic.[8] This suggests that discrimination also exists *in practice*, that is, in arresting, charging, and prosecuting drug offenders.

The extreme overrepresentation of African Americans among those prosecuted for crack, combined with the prescribed difference in sentencing, means that African American cocaine offenders spend substantially longer in prison than either whites or Hispanics. The median federal sentence for crack cocaine offenses of all kinds is now ninety-six months, compared with sixty-three months for powder cocaine (U.S. Sentencing Commission 2010). This sentencing rule is the key factor behind the gap between the prison sentences of African Americans and other groups, which began to widen dramatically in 1986 (the year the rule was imposed).

Table 3.1. Demographic Characteristics of Federal Drug Offenders, 2009

	Powder Cocaine		*Crack Cocaine*		*Methamphetamine*	
	Number	*Percent*	*Number*	*Percent*	*Number*	*Percent*
White	1,031	17	558	10	2,158	52
Black	1,684	28	4,476	79	118	3
Hispanic	3,202	53	584	10	1,577	38
Other	103	2	51	1	265	6
Total	6,020	100	5,669	100	4,118	100

Source: Adapted from table 34, United States Sentencing Commission 2010.

Though sentences are shorter for powder cocaine offenders, both blacks and Hispanics are overrepresented among those sentenced for these offenses as well. According to the NSDUH, whites are about 74 percent of powder cocaine users, African Americans 5 percent, and Hispanics 16 percent. As table 3.1 illustrates, however, Hispanics were 53 percent of those prosecuted in federal courts for powder cocaine offenses in the year 2009, with African Americans at 28 percent. This means that Hispanics are overrepresented among those prosecuted by a factor of three (they are 16 percent of users but 53 percent of those prosecuted), African Americans by a factor of six. Assuming NSDUH estimates are even close in capturing patterns of use by race, more than four times as many whites should be prosecuted than the current number.

The situation is somewhat different in the case of methamphetamine, in which sentencing practices have also toughened. Median sentences for those convicted of offenses in this category are seventy-two months (in contrast, the median sentence for heroin offenders is fifty-seven months). Whites are a majority (52 percent) of those prosecuted for these offenses. This reflects in some ways the regional distribution of methamphetamine use, which is more likely to be found in the West and Midwest. Even so, whites are underrepresented as defendants; data from the NSDUH indicates that whites are 78 percent of methamphetamine users. Hispanics, on the other hand, are dramatically overrepresented as defendants. Hispanics were 38 percent of those prosecuted on methamphetamine charges in 2009, yet they represent only an estimated 12 percent of all users.[9] More than three times as many Hispanics are prosecuted as one would expect given their distribution in the user population. The percentage of African Americans among those prosecuted (3 percent) roughly matches their estimated proportion among users (2 percent).

Federal mandatory minimums thus provide a particularly clear example of legal discrimination both *by effect* and *in practice*. Though the law is racially neutral on its face, it reserves harsher penalties for crack cocaine users, who are in turn disproportionately likely to be African American.[10] Sentencing statistics tell us that enforcement of the law has been discriminatory *in practice*; in terms of raw numbers of defendants, African Americans are eight times more likely than whites and Hispanics to be prosecuted for possession and distribution of crack cocaine. These statistics confirm that crack cocaine has been almost completely *racialized* in the eyes of the system (as well as in mainstream culture). The archetype of the crack user is the poor black man or woman, despite widespread use by whites, and this stereotyping affects enforcement at all levels of the system. Indeed, studies of police practices show that police focus on African American crack users and dealers with disproportionately greater intensity than on those who use and sell other drugs or on drug markets in white neighborhoods (Beckett et al. 2005). We see a similar pattern with Hispanics and powder cocaine. Hispanics are almost three times more likely than whites and about twice as likely as African Americans to be prosecuted for these offenses—a fact that is especially striking when we consider that whites make up about 75 percent of powder cocaine users.

There is little question that mandatory minimum sentences for drug offenses discriminate in effect as well as in practice. They have, in fact, been the target of considerable criticism by those who argue, in the case of the disparity between crack and powder cocaine, that the distinction between two forms of the same drug is both arbitrary and discriminatory (see, for example, www.famm.org). More generally, mandatory minimums have been attacked as expensive and ineffective strategies, the brunt of whose negative effects falls disproportionately on the most disadvantaged groups (United States Sentencing Commission 2004). Many judges have joined the ranks of those opposed to mandatory minimums, with some even resigning from the bench in protest at the law's inflexibility and restriction of judicial discretion. As of late 2010, President Obama signed into a law a bill reducing the disparity between crack and powder cocaine sentences to eighteen to one. Though certainly this represents a substantial change from the hundred-to-one disparity originally specified by Congress, the fact remains that those who are prosecuted in the federal courts for crack cocaine still face tougher penalties than those sentenced for powder cocaine offenses. Moreover, the underlying strategy of imposing mandatory minimum sentences remains in place.[11]

GENDER INEQUALITY AND THE CRIMINAL JUSTICE SYSTEM

Like race, class, and sexuality, sex and gender have also historically served as the basis for explicit discrimination in criminal law. Historically, states criminalized a variety of behaviors in the case of women, morals offenses like saloon visiting and "waywardness," that were not crimes if engaged in by men. Though these laws discriminated on the basis of sex—they made a distinction between biological men and women—in reality they attempted to regulate gender, enforcing the bounds of behavior those in power believed appropriate to (white, middle-class) femininity. These statutes criminalized women in a generic sense; in theory any woman could be charged with such offenses. In reality, however, there is no such thing as a generic woman. African American women, for example, bore—and still carry—the burden of discrimination on the basis of race *and* sex and were hence subject both to the criminal laws that enforced the behavior of "ladies" as well as those that prescribed separation and difference between the races.

As with race and class, most criminal statutes that made categorical distinctions on the basis of sex and gender have largely disappeared. What remains instead is gender inequality perpetuated by effect and through practice. In the rest of this section I provide a broad overview of what we know about the criminal justice system and gender inequality in the law itself, as well as at the stages of arrest, charging and prosecution, and incarceration.

Gender Inequality and Current Criminal Law

We can see gender discrimination by effect in a number of instances in the criminal statutes. Probably the most straightforward lies in most states' laws on prostitution. In all states (with the exception of a few counties in Nevada), both purchasing the services of a prostitute and selling such services are criminal offenses. The laws are sex-neutral; both men and women can be arrested for buying or selling sexual services. States generally penalize selling sex more harshly than purchasing it, however, a decision that invariably singles out women for the most serious punishments. Most prostitutes are women and almost without exception customers are men—whether the prostitutes are male, female, or transgender. The framing of the law thus means that in effect women who sell sex are punished more severely than the men who buy it. The enforcement of laws on prostitution also leads to clear discrimination in practice. Prostitutes are much more likely to be arrested than are their customers (without whose demand there would be no prostitution). In 2009, only about 30 percent of those arrested for involvement in prostitution were men (Federal Bureau of Investigation 2010). Some of these individuals were undoubtedly prostitutes themselves, which means that customers are quite significantly underrepresented among those singled out by the law for charging and punishment.

Prostitution accounts for less than 2 percent of women's arrests, however. Drug offenses, on the other hand, rank among the top arrest categories for women. About 10 percent of women arrested per year are charged with drug crimes—a number that amounted to 242,414 in 2009. I have demonstrated some of the ways that drug laws discriminate on the basis of race, but several features also uniquely disadvantage women as a group. One striking example lies in the legal expansion of child abuse statutes as part of the war on drugs. Over the past twenty-five years, a number of states passed laws that allow pregnant women who use drugs (and who are generally addicted) to be charged with felony child abuse for exposing their fetuses to drugs. In fact, in some states pregnant women can be charged with homicide if their babies are stillborn or if they miscarry. The scientific rationale for these charges—the notion of the developmentally disabled "crack baby"—is the subject of considerable debate among experts, but the emerging consensus is that cocaine, in particular, is no more harmful to fetuses than poor nutrition, lack of prenatal care, or other circumstances commonly encountered by poor mothers (Flavin 2008; Flavin and Paltrow 2010).[12] This is an example in which the law discriminates quite explicitly on the basis of sex—the fathers of these babies cannot be prosecuted for child abuse for delivering drugs to fetuses in utero.

Another less explicit example can be found in federal laws prescribing punishments for drug conspiracies. As I noted in chapter 2, women's participation in drug markets is usually marginal. Studies tell us that women are less likely to control these markets, that they are involved in selling to a lesser degree and at lower levels than men, and that often their connection to drug selling comes through an associated man, often a husband or boyfriend (e.g., Maher 1997; Evans, Forsyth, and Gauthier 2002; Lopez, Jurik, and Gilliard-Matthews 2009).

Before the passage of "get tough" laws such as mandatory minimums, judges had considerable discretion to consider women's role and mitigate or suspend their sentences if they felt that a woman should be held less responsible in a particular case. In 1988, however, Congress passed the "Anti-Drug Abuse Act," a statute that provides, among other things, that all persons involved in a conspiracy to sell drugs are held responsible for the full amount of the substance involved, regardless of their role (Nagel and Johnson 1994). The word *conspiracy* has been interpreted quite loosely prosecutors and the courts; members of a conspiracy might include d kingpins, street-level sellers, or even those who do not sell drugs but are nonetheless associated with those who do. As written, this law is neutral. In application it has meant that wives and girlfriends have been charged in major drug cases in which their only roles were asso with the men who actually controlled a selling operation.

One such case is that of Tammi Bloom, an African American wo rently serving a sentence in federal prison for drug distribution. husband distributed cocaine, primarily from an apartment he sh his mistress in another city. Though there were drugs in the hous with Tammi and their two children, they were hidden—even f a septic tank in the back yard. According to the testimony witness, a confidential informant, Tammi's sole participatio selling operation was her presence at one of the drug sale ring which her husband directed her to count the mone had no prior criminal convictions of any kind. In nspiracy statutes, however, she was held r gs seized at the house and the co Her sentence was further i eized from the hous minimum s enter wthan her husband's sentence of seventeen years and six months or his mistress's six-year, six-month sentence. Both the husband and the mistress plea bargained their cases, which resulted in lower sentences. Tammi's sentence was conversely increased by an obstruction of justice charge applied because she argued for her innocence at trial (Families Against Mandatory Minimums undated). Women's lesser role in drug markets means that any law holding minor players as accountable as major ones will have a disproportionate impact on women. The case of Tammi Bloom and literally thousands of others like her illustrates this in sharp detail.[13]

Moreover, criminal law does not exist in a vacuum. Its effects are amplified by other bodies of statutes. For example, laws in thirty states deny the right to vote to convicted felons on parole or probation; two disenfranchise felons for life. These laws have excluded an estimated 5.3 million people ᵒm voter rolls, denying the vote to about 13 percent of black men in ᵉ United States (Manza and Uggen 2006; Sentencing Project 2010). For ᵉn, one area of convergence that has had particularly negative effects ᵉn that between the criminal law and administrative rules governing ᵉlfare policy. Women, especially single mothers and their children, 90 percent of those who receive government assistance such as ᵉsidies, food stamps, and direct welfare assistance (now known Aid to Needy Families, or TANF). The Personal Responsibility ᵣtunity Reconciliation Act (PRWORA), passed by Congress the welfare system, instituted a lifetime ban on public ᵒr otherwise eligible recipients convicted of drug felo-193, section 115). Additional stipulations bar those ᵗion violations for any crime. Taken together, these 100,000 women from federal assistance (Haney already know about who is most affected by ᵉs and sentencing guidelines, it is obvious ᵒor women of color and their children, are ᵉs (Allard 2002).

ᵢslation that has followed in its wake ᵒf laws that perpetuate gender (and *in practice*. With the exception of ᵒf these laws singles women out the net of social control to ᵒse who associate wit ᵗions to th

incarceration. In the next sections I review what we know about gender inequality in the practices of actors and institutions at each of these levels.

Gender Inequality in Policing

When it comes to gender and the police, one of the most enduring images in the public imagination is that of the apocryphal traffic stop in which a crying woman is let off the hook by the sympathetic male officer. This mythical vision is at the heart of chivalry theory, which is the notion that women are treated more leniently by the police—and by the criminal justice system generally—than are men. Decades of research on police discretion have, in some instances, contradicted this notion. At the very least what we now know about gender and the everyday practices of police complicates this image considerably.

At first glance, chivalry does indeed seem to rule the day. Men are in fact more likely to be arrested than women; as I note in chapter 2, about three times more men are arrested than women in any given year. But this fact alone tells us little. It may be that men are simply three times more likely than women to commit crimes, or that they commit more serious infractions than women and so are more likely to be arrested. Information collected from self-report surveys, in which individuals are asked to report on their own criminal activity, confirms that men do indeed commit significantly more crime than women and that they heavily predominate among serious violent offenders. This means that differences in arrest rates may not confirm the presence or absence of chivalry.

Data on traffic stops—the scenario that epitomizes chivalry theory—also indicate that among those adults who drive a car at least a few times a year, men are more likely than women to report being stopped. According to a survey conducted by the United States Department of Justice (Bureau of Justice Statistics 2008), 10.8 percent of men reported being stopped by the police in 2005, versus 6.9 percent of women. Table 3.2 depicts data on the outcome of these stops. As the table indicates, women are somewhat more likely than men to receive warnings and less likely to receive tickets. These differences are on the order of less than seven percentage points, and the majority of both men and women receive tickets. At best we find mixed evidence for chivalry—though men are somewhat more likely to be stopped, they are only slightly less likely than women to receive warnings, a fact that generally belies the myth of the crying woman and the chivalrous officer. There is much these data do not tell us, however. They provide no information, for example, on whether men are simply more likely to be driving (and we know that men do, in fact, drive more frequently), or speeding, than women. What they do demonstrate is that once a driver has been pulled over, the decision to ticket is essentially neutral on the basis of sex.

Table 3.2. Traffic Stops by Percentage of Population, 2005

	Total Pop.	Men	Women	White	Black	Hispanic
Stopped	8.8	10.8	6.9	8.9	8.1	8.9
Warning	25.8	23.2	30.1	27.4	21.4	19.5
Ticket	57.1	59.7	52.9	55.8	55.8	64.6
Searched driver or vehicle	4.6	6.5	1.5	3.4	9.0	8.7
Handcuffed driver	2.5	3.4	0.9	2.1	3.9	3.6
Arrested driver	2.3	3.1	1.1	2.0	4.2	3.3
Use of force	0.8	1.1	0.4	0.6	1.8	2.1
Excessive use of force	0.5	0.8	0.1	0.4	1.1	1.4

Source: Author calculation, Bureau of Justice Statistics 2008.

The more serious outcomes of traffic stops—being searched, handcuffed, arrested, or being the recipient of force on the part of police, are also shown in table 3.2. Men are more likely than women to experience all of these police behaviors. This finding is undoubtedly confounded by race, however; it seems likely that all men do not experience these consequences proportionately. While whites, blacks, and Hispanics are about equally likely to be stopped, Hispanics and blacks face the most serious consequences of traffic stops; they are less likely to receive warnings, and Hispanics in particular are much more likely to be ticketed. African Americans and Hispanics are, on average, about two to three times more likely than whites to experience the other, more serious events depicted in the table.

The BJS does not report data on traffic stops by sex *and* race. It is not possible to know from this table whether white men are less likely to be stopped or ticketed or searched than black men, for example, or whether white women benefit from chivalry more than Hispanic women. It is reasonable to suspect that differences of this kind exist. The mythical crying woman by the side of the road is both a gendered and a racialized image—she is a white woman, relying on traditional femininity to manipulate the officer at her window. Similarly, notions about dangerous and criminal populations are built on race and gender stereotypes; black and Hispanic men have come to represent, for mainstream white America, archetypal images of violent, uncontrollable masculinity.

Because data collected in government surveys are available to the public, it is possible to test this notion; table 3.3 displays the results of such an analysis. As in table 3.2, all groups of women are less likely to be stopped than are men, but these differences are on the order of no more than four percentage points. Once drivers are stopped (though the majority in all groups receive tickets), white women and African American women are

Table 3.3. Traffic Stops by Percentage of Race/Sex Group, 2005

	White Men	*Black Men*	*Hispanic Men*	*White Women*	*Black Women*	*Hispanic Women*
Stopped	10.9	9.9	10.7	7.0	6.5	6.7
Warning	24.9	16.8	18.4	31.3	27.8	21.5
Ticket	58.3	59.0	65.6	52.0	51.5	62.7
Searched driver or vehicle	4.8	13.7	12.4	1.3	N/A	N/A
Handcuffed driver	2.8	5.9	5.6	1.0	N/A	N/A
Arrested driver	2.6	5.8	5.0	1.0	N/A	N/A
Use of force	0.8	3.1	2.6	0.4	N/A	N/A
Excessive use of force	0.5	1.8	2.1	N/A	N/A	N/A

Source: Author calculation, Bureau of Justice Statistics 2008.

N/A indicates estimate would be based on ten or fewer sample cases.

least likely to be ticketed. Those most likely to receive tickets are Hispanic men, followed very closely by Hispanic women.

In terms of the other police behaviors tracked by the survey, black and Hispanic men are significantly more likely than other groups to be searched, handcuffed, arrested, and have force used against them. Many of these differences are quite large; for example, only 5 percent of white men were subject to searches by police, versus 14 percent of black men and 12 percent of Hispanic men. Given this disparity, it is definitely worth noting that additional data (not reported in this table) also show that police found *no incriminating evidence* in 87 percent of such roadside searches. In fact, the likelihood of finding such evidence was about equal for black male drivers (19 percent of searches) and white male drivers (16 percent) and least likely for Hispanic men (10 percent).

Do we see chivalry at work here? At best, we can say that the picture painted by these data is a complicated one, and that the probability of traffic stops and their outcomes is highly dependent on both the race and sex of the driver. Women of all races are less likely to be stopped, but these differences are quite small and probably have much to do with the fact that they drive less frequently than men. Once they have been stopped, Hispanic drivers, both men *and* women, are most likely to be ticketed, while white women, black women, and white men are most likely to receive warnings. Among women in particular the differences across groups are substantial—Hispanic women drivers are almost ten percentage points less likely to receive warnings and ten percentage points more likely to receive tickets than are white women.

The clearest effect revealed by this analysis is the much higher likelihood of aggressive police treatment for black and Hispanic men. White women are the least likely of all groups to experience these tactics; small sample sizes do not permit conclusions about other groups of women. Hence it is accurate to say that the intersection of race *and* sex matters—the group with the most consistently positive experiences is white women (though in fact black and Hispanic women are slightly less likely to be stopped), while black and Hispanic men fare worst regardless of the outcome. If chivalry exists, it appears to benefit white men as well as white women.

Useful though these data are, there is much they do not tell us. There are obviously many venues other than traffic stops in which citizens interact with the police. We also have no way of knowing from simply looking at these statistical tables how suspects behaved before and after they came into contact with the police or the circumstances under which they encountered police. And finally—and most importantly for the present purposes—the data can tell us only about *sex*, not gender. We know that males and females are treated differently, but we can only guess at the role that ideas and enactments of masculinities and femininities play in this process.

There is a very large volume of research on citizen encounters with the police that sheds light on these issues, however. Researchers using a variety of methods have found that both *legal* and *extralegal* factors shape the likelihood and the outcomes of such interactions. *Legal* factors center on the seriousness of the offense committed, as well as elements such as the presence of a weapon, injuries sustained by the victim, and other relatively objective elements of a crime. We might expect, for example, that police would react more harshly to a suspect fleeing the scene of a murder than to a youth caught shoplifting small items in a department store. Research indeed confirms that offense seriousness matters in just this way. Regardless of the study or method, we find that legal factors are generally the most important predictors of police behavior.

Extralegal factors—such as suspect conduct, race, gender, and age—matter as well, however. Police perceptions of suspects and citizens are shaped by cultural stereotypes, a fact that can lead to discrimination in police practice. Consonant with the data on traffic stops, research demonstrates that black men in particular bear the brunt of police suspicion and negative treatment, a pattern that is especially pronounced in poor inner-city communities. Here race and gender combine powerfully in the stereotype of the "criminalblackman" (Russell-Brown 1998, 3), a rhetorical equation in which blackness and masculinity come to equal (presumed) criminality in the eyes of the police (see also Anderson 1992; Hawkins 1995; Jones 2009; Mann and Zatz 1998; Miller 1996; Browning et al. 1994; Fagan and Davies 2000; Hurst, Frank, and Browning 2000; Mastrofski, Reisig, and McCluskey 2002; Smith and Holmes 2003; Terrill and Reisig 2003; Weitzer 1999).

And, as in the analysis of traffic stops, Hispanic men are also often disproportionately the targets of aggressive police enforcement tactics. An analysis of "stop and frisk" encounters between police and citizens in New York City in 2009 found that African Americans and Latinos were more than nine times as likely to be stopped by the police, but once stopped, they were *no more likely* to be arrested than whites. About 6 percent of all such stops—more than one hundred thousand in all—resulted in arrests. Though police claim that the tactic is a particularly effective one in getting guns off the street, about 1.1 percent of African Americans were found to be carrying weapons, while the percentage of whites carrying weapons was larger, 1.7 percent (Baker 2010). Recent changes in immigration law, like SB 1070 in Arizona, which allows police to stop and question anyone they suspect is in the country illegally, essentially guarantee that Hispanics will be subject to ever-more aggressive police enforcement tactics. Conversely, all of these cases illustrate what the bulk of the research also demonstrates, which is that white men experience much more lenient treatment at the hands of police than do their black and Hispanic counterparts (Fine et al. 2003).

Extralegal factors play a role in women's interactions with the police as well. One of the first major studies to examine this topic was conducted by Christy Visher in 1983. Visher found that demeanor—a citizen's behavior during an encounter with the police—was particularly important in shaping women's contacts with the police. Police leniency was a relatively uncommon occurrence in this study, but where it occurred it tended to be directed toward women more often than men, an outcome that apparently supports the claims of chivalry theorists. Not all women benefited equally, however. Specifically, Visher found that "chivalry exists at the stage of arrest for those women who display appropriate gender behaviors and characteristics" (1983, 5). Women who best fit the norms of traditional mainstream femininity, those who were white, appeared to be middle class, deferred to the police, and were older—in general, those whom the police judged to be "ladies"—were most likely to be shown leniency. Younger women, women of color, and those who failed to defer appropriately (both men and women) often received particularly harsh treatment, a finding that has been replicated in numerous studies since the publication of Visher's groundbreaking research (e.g., Engel, Sobol, and Worden 2000; Lundman 1994, 1996, 1998; Lundman and Kaufman 2003; Worden and Shepard 1996; Stolzenberg and D'Alessio 2004).

Gender Inequality and Sentencing

The issue of bias in sentencing men versus women has been an extremely contentious one among scholars. This is because there is little agreement on what equity would look like, how it might be achieved, or whether it is even a desirable goal. At first glance, testing for the existence of equitable treatment looks quite simple—just take men and women convicted of exactly the same crimes and see whether their punishment, for example, decision to incarcerate or sentence length, is the same. There are problems with this approach, however. First, pursuing this strategy inevitably takes men as the standard—treatment is "fair" when women receive the same punishment as men. Yet it is entirely possible that men's and women's sentences might be exactly the same and these sentences might still be unfair. As Maureen Cain notes: "[We must] question whether or not even absolutely equal sentences might be unjust . . . too high or too low in themselves, or [whether a given] behaviour . . . should not, from some standpoints at least, be subject to penalty" (1990, 2–3). Simple comparisons of this kind have the effect of justifying sentences given to men without considering the justice of the sentences in themselves.

Another problem has to do with the very different contexts of men's and women's crimes. The example of death penalty sentencing illustrates this particularly clearly. Women made up about 6 percent of those serving time for murder in American prisons in 2008 (Sabol, West, and Cooper 2009), yet they made up only 1.7 percent of the 3,279 individuals under sentence of death (Finns 2009). Of the 1,168 people executed since the reinstatement of capital punishment in 1976, only eleven have been women (Finns 2009). At first glance this seems a clear example of what most Americans take as an article of faith—courts are reluctant to sentence women to death, and even once they are sentenced, judges and public officials are too chivalrous to carry out the prescribed punishment.

As Rapaport (1991) first noted more than fifteen years ago, this seemingly straightforward assessment ignores a fundamental fact—the circumstances of men's and women's homicides vary dramatically. The main reason women are less likely to receive the death penalty is that they commit different kinds of murders than do men. Capital murder—murder eligible for death penalty sentencing—is defined by the various states and the federal system essentially as aggravated first-degree homicide. What this means is that the murder has to have been premeditated and intentional (hence first-degree) and must have been committed in combination with some other act that made it a particularly heinous crime. In many states, the killing of a law enforcement officer automatically qualifies as capital murder, as does murder committed in the course of another serious crime, such as rape, armed robbery, or kidnapping (the latter are called felony murders). Women are particularly unlikely to commit these kinds of homicides. Of all felony murders in 2009 for which the offender's sex was known, men committed about 90 percent (Federal Bureau of Investigation 2010). When women kill, their victims are disproportionately husbands and boyfriends whom they murder in the context of arguments and/or after long histories of abuse. These homicides do not qualify as capital murder, and this is true whether women or men commit them. Women's lower rates of death penalty sentencing are thus a consequence of the *kinds* of murders they commit, not a chivalrous judicial system.

In fact, punishments for homicide discriminate in a paradoxical way against women *victims* (Rapaport 1991). The law punishes crimes committed between strangers much more harshly than those in which the victim and offender know each other; generally speaking, we find that the severity of punishment varies inversely with the closeness of the relationship between the offender and the victim. This means that crimes committed between intimates, including homicides, are treated more leniently by the law regardless of the sex of the offender. In 2009, 56 percent, or 1,081 of the 1,928 female murder victims (in single-victim/single-offender incidents), were killed by their husbands or boyfriends, making this the single largest category of homicide victimization for women. By contrast, only 6 percent, or 279 of the 4,638 male murder victims, were killed by their wives or girlfriends (men are most likely to be killed by male acquaintances or by strangers) (Federal Bureau of Investigation 2010). Given that the law treats murders between intimates more leniently, this in effect means that murders of women are punished less severely than are those of men.

Homicide is relatively rare, however, and its seriousness means that we would expect any gender differences in sentencing to be minimal. Research focusing on bias in sentencing for a wide array of other crimes has generated conflicting results. In their review of dozens of studies conducted the past two decades, Daly and Bordt (1995) find that about half find no bias or mixed results and the other half show some leniency in favor of women (see also Steffensmeier, Kramer, and Streifel 1993; Steffensmeier, Ullmer, and Kramer 1998; Spohn and Holleran 2000; Koons-Witt, Where leniency exists, however, it tends to occur at the level of the decision to incarcerate (or not), rather than in sentence length, and varies by offense types, with less leniency for violent offenders (Zatz 2000; Spohn, Curry, and Lee 2006). Once a judge chooses to incarcerate an offender, sentence is essentially the same, regardless of whether that offender is male or female (Steffensmeier, Kramer, and Streifel 1993; Wooldredge 1998; see also Farnworth and Teske 1995). Perhaps not surprisingly, given what we have already discussed about gender bias in policing—not all women benefit equally, nor are all men disadvantaged. Those treated most harshly by courts are African American and Hispanic men; white women most benefit.[14]

In sum, then, it is apparent—if limited—chivalry does exist. Women are almost always treated more leniently by courts. Men's crimi-

to be longer, and more violent, men's and women's roles in committing crimes are often very different, and women are much more likely than men to have experienced physical and sexual abuse in their relationships. All of these factors may influence sentencing decisions, yet they are often difficult to control in large-scale statistical research. For example, a study of federal drug prosecutions (Nagel and Johnson 1994) found that women are more likely than men to receive downward departures under federal sentencing guidelines (see also Ferrell 2003 and Mustard 2001). Downward departures are judicial decisions in which a defendant is punished less harshly than the mandatory minimums require, and judges may, under severely restricted circumstances, grant these to defendants due to mitigating circumstances. Nagel and Johnson (1994) conclude that the greater likelihood of downward departures for women is clear evidence of discrimination against men. Ultimately, they argue for complete equality of treatment (defined in terms of how men are punished). Yet consider the case of Tammi Bloom, discussed earlier. Her connection to crime through a male associate is far uncommon for women offenders, and here we see an instance of treatment (relatively—her punishment was actually more severe) for and a woman convicted of the same charges. Surely a judge would justified in considering a downward departure in this case. This ne of the problems with large-scale quantitative research like d by Nagel and Johnson (1994); such studies tend to miss the plicate cases in which defendants may have received exactly It is in these details that the effects of gender often lie.

tion

f the war on drugs in the 1980s, the United States s have aptly labeled an incarceration "binge." w larger than at any point in our history, and of our citizens than does any other nation an 1.5 million people held under state or 2009 (Maguire undated).[15] The growth illustrated in figure 3.1. The most no- curve on the right, an upward trend relative stability in prison popula- in an era in which the political ome insatiable. tion rates expl ne ha

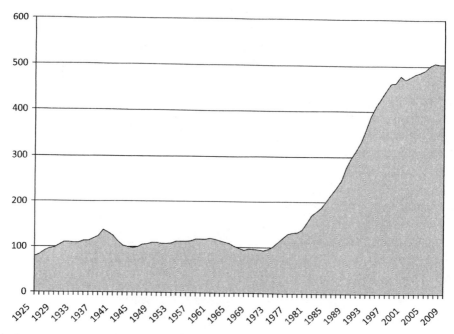

Figure 3.1. U.S. Incarceration Rate, 1925–2009

Source: Maguire (undated), table 6.28.

rates have declined approximately 20 percent since the mid 1980s; arrests for serious (index) crimes have fallen even more sharply.

How is it possible that incarceration has risen sharply while arrests have fallen? The reason lies in the fact that offenses that were once considered relatively minor by legislatures and the courts, offenses that would not have carried a punishment of incarceration, now routinely result in time in prison. Many of these offenses are drug related, like simple possession of marijuana. Other laws prescribe harsh punishments for first-time and petty offenders. At the same time, average prison sentences have increased in the wake of the abolition of parole in many states and the adoption of determinate sentencing schemes such as the "three strikes" and "hard forty" rules for recidivists.[16] In direct terms, the increase in our prison population is due to a rising tide of *criminalization*, rather than a rise of crime—a process in which more and more minor offenders are being drawn into the net of formal social control. As we will see, this has had especially negative effects on women, who are disproportionately found among the ranks of minor criminal offenders.

Of those in prison at the end of 2008, about 93 percent were men and 7 percent were women (Sabol, West, and Cooper 2009). Women are much less likely than men to be incarcerated, a fact that reflects their lower arrest rates and the kinds of offenses for which they come into contact with the system. Women's incarceration rates have recently been rising much faster than men's, however; having risen 240 percent since 1986, as compared with an increase for men of 132 percent. Most scholars agree that the faster pace for women indicates the net widening now taking place across all levels of the system; as pettier offenders are targeted, more women are drawn into the system.

In terms of race, differences at the level of arrest translate into stark racial inequality in the likelihood of incarceration. Table 3.4 depicts the U.S. prison population by both sex and race. African American men have the highest rate of any group; they are six and one-half times more likely to be in prison than are white men, about two and one-half times more likely than are Hispanic men. Though women's rates are much lower overall we see a similar pattern of racial disparity. Black women are three times more likely to be in prison than are white women and twice as likely to be incarcerated as are Hispanic women.

Those who occupy our prisons also come from the lowest socioeconomic classes in society. Though 73 percent of men and 58 percent of women report having been employed prior to their admission to prison, their incomes were very low; for men, the median income was less than $18,000 per year; for women, $12,000 (author calculation, Bureau of Justice Statistics 2007). This means that those who are in prison are disproportionately likely to have been living below the poverty line ($18,850 for a family of four in 2004, the year these data were collected) before their conviction.

As table 3.5 indicates, women in prison differ from their male counterparts in other significant ways. They are less likely to be incarcerated for violent offenses, more frequently serving time for property offenses and drug crimes. Women have shorter criminal records than men, and they are far less likely to have been incarcerated for a prior (or current) violent crime. It is worth noting that all of these data contradict the perceptions of the officer quoted at the beginning of this chapter—women in prison are in fact

Table 3.4. Prisoners in 2008

	Number Incarcerated	Incarceration Rate
Total men	1,434,784	952
White men	591,900	487
Black men	528,200	3,161
Hispanic men	313,100	1,200
Total women	105,252	68
White women	50,700	50
Black women	29,100	149
Hispanic women	17,300	75

Source: Sabol, West, and Cooper 2009, tables 1 and 2.

less violent, and they have shorter criminal records than men. The majority of both men and women in prison are parents, but women are more commonly custodial parents; 45 percent of women, versus only 27 percent of men, lived with their children prior to their entry into prison. And finally, as the table demonstrates, one of the most noteworthy differences between men and women lies in their histories of abuse. Women are nine times more likely to have been both physically and sexually abused in their lives and more than thirty times more likely to have experienced that abuse at the hands of an intimate (defined as a spouse, boyfriend, or girlfriend).

And as men and women in prison differ, so too do men's and women's prisons. As we would expect, there are far fewer women's prisons than men's—as of the most recent prison census in 2005, there were 1,061 prisons in the United States that housed men, versus 192 that housed women. Women's prisons tend to be smaller, with a median population of 214 inmates, compared with 958 in the men's prisons. They are also much less likely to experience serious violence; women's prisons experienced no staff deaths in 2005, versus nine in men's prisons, and there were more than 22,000 physical or sexual assaults of inmates by other inmates in men's prisons, compared with fewer than 1,800 in women's facilities. And finally, the population of officers in men's and women's prisons differs; about 80 percent of officers in men's prisons are men; 60 percent of officers in women's prisons are women (Bureau of Justice Statistics 2009). This means that the work environment in men's prisons is more segregated than that in women's prisons, a topic to which we will return in chapter 5.

Table 3.5.   Profile of Men and Women in State Prisons

	Women (%)	Men (%)
Offense and Criminal History		
Incarceration offense violent	30	49
Incarceration offense property	29	18
Incarceration offense drug	31	21
Any prior incarceration	41	55
Recidivist—prior violent	22	45
Social Characteristics		
Income less than $15,000/year prior to arrest	65	49
Have children under 18	62	51
Children living with prior to incarceration	55	36
Child's current caregiver is other parent	37	88
Physically abused	49	14
Sexually abused	42	6
Both physically and sexually abused	30	3
Sexual abuse by family or adult intimate	27	3

Sources: Author calculation, Bureau of Justice Statistics 2007, and Glaze and Maruschak 2008.

Taken as a whole, these data on incarceration tell us that sex is an extremely important characteristic affecting the probability that one will spend time in prison—men are almost fourteen times more likely to be incarcerated than are women. The effects of race and class, however, are relatively constant across sex—poor men and women, and African American or Hispanic men and women, are more likely to be in prison than are their middle-class and/or white counterparts. But what role does *gender* play? Table 3.5 begins to answer this question. Gender matters, for example, in influencing the kinds of offenses for which men and women are sentenced—women are less likely to be serving time for violent offenses (30 percent of women versus 49 percent of men) and more likely to be sentenced for property and drug crimes. Men have longer and more violent criminal histories—they are more likely than women (55 percent versus 41 percent) to have served time in prison previously and are twice as likely to be violent recidivists.

In terms of their social characteristics, gendered inequality in the labor market means that women's incomes are lower than those of similarly situated men—of those who reported any income in the month before arrest, 49 percent of men, but 65 percent of women, earned less than fifteen thousand dollars per year. Gender also plays a powerful role in shaping women's relationships with their children, specifically their status as custodial parents. Women in prison are more likely to be parents (62 versus 51 percent) and to have had children living with them before incarceration (55 versus 36 percent). Other research suggests that women in prison engage in active mothering (to the extent that they are able) more than men serve as active fathers, a fact that creates stresses for women inmates that most men simply do not face (Enos 2001). Among other things, this difference may be due to the custody arrangements of children whose parents are in prison—for 88 percent of men in prison, children are in the custody of the other parent; this is true for only 37 percent of women.

Gender also constructs an interpersonal context in which women are more likely to have been victims of abuse, particularly from those closest to them. Women in prison are more than three times as likely to have experienced physical abuse and seven times as likely to have experienced sexual abuse as men. This abuse comes disproportionately at the hands of intimates—in the case of sexual abuse, women are nine times more likely than men to report that they were abused by a parent, relative, spouse, ex-spouse, or boyfriend.[17]

Taken together, all of these facts paint a picture that fits with what we know about the way gender shapes the lives of men and women in a more general sense—women are generally less violent than men, earn lower salaries, are more likely to actively parent, and are more likely to experience physical and sexual abuse. As it does in organizations more generally, gender also plays a role in shaping prison environments—men's prisons are larger, more violent, and much more likely to be staffed by male officers than are women's institutions. This is a topic I explore in more depth below.

The Prison as a Gendered Organization

As I note in chapter 1, gender is not only a characteristic of individuals. Gender shapes organizations, which at the same time may both reflect and reproduce gender. Prisons are deeply gendered institutions, having been formed from their first appearance in this country by their founders' ideas about the reformation of gendered (and raced, and classed) subjects. The first disciplinary regimes imposed in prisons were in fact designed for men, emphasizing military regimentation and industrial labor and the reformation of inmates in the mold of the sober, white, male, middle-class citizen (Butler 1997; Dumm 1987; Hirsch 1992). In these early prisons, women were an afterthought, first housed with men and then separated and held in whatever makeshift quarters were available. At New York's Auburn prison, opened in 1819, women were initially kept in an overcrowded, unventilated, third-floor attic above the institution's kitchen. In 1842, women inmates in one Illinois prison were kept "in the cook house in the day time and in a cellar [under the warden's house] at night" (quoted in Dodge 1999, 911). Between 1870 and 1896, women inmates at another Illinois institution were kept on the fourth floor of an administration building and allowed out only for a once-yearly stroll in the prison yard (Dodge 1999).

Penologists and prison reformers of the early nineteenth century held very different ideas about men and women criminals. Men, they believed, could be returned to their inherent rationality through the application of harsh discipline. A woman prisoner, on the other hand, behaved "more . . . like a madwoman than a rational, reflecting human being" (quoted in Butler 1997, 27). And indeed it was the seemingly irredeemable nature of women (combined with their relatively small numbers) that justified their placement in makeshift quarters and their exclusion from the disciplinary regimes imposed upon men.

It was not until the mid nineteenth century that this view changed, largely as a result of the work of women's prison reformers, who advocated separate institutions for women and "reformatory" *treatment* that would transform them into models of appropriate femininity. This was to be accomplished in institutions based on a "cottage" design, in which women would live in a sort of family structure. The reformers' ideal is expressed in a report on the Hudson House of Refuge, established in 1887:

> The idea of a family and home life is carried out as far as possible in the cottages. In the evening [the inmates] are gathered together in a circle, of which

the supervisor and the assistant form the center. . . . The girls, while knitting or sewing, profit by some appropriate reading or oral instruction. (quoted in Freedman 1981, 57)

Reformers believed that women would respond best to a family structure and that proper femininity was the key to their reform. To that end, women in reformatories were instructed in the correct performance of domestic tasks. At one such institution an expert was brought in to teach the women "the secrets of starch, ironing," and other important household skills (quoted in Freedman 1981).

Those spearheading the men's reformatory movement, which also began in the mid-nineteenth century, expressed very different ideas about the rehabilitation of male inmates. Men's reformatory advocates argued that to reform men, "The prisoner's self-respect should be cultivated to the utmost, and every effort made to give back to him his *manhood*" (quoted in Pisciotta 1994, 158, emphasis mine). The prime architect of the men's reformatory movement, Zebulon Brockway, in fact explicitly described his aim as the production of "Christian gentlemen." To this end he advocated military drill and discipline and instruction in masculine trades.

The reformatory movement did succeed to some degree; dozens of institutions based on these ideals did open during the late nineteenth and early twentieth century, particularly in the Northeast, Midwest, and West. In fact, their descendants are still with us in the form of institutions for youthful adult offenders. If reformers had an ideal man or woman in mind as the epitome of the successful inmate, however, they also had very clear notions about the raw material with which they intended to work. Both men's and women's reformatory advocates did not see black inmates, in particular, as amenable to treatment, and during the early days of the reformatory movement, most remained in existing state prisons (Rafter 1990; Pisciotta 1994).

Most black inmates were held in the South, however, where the reformatory movement made little headway. As I note in chapter 1, during the years following the Civil War, the most common system in this region was neither prison nor reformatory based, but instead involved the *leasing* of inmates to private farmers and business owners. Black inmates, men, women, and children, were held in mass leasing camps in which conditions were abominable. In Mississippi, for example, not a single leased convict lived long enough to serve a sentence of ten years or more (Oshinsky 1997). Scandals around the brutalities of the leasing camps led at the turn of the twentieth century to the development of large state-run prison farms, in which inmates worked largely as plantation laborers. Advocates for convict leasing and later, for prison farms, believed agricultural labor to be well suited to the "essential nature" of the black inmate, for whom a more intellectual sort of reform would simply be a waste of time (Oshinsky 1997).

Women were first housed with men on prison farms, separated into their own camps, but by the middle of the century they were being moved to women's institutions. Prison farms still dot the South; at institutions such as Louisiana's Angola State Prison and Mississippi's Parchman Farm, men in prison uniforms still work the fields just as their counterparts did a century ago.

This brief review of prison history tells us that notions about gender, race, and class have shaped the actual physical structures of prisons and their disciplinary regimes from the outset. But this is not simply an artifact of history; modern prisons continue to reflect and reproduce these dimensions. Women's prisons remain afterthoughts in most correctional systems, at the bottom of the priority list for limited state resources. Women inmates in many states have had to sue to get access to the same programs and opportunities routinely offered to men, and work assignments and vocational training continue to reflect gendered notions. Sewing and cosmetology courses are still among the most common offerings at women's institutions (Britton 2003).

The cultures of contemporary men's and women's prisons are also shaped by ideas about gender. For my book *At Work in the Iron Cage* (Britton 2003), I interviewed correctional officers about (among other things) their views on inmates. Their comments reveal clear differences in their perceptions of women and men in prison, ideas that are in some ways surprising but that nonetheless fit well with prevailing stereotypes about gender. In line with what others have found, I discovered that almost all of the seventy-two officers to whom I spoke—men and women—expressed a preference for working with men inmates. This may seem paradoxical at first, but their reasons align well with gendered notions that mark women as emotional, irrational, and unpredictable. This woman officer explains:

> I would much rather work with the men! I mean, that's awful to say that . . . but it's very true. I'm just not real good at babying, and the females need a lot more attention. They need a lot more coddling, and that's just kind of our gender. That's the way we are. They tend to cry if we go over and talk to them, where you're not going to get that with the men. I just don't deal with that well. I just personally would rather work with the men. (quoted in Britton 2003, 118)

This sentiment was not uncommon; one man noted, "When I came here they handed me a pair of handcuffs. I couldn't understand why. What they really need to give you is a pack of tissues!" (quoted in Britton 2003, 117). For almost all officers, women's perceived greater emotionality served as a primary reason for preferring work with men.

But what of men's greater potential for violence? Though officers readily admitted that men could be more violent, most saw dealing with women's emotions as a more onerous, complicated task. They also believed that women's violence, though less frequent, could be more difficult to handle. These officers reflect this point of view:

> A male inmate and a female inmate are two different types of inmates. A male inmate is easier to manage because they're not as emotional as female inmates. And the risk factor in dealing with males is not as serious as it is with females when it comes to a confrontation. (male officer, quoted in Britton 2003, 121)

Similarly, this woman observes:

> Women [inmates] are more emotional. They fly off the handle a lot faster. They don't think, they just react. They just do. The men, some of them do, but most of them think a little bit before they react. So, that's the true difference right there. (quoted in Britton 2003, 121)

For both of these officers, and many of their counterparts, women's violence is more dangerous because of women's irrationality and unpredictability. Men's violence is based on rational complaints, but women's violence is irrational and hence cannot be anticipated. As one officer put it, "When males come to you with problems they're real problems"; women, by contrast, are pettier and more likely to explode over trivial issues (Britton 2003, 126).

I discuss the reasons behind these perceptions at length elsewhere (Britton 1999, 2003). For the current purposes it will perhaps suffice to note that these ideas are obviously gendered and in many ways reflect various aspects of the notions that prison reformers have held about men and women prisoners through the past two centuries. Modern prisons echo with the notions that men can be returned to rationality; women are by contrast emotional and irrational. Women need domestic environments and "womanly" occupations, and men need vocations. Ideas about gender shaped the earliest prisons; it is perhaps not surprising that they continue to shape regimes, policies, and culture in their modern descendants.

THE CRIMINAL JUSTICE SYSTEM ENGENDERED

Though laws rarely now explicitly discriminate on the basis of distinctions such as gender, race, and class, the criminal justice system is deeply inscribed by social inequality. Men—and particularly poor African American and Hispanic men—are more likely to come into contact with the system than are women, and they correspondingly receive its harshest punishments. Women are arrested less often and by comparison make up a relatively small (if rapidly growing) proportion of our burgeoning prison population. The "benefits" of gender are not equally available, however. Poor African American and Hispanic women bear the brunt of the system's punishments. Sex, race, and class all matter in determining whom the system will punish, for what offenses, and in what measure.

Gender matters as well, and at all layers of the system. I opened this chapter by introducing the notion of chivalry theory, a bit of folk wisdom which holds that—due to our ideas about femininity—women are treated more leniently by the criminal justice system than are men. Yet as we have seen, to the extent that chivalry exists, it appears to work only for those who most closely fit prevailing definitions of "acceptable" femininity—older, white, heterosexual, middle-class women. Those who deviate from this mold are likely to be treated the same as their male counterparts; to the extent that they actively reject femininity, they may be punished even more harshly (Chesney-Lind and Irwin 2008; Carr et al. 2008; Morris and Wilczynski 1995). White men apparently share in the benefits of chivalry in many ways as well. Racialized stereotypes concerning African American and Hispanic men are undoubtedly important in shaping the system's responses to them (as in the traffic stop data discussed earlier; for a discussion of another context, see Ferguson 2001). Gendered family and relationship systems shape women's (and men's) involvement in crime and the punishments they receive, as we saw in the case of Tammi Bloom.

Gender, race, and class have—historically and into the present—played key roles in the structure and culture of our prisons as well. In many ways the current situation represents a continuation of historical trends. Since the first prisons were established in this country, they have always been filled with those at the bottom of the social and economic ladder and they have invariably held many more men than women (Colvin 2000; Rafter 1990). It is not random chance that our prisons are populated by the least advantaged members of our society. The recent dramatic rise in incarceration has simply magnified these divisions to an extent unprecedented in our history.

This incarceration binge is a clear demonstration of the fact that criminal justice policy is not a simple, mechanistic response to rising crime rates. It is in fact a consciously crafted social policy in which legislators and policy makers have turned to incarceration as the prime—and some would argue the only—solution for a wide variety of social problems at the intersection of race, gender, and class, from unemployment, to poverty, to homelessness. Viewing the criminal justice system from a perspective that takes gender, and race, and class seriously is the only way to begin a meaningful conversation about whether the crime-processing system in this country deserves to be called justice.

4

Gender and Crime Victimization

Rape was, in the words of one Vietnam veteran, "pretty SOP"—standard operating procedure, and it was a rare GI who possessed the individual courage
or morality to go against his buddies and report, let alone stop, the offense.
"They only do it when there are a lot of guys around," veteran George Phillips
told writer Lucy Komisar. "You know, it makes them feel good. They show
each other what they can do—'I can do it,' you know. They won't do it by
themselves."

"Did anybody report these incidents?"

"No. No one did. You don't dare. Next time you're out in the field you won't
come back—you'll come back in a body bag. What the hell, she's only a dink,
a gook, this is what they think." (Brownmiller 1975, 110–111)

In the early morning hours of Feb. 27, 1999, Lisa King performed as an exotic
dancer during a Delta Chi fraternity party at the University of Florida. . . . King
charged that she was later raped by fraternity member Mike Yahraus while
two or more men watched, assisted and videotaped the rape. After the attack,
King ran naked to another fraternity house and called her mother, who called
the University Police Department (UPD). King was taken to a hospital on a
stretcher in a neck brace. On March 1, less than two days after the report was
filed, the UPD arrested, handcuffed and took Lisa King to jail for "falsifying
a police report." The UPD and the state attorney's office maintained that the
videotape (edited by Delta Chi members) demonstrated consensual sex even
though the word "rape" is chanted several times. King claimed that Yahraus
said he would "break her neck" if she fought. The men titled their videotape
The raping of a white-trash, crackhead bitch. . . . King, ultimately charged with
soliciting prostitution and performing lewd acts, served six months' probation
after pleading guilty to one of three misdemeanor counts against her. . . . Six
Delta Chi brothers were charged with solicitation of prostitution and two other

misdemeanor charges. Four pleaded guilty. Charges were deferred against another. Those found guilty received a sentence of probation and community service.[1]

The Milwaukee Bucks on Thursday acquired [Ruben] Patterson from the Denver Nuggets. . . . The athletic 6-5 swingman averaged 12.1 points and 3.4 rebounds in 71 games last season. "Adding Ruben gives us added strength at the small forward position," Bucks general manager Lenny Harris said. "He's a tough, defensive-minded player who has shown an ability to score." Nicknamed "Captain Chaos," Patterson has had a history of off-court problems, including a felony domestic assault charge against his wife in 2002. He also was suspended for the first five games of the 2001–2002 season after a charge of attempted rape. "We know that Ruben's path through the NBA has been a difficult one at times," Harris said. "But we're confident that he has learned from those experiences and that he's ready to contribute to helping our team win." (espn.com, October 2006)

Women are underrepresented as criminal offenders and at all levels of the criminal justice system. So, too, are they underrepresented as victims. Contrary to media accounts and perhaps public preconceptions, the most common victims of crime in America, particularly violent offenses, are men. Women are much more likely than men to be targets of certain kinds of victimization, among them rape and domestic violence (though there is a debate about the latter, discussed below). Regardless of whether a victim is a man or a woman, however, acts of victimization take place and are interpreted by victims and observers in a context that is fundamentally shaped by gender. For men, victimization often occurs in conflicts that escalate due to expectations about violence and masculinity. And as the cases above illustrate, when men victimize women, these same norms—held by offenders, agents of the criminal justice system, outside observers, and sometimes even victims themselves—can lead to the minimizing and even erasure of these acts. Rape becomes "standard operating procedure," or an "experience" that need not impair one's ability to "[help the] team win." In some instances, women who are victims find themselves held—and sometimes hold themselves—responsible for having been in the wrong place at the wrong time, engaged in seemingly risky behavior, or having enticed their offenders, rationalizations that have much to do with cultural norms about femininity and heterosexuality.

In this chapter I turn a gender lens on crime victimization, examining how gender (and sex and race and class) shapes the probabilities, contexts, and outcomes of victimization. I begin with a review of official statistics on victimization and then turn to some controversies over the extent of women's victimization. In the second half of the chapter I examine mainstream theories of victimization and finally offer a sociological perspective on victimization that takes into account the gendering of social contexts. I conclude by considering the implications of a contextual and cultural approach.

SEX, GENDER, AND VICTIMIZATION—WHAT
THE OFFICIAL STATISTICS TELL US

For criminologists, the most widely used official source of victimization data is the National Crime Victimization Survey (NCVS). The NCVS is an annual survey conducted by the Bureau of Justice Statistics in cooperation with the U.S. Census Bureau and has been administered annually since 1973. In 2007, 41,000 households and 73,650 individuals twelve years and older were interviewed.[2] The NCVS asks respondents about whether they have been victims of a wide variety of crimes during the past year, from personal offenses such as rape and assault to household crimes such as burglary. Respondents are also queried about whether they reported these victimizations to the police and their reasons for making the decision to report or not. Like any survey, the NCVS is only as good as respondents' memories and their willingness to be honest. We do know that the NCVS captures more information about crime than measures such as the UCR (discussed in chapter 2) that rely on only police reports. Of all of the offenses reported to NCVS interviewers, respondents say that they reported only a fraction to the police—about 49 percent of violent crimes and 40 percent of property crimes in any given year.[3] This means—at a minimum—that the UCR can give us no information at all about 60 percent of the crime committed in the United States.

Table 4.1 displays the most recent estimates of crime victimization from the NCVS.[4] The rates depicted in this table are calculated by taking the total number of offenses reported in the sample, extrapolating to the total population of a particular group, dividing the total by the number of people in that population group twelve years of age and older, and then multiplying by one thousand to create numbers that are easier to interpret. This means that the rates depicted here should be interpreted as the number of victimizations that are projected to have occurred per one thousand members of a particular population group. So, for example, using the data in the table for men's victimization by violent crime as a whole (depicted in the first column), this means that 22.5 out of 1,000 men twelve years and older were victimized by a violent crime in 2007 (or 2.25 percent). By comparison, 18.9 out of 1,000 women were victimized (or 1.89 percent).

These data make it readily apparent that with the exception of rape, men are more likely than women to be victims of all violent crimes. This is a pattern criminologists have observed since the first victimization surveys were conducted. Scholars differ about why, but some of the reasons are

Table 4.1. Crime Victimization as Measured by the NCVS, 2007

	Violent Crime Total	Rape	Robbery	Aggravated Assault	Simple Assault	Personal Theft	Burglary
Sex							
Male	22.5	0.1*	3.4	4.5	14.5	0.9	N/A
Female	18.9	1.8	1.4	2.4	13.2	0.7	N/A
Race							
White	20.5	1.0*	1.9	3.2	13.9	0.6	25.1
Black	26.1	0.5*	4.9	4.4	14.4	1.9	37.2
Hispanic	18.6	0.1*	3.9	3.0	11.4	1.0*	30.8
Other race	11.4	1.2*	1.8*	2.7	5.7	1.1*	22.8
Age							
12–15	43.4	1.0*	4.2	2.8	35.5	0.8*	N/A
16–19	50.1	2.4	6.4	7.2	34.2	1.6*	N/A
20–24	35.2	2.9	3.5	7.5	21.2	1.1*	N/A
25–34	24.7	1.2	3.4	4.8	15.3	1.1	N/A
35–49	17.7	1.0	1.4	3.2	12.1	0.6	N/A
50–64	11.6	0.3*	1.7	2.3	7.2	0.3*	N/A
65+	2.5	0.1*	0.6*	0.3*	1.5	0.8*	N/A
Household Income							
Less than $7,500	50.7	2.5*	4.1*	5.4	38.7	2.0*	57.6
$7,500–$14,999	39.0	1.5*	6.7	6.6	24.0	1.9*	51.2
$15,000–$24,999	25.9	1.5*	3.3	3.5	17.6	1.3*	33.5
$25,000–$34,999	27.5	0.5*	2.7	4.6	19.7	0.6*	25.2
$35,000–$49,999	21.7	1.5	3.0	3.5	13.6	0.4*	28.3
$50,000–$74,999	19.8	0.5*	1.1	3.3	14.9	0.5*	21.8
$75,000 or more	14.1	0.4*	1.3	2.6	9.9	0.6	17.2

Source: Maston 2010, adapted from multiple tables.

*Estimate is based on ten or fewer sample cases and should be interpreted with caution.

undoubtedly connected to gender—assaults and other interpersonal crimes tend to happen between men who know each other, often in the context of arguments about money or property. Men are also far more likely than are women to carry guns—a fact that figures in rates of aggravated assault and homicide victimization—and it is also the case that men are simply more commonly present in locations—such as bars and on the streets—where assaults take place. Robbery, too, is a gendered offense, as we discussed in chapter 2—men rob other men to boost their own masculinity, or as one offender interviewed by Jody Miller (1998) noted, because "that's who has the money." Gender, on the other hand, may "protect" women from some victimization (i.e., because women carry less money or are less likely to be on the streets alone), making them less likely targets for this kind of masculinized violence.

Race and class also strongly influence the probability of victimization. Generally speaking, African Americans are more likely to be victimized for all offenses than are either Hispanics or whites. Rates for Hispanics do not reveal a clear pattern; for some offenses they fall between blacks and whites, and for others their rates of victimization are lower. The effects of social class are much clearer. The poor are much more likely to be victimized than the rich. This is true not only for violent crimes such as assault, but also for property crimes such as "personal theft" (essentially, pocket picking and purse snatching) and burglary.[5] And though age differences in victimization are not a central focus of this chapter, it is worth noting that young people are more likely to be victimized by all crimes; those over 65 are conversely least likely to be victims of crime.

Race and class intersect in complicated ways in shaping the chances of victimization. Those most likely to be victims of crime are poor African Americans, who are more likely than whites to be highly residentially segregated into economically depressed urban areas. We know that the chances of victimization in these communities are much higher than in the suburbs or in rural areas.[6] Violent crime victimization rates in urban areas were more than 60 percent higher in 2005[7] than those in rural or suburban locations, a difference that has been relatively constant over time. Patterns of residential segregation also help to explain the seemingly paradoxical findings of the NCVS about personal theft and burglary. It seems logical to expect that those who have the most would be most at risk for losing their property, yet crime statistics consistently demonstrate that this is not the case. Burglary, like most crimes, is usually committed near the offender's residence or in a neighborhood with which he or she is familiar. Techniques such as geographic (GIS) mapping of crime patterns across cities enables detection of these patterns. As the poor are more likely to be burglary offenders, so, too, are their victims living nearby equally likely to be poor. Though the well-off may imagine their homes as the most likely targets for thieves, the poorest members of their communities are more than twice as likely to be burglarized.[8]

The NCVS is one of the few sources of official statistics to provide data about social class; it is also unique in that it reports data on victimization by race *and* sex. These statistics appear in table 4.2. For violent crime overall and for most specific offenses, black men report the highest rates of victimization. Patterns for Hispanic men are not consistent—for some offenses their rates are intermediate, between blacks and whites; for others, their rates are lowest. Among women, whites generally have the lowest rates of victimization, and their rates are similar to those for Hispanic women.

The most striking differences in the table are those by race. Across categories and years of the survey, black men consistently experience the highest rates of criminal victimization. Beyond the effects of racially segregated residence, black men are more likely to be found in the locations—like the streets and in bars in urban areas—where violence occurs; they are also more likely to come into contact with potential violent offenders. As Miller (2008) indicates, street culture is deeply masculinized, and violence is a normatively accepted resource for dealing with conflicts (see also Anderson 2000; Brezina et al. 2004). These factors combine to place black men particularly at risk of violent victimization.

Though there have been many studies of violence among men in segregated urban communities (e.g., Anderson 1999; McCall 1994), criminologists have paid far less attention to persistently high rates of victimization among black women. As table 4.2 indicates, black women's rates of violent victimization are 30 percent higher than white women's, and for violent crimes as a whole—robbery, simple assault, and personal theft—their rates of victimization are actually higher than white men's. Jody Miller (2008) has recently linked black women's rates of victimization to the disadvan-

Table 4.2. Victimization Rates by Race and Sex, NCVS 2007

	Violent Crime Total	Rape	Robbery	Aggravated Assault	Simple Assault	Personal Theft
Men						
White	21.9	0.1*	2.6	4.5	14.7	0.7*
Black	25.3	0.0*	7.6	4.7	13.0	2.2*
Hispanic	21.1	0.0*	5.8	4.6	10.7	1.1*
Women						
White	18.0	1.8	1.3	1.9	13.1	0.5
Black	23.4	0.9	2.6	4.2	15.6	1.6*
Hispanic	16.1	0.6*	1.9*	1.5*	12.1	0.9*

Source: Maston 2010, adapted from multiple tables.

*Estimate is based on ten or fewer sample cases and should be interpreted with caution.

taged community contexts in which they are disproportionately likely to live. These are neighborhoods in which

> Other forms of violence are widespread, community and personal resources are limited, collective efficacy is difficult to achieve, and young men are faced with a masculine street code that emphasizes respect, interpersonal violence, and heterosexual prowess demonstrated via sexual conquest. (2008, 191)

In such settings, violence against women becomes endemic and women have few strategies other than staying indoors and at home. Even then, however, they face violence by intimates, violence that is often framed as a private matter.

As the NCVS is an in-person survey of victims, it cannot track homicide victimization. These data are gathered as part of the FBI's Uniform Crime Reporting program, and they reveal differences by sex and race that are among the most dramatic of those for any crime. In 2009, for example, the overall homicide victimization rate for men was approximately 7 per 100,000 men in the population. For women, the comparable rate was 2, lower by a factor of more than three. The group with the highest overall level of victimization is African American men, with a rate of 30 per 100,000 black men in the population. They are followed by black women, with a rate of 5, white men (4), and white women (2).[9] In fact, black men made up the single largest group of homicide victims in 2009—5,561 out of a total of 13,636. Differences in rates for young victims, between the ages of eighteen and twenty-four, reveal what has been justifiably called an "epidemic." In 2005, the homicide victimization rate for black men in this age group was 102 per 100,000—about nine times higher than the rate for white men age twenty to twenty-four, of whom twelve in one hundred thousand were victimized. For black women the rate was 11, for white women, 3. In terms of lifetime exposure to potential homicide victimization, black women are actually at *higher* risk than are white men.

All of these differences by race and sex reflect the fact that most crime ___ ___tween people of the same race and class. White offenders tend to ___ ___ assault, white victims. *The poor* prey on the poor (though ___ ___hat the rich prey on everyone!). Again, patterns of social ___ ___n undoubtedly help to *explain* this phenomenon. ___ ___y with whites in social *and* community life; ___ ___anics. Neighborhoods are generally not ___ ___ding are stratified across race and ___ ___ical to expect that victimiza- ___ ___ is is what we find. ___ ___d by sex, however. ___ ___ders are over- ___ ___known offenders, men were responsible for the murders of 88 percent of all male victims and 89 percent of female victims. As I discussed in chapter 2, criminal offending is deeply gendered; masculinity is entwined with the cultural prescriptions about the use of violence. Mastery of violence remains, in fact, one important way men can achieve masculine status, can show themselves to be "real men" (Messerschmidt 1993, 2000). Some criminologists have speculated that this might be particularly true for men who have few other resources—that is, those boys and men who do not have access to legitimate power (like money or status) turn to illegitimate means, such as the use of violence, to prove their manhood (cf. Reiman 2006).[10]

Studies of homicide, for example, have shown that the most common situation that leads to murder involves what some criminologists call victim precipitation (Wolfgang 1958). This phrase describes an interactive process in which two parties are engaged in an argument in which words and insults escalate on the part of both victim and offender until lethal violence results. While the homicide is not justifiable, it is accurate to say that the victim played a role in the violence that ultimately resulted in homicide. My local newspaper recently carried a report on a murder of just this kind in which two men who knew each other got into a fight at a party, and the fight escalated until one man eventually drew a gun and shot the other five times. In 2009, the FBI reported that about half of all nonfelony murders (those not committed during the commission of other felony crimes) happened in the context of arguments.

Though criminologists have rarely been explicit about the gender component of this process (for an exception, see Messerschmidt 1993), the concept of victim precipitation essentially describes a masculinity contest. Such homicides occur most frequently when two men who know each other engage in an interactive process in which backing down becomes an ever-increasing threat to manhood. The ultimate choice becomes one to back down and risk being seen as a "wimp" or to escalate violence to the point of lethality. Logically, it makes little sense to talk about conflict between women as "femininity contests," nor does the use of vi carry positive associations for women as it does for men. And few women are murdered each year by other women; th 182 women in 2009, about 10 percent of all wom known offenders.

About a third of the total number of versus about 2 percent of male victi In 2009, this amounted to 1,0 of 3,122 total women (of 14,496 men) tion in which priate (I

cisely because each party has legitimate reason to fear lethal violence from the other—in the typical homicide, gendered norms governing the ability and acceptability of the use of violence ensure that there is a certain equality between the male victim and male offender. In the context of heterosexual intimate homicides of women victims, gender on the other hand exacerbates inequality between men and women—men who kill their intimate partners almost never claim to have done so because they felt threatened by them. The opposite is true in intimate homicides of men by women, however. Victim precipitation is common—decades of studies have shown that women who kill intimate partners usually do so after years of escalating physical violence (Campbell 1992; Mann 1998; Goetting 1995; Rosenfeld 1997; Swatt and He 2006).

As homicide victimization is gendered, so, too, is victimization from other offenses. One of the clearest and most consistent findings to come from the NCVS is that the relationship between victims and offenders differs sharply by sex; men are much more likely to be victimized by (male) acquaintances or strangers, women by (male) intimates. Victimization for women is hence a more *personal* phenomenon than it is for men. NCVS data on victim-offender relationships, depicted here in table 4.3, demonstrate this quite clearly. For violent crime as a whole, strangers commit 52 percent of all victimizations of men. Fewer than a third of women's victimizations occur at the hands of strangers. Though these data undoubtedly underestimate the prevalence of acquaintance and marital rape (and intimate victimization generally), they still provide compelling evidence that most women are sexually assaulted by someone they know; 79 percent of all sexual assaults of women are committed by a nonstranger, 39 percent by a "friend or acquaintance." Forty-one percent of sexual assaults of women reported to the NCVS are committed by intimates (defined as a current or former husband or boyfriend). A very similar pattern holds for both simple and aggravated assault. For both of these offenses, about 50 percent of offenders for men are strangers, compared with less than a third for women. Women are also many times more likely than men to be assaulted by intimates in particular. Eighteen percent of women victims of aggravated assault report that they were assaulted by an intimate, versus only 6 percent of men (though the small sample size in this latter category means we should be cautious about this figure), and the comparable figures for simple assault are 28 percent and 6 percent, respectively. Even robbery is sex-differentiated in this way. About half of all women robbery victims reported that their offender was someone they knew; the same is true for about only a third of men.

Violence for women is hence very much a gendered experience. It typically arises in the context of relationships with male friends, acquaintances, and intimates, contexts that are themselves shaped by norms concerning

Table 4.3. Victim-Offender Relationships by Offense, NCVS 2009

	Violent Crime Total		Rape		Robbery		Aggravated Assault		Simple Assault	
	Number	Percent	Number	Percent	Number	Percent	Number	Percent	Number	Percent
Male Victims										
Total	2,283,200	100%	19,820	100*	329,070	100	529,550	100	1,404,760	100%
Nonstranger	1,029,710		5,090	26*	108,130	33	247,800	47	668,690	48%
Intimate	117,210	5%	—	NA**	—	NA**	33,150	6*	84,050	6%
Other relative	130,530	6%	–	NA**	22,380	7*	—	NA**	108,150	8%
Friend/acquaintance	781,980	34%	5,090	26*	85,750	26	214,640	41	476,490	34%
Stranger	1,180,000	52%	14,720	NA**	205,800	63	275,920	52	683,560	49%
Unknown	73,490	3	—	NA**	15,140	5*	5,840	1*	52,510	4%
Female Victims										
Total	2,060,250	100	106,100	100	204,720	100	293,790	100	1,455,650	100%
Nonstranger	1,390,720	68	84,240	79	94,890	46	189,610	65	1,021,980	70%
Intimate	538,090	26	43,200	41	41,590	20	52,350	18	400,950	28%
Other relative	181,670	9	—	NA**	21,710	11*	19,850	7*	140,110	10%
Friend/acquaintance	670,960	33	41,040	39	31,590	15*	117,410	40	480,920	33%
Stranger	633,850	31	21,860	21*	97,250	48	104,180	35	410,550	28%
Unknown	35,690	2*	—	NA**	12,570	6*	—	NA**	23,110	2%*

Source: Truman and Rand 2010, table 7.

* Estimate is based on ten or fewer sample cases and should be interpreted with caution.

** Rounds to less than 0.5 percent; value not reported.

Values may not sum to 100 percent due to rounding.

gender and sexuality. As I noted in chapter 2, researchers who have interviewed male rapists have found that, for them, rape often serves as confirmation of masculinity and power. Similarly, violence committed against one's girlfriend or spouse may serve as a way of reasserting masculine power in a relationship, or offenders may simply perceive the use of violence as their right, as just another resource in managing interpersonal conflicts or enforcing their will (e.g., Miller 2008). Regardless of the motivation, such violence arises against a backdrop of notions about masculine power and feminine passivity and has the unquestionable effect of reinforcing these normative expectations.

The picture painted by official statistics on crime victimization is one that mirrors quite closely what we know about other forms of social inequality. Those groups at the bottom rungs of society's ladder of racial and economic privilege are also most likely to be victimized by crime. Black men in particular are facing a crisis of epidemic proportions in America's urban areas, with homicide victimization rates more than eight times higher than those of any other group. Among women, we find that black women are also more likely than are other women to be murdered or to face other forms of violence. Women find themselves with frightening frequency to be the victims of those (men) they know and love; men's victimization is conversely much less personal. And though the poor possess the least, they are most likely to lose the little they have to burglary and theft. Chances of victimization are thus strongly affected by one's standing on the social ladder. As in the case of most social ills, those who are most privileged are least affected.

GENDER AND VICTIMIZATION—WHAT THE OFFICIAL STATISTICS DO NOT TELL US

No method of data collection is perfect, of course. In many ways the NCVS is an improvement over the UCR in that it captures considerably more information about crime and can tell us something about offenses that people are unwilling to report to the police.[11] For example, the UCR reports a total of 88,000 rapes in 2009, a rate of approximately 0.5 per 1,000 women in the population. The NCVS, on the other hand, counts 125,910 rapes, for a rate of approximately 1.0 per 1,000 women over the age of twelve, about twice the UCR statistic. This difference is due to the fact that the NCVS surveys victims directly, while UCR data come from police agencies. The NCVS is hence able to capture rapes that victims did not report to the police, as well as rapes that might have been reported but not founded or investigated by the police.

The NCVS is far from perfect, however, and there is evidence that it may be a particularly poor instrument for capturing the kinds of victimization women are most likely to experience. The NCVS has in fact changed over the years in response to critics who have made just such arguments, and the results of these changes tell us a lot about how gender shapes victims' responses. Before 1992, the NCVS did not ask sample respondents specifically about rape or sexual assault. The instrument instead posed generic questions about whether respondents had been "beaten up" or attacked in other ways. Nor did the survey specifically ask about victimization in the home, inquiring only whether "anyone" had committed violence against the respondent. A redesign process, prompted in part by criticisms from feminist advocacy groups, led to the inclusion of questions specifically about rape as well as an item addressing victimization in the home. After the redesign, rape and sexual assault victimization rates increased by 157 percent. The new instrument also produced a 72 percent increase in women's reporting that they had been victimized by intimates and a 155 percent increase in reports of victimizations by other relatives (Bachman and Saltzman 1995).

This dramatic change confirms that women may not think of themselves as legitimate victims of violence in a generic sense, nor do they generally think of intimates as "typical" abusers. The picture provided by the NCVS is unquestionably more accurate as a result of the redesign. But limitations remain. People may simply be unwilling to report victimizations to interviewers (a problem with any survey), or they might in fact be reluctant to admit even to themselves that they have been victimized. There is good reason to expect that these omissions are systematic, that is, that they affect the statistics for some kinds of victimization and for some groups more than others. Rape, for example, is a heavily stigmatized experience, one that women might be unwilling to discuss with anyone (Weiss 2010). The same is true for physical assaults committed by intimates, or "domestic" violence.[12]

Activists who focus on the issue of violence against women have in fact argued that data gathering from police reports or surveys like the NCVS are poorly adapted for understanding the true extent of women's victimization. Unlike victims of assaults by strangers, women who experience victimization at the hands of intimates and acquaintances live their lives in the context of a host of social institutions—the family, popular culture, and religion—that work to minimize their victimization and make at least some abuse seem like a normal part of life. Women victimized by date rape may see the experience as a result of their own actions—for example, in wearing revealing clothing, going to a bar with a man, or accepting a ride. Wives who are battered by husbands may see this as their own fault for making him angry or failing to perform their domestic responsibilities appropriately. Wives who are raped by their husbands may see this as a normal part of marriage, or as one of the rights husbands legitimately exercise in marriage. As a result, victims of rape and battering are often persuaded that such things are either normal or justified, and their victimization may not be apparent even to themselves. Those who are victimized by strangers, on the other hand, have far less difficulty believing that they are legitimate victims. This poses an obvious problem for empirical research, which requires at a minimum that victims be able and willing to recognize themselves as such.

For all of these reasons, few would disagree that official statistics on women's victimization understate the magnitude of the problem, though no one can say precisely to what extent. It is this uncertainty that has given rise to an ongoing and bitter controversy in criminology—and in the larger culture—over statistics on women's victimization. On one side are antirape and antibattering activists, largely feminists, who argue that the official statistics dramatically underestimate women's victimization. From rape crisis and battered women's shelters come estimates that one-fourth or even one-third of women may be raped or battered in their lifetimes, an estimate many times higher than those produced by any official data source. On the other side of this debate stand some mainstream criminologists, social scientists, and cultural commentators who argue that activists are alarmists with a vested interest in inflating the statistics to advance their own cause.[13] This debate has exploded around a number of issues; I will examine the rhetoric on sexual assault and domestic violence.

She Never Called It Rape:[14] Estimating the Extent of Sexual Assault

Though certainly improved by the redesign instituted in 1992, the NCVS continues to ask victims specifically about "rape" and "assault," a fact that activists suggest depresses rates of reporting for those victims who are unwilling to label their experiences in this way. A victim of an acquaintance rape might, for example, be less likely to label her experience as a rape than as a date that "got out of hand." Wives raped by their husbands face even stronger barriers to viewing their experiences as assaults. Given this, studies that rely on a legalistic operationalization of rape—that is, that ask respondents whether they have experienced this specific act by name—are likely to miss substantial numbers of assaults that nonetheless fit the legal definition. The following excerpt is from an interview as part of a study of marital rape conducted by Diana E. H. Russell:

> Always when [my husband] was drunk he wanted sex. I was afraid of him. He used to accuse me of looking at other men. *Did you have any unwanted sexual experiences with him?* Yes I did—to keep myself from getting banged. He never forced me. He just did the normal things a husband and wife do together.

There was nothing abnormal or unnatural about the sex we had. It was just that I didn't at all want to have it. (quoted in Russell 1982, 44)

By any legal definition of rape, this clearly qualifies. The husband in this case relies on fear, force, and threat of force, and the wife indicates that she "didn't at all want to have [sex]." Yet other elements of this story tell us that this woman is unlikely to call this rape. Indeed, she sees what happened to her as a "normal thing," "nothing abnormal or unnatural." It is even less likely that this woman would report her repeated assaults to the police (and in fact she did not). Russell found that while 14 percent of the women she interviewed described experiences that fit the legal definition of rape, only 7 percent of these women labeled these acts as rape.[15] None ever reported their victimization to the police.[16] This creates a clear problem for those interested in documenting the extent of rape and assault and exposes the heart of the debate over rape statistics—should we call such experiences rape or not?

For feminist criminologists and sociologists, the answer to this question is yes, and the key obstacle is crafting a way to document assaults that victims themselves may not label in this way. The solution to this problem has so far been to construct surveys and interview questions that describe rape in behavioral and definitional terms. Such instruments ask respondents in more general terms if they, for example, have had sex against their will due to force or threat of force or incapacity to consent. Diana E. H. Russell (1984) was one of the first American academics to conduct such research in a sample of the general population. Her work was followed by a number of studies of college-age women by Mary Koss and colleagues (e.g., Koss, Gidycz, and Wisniewski 1987). More recently, a large study of college women (N = 4,446) funded by the U.S. Justice Department (Fisher, Cullen, and Turner 2000) defined victims of completed rape as those who answered "yes" to a series of four questions. Taken together, the question defining rape was essentially this: "Did anyone ever make you have vaginal, oral, or anal intercourse—including penetrating you with a penis, a finger, or a foreign object—by using force or threatening to harm you?" The act described here meets the legal definition for rape in almost all states, yet never specifically asks victims if they were "raped." Researchers call this approach a "behavioral" definition of rape, as it invokes the behaviors defined as rape, rather than naming the act itself.

This particular study, like all others using a behavioral approach, yielded estimates of the prevalence of rape much higher—in this case more than ten times higher—than those reported by the NCVS. In a given year, this study found, about 5 percent of college women report being victimized by completed or attempted rape. Projecting this rate out over a typical college career of five years, the number of victims at any given time on a college campus might rise to between one-fifth and one-quarter of all women students. This estimate is consistent with those of other studies (e.g., Koss, Gidycz, and Wisniewski 1987; Michael et al. 1994; Tjaden and Thoennes 2000, 2006), a fact which suggests that this is a relatively reliable estimate of the prevalence of sexual assault among college women. Comparing these findings to official police counts is instructive; according to this research, a campus of ten thousand students should expect to experience more than 350 rapes in any given year. On my campus of about twenty thousand students, there should by this reckoning have been seven hundred victims during 2009. Campus police report that a total of five rapes occurred during this period.

The roots of the controversy over rape statistics lie in the gap this research and other studies using a behavioral approach reveal between victims' labels of their experiences and the prevalence of acts that meet the legal definition of rape. Of the victims of completed rape surveyed by Fisher, Cullen, and Turner (2000), 49 percent said "no" when asked whether they had been raped, 47 percent said "yes"; the remainder were "not sure." Similarly, though Koss found that 28 percent of the women in her sample of college women reported acts that fit the legal definitions of completed or attempted rape, only 27 percent of those (or 7.6 percent of the total sample) labeled their experiences as rape (Koss 1988; Koss et al. 1987).

Critics have argued this gap indicates that research employing behavioral definitions of rape is little more than advocacy disguised as science. Feminists, they suggest, have used wildly inflated statistics to draw attention to a problem that simply does not exist, at least not on the scale these studies indicate. Their critiques have ranged from the flippant—for example, Katie Roiphe's (1993) remark "If 25 percent of my women friends were really being raped, wouldn't I know it?"—to more serious interrogations of the methods of behavioral studies (e.g., Gilbert 1997). Critics have essentially argued that it is inappropriate to count acts as rape that victims themselves do not label in this way. As Christina Hoff Sommers, another prominent critic, puts it: "The women were there, and they know best how to judge what happened to them" (1995, 214).

This critique misses at least two fundamental points. All data collection about crime relies on legal definitions of particular acts. This is true for rape, robbery, and all of the other offenses tracked by official statistics. If in fact behavioral surveys are defining acts that meet the legal definition of rape (there is some debate about this, though the issue is less contentious), then these acts should be counted as rape. The law does not require that a victim be aware that she or he has been victimized—it focuses on whether the actions of the offender meet the legal definition of a crime. Indeed, such a requirement would contradict the basic logic of criminal law, which presumably identifies acts that *society* (in the guise of its legislators) has identified as harmful and contrary to social order. There is in fact a large category of offenses that have no immediate victims at all, beyond perhaps the offenders themselves (e.g., prostitution, drug use), yet such acts have nonetheless been defined as crimes.

The second problem with this reasoning is that the kinds of victimization that happen disproportionately to women occur in a gendered context of inequality that, as I have noted, works to normalize such experiences. If rape can become, as one of the quotations opening this chapter suggests, "standard operating procedure," or if women raped on videotape can themselves serve time for soliciting prostitution, then we have every reason to expect that victims will resist labeling themselves as such. Indeed in the current legal and cultural context, one might argue that it is quite rational for them to resist these labels.

Whatever side of this debate one finds most persuasive, the most interesting and important question it raises is that of the real-life effects of our definitions. If one defines rape narrowly, as the UCR or NCVS do, as those acts the police or victims are willing to label explicitly as rape, then we certainly face a problem of smaller magnitude; for example, according to police my campus of twenty thousand students was the site of only five rapes in 2009. We are more likely to see rape as an infrequent occurrence, one that occurs primarily between strangers. And we will see victims' unwillingness to label their experiences as rape as confirmation that what occurred really was a "miscommunication" rather than a crime.

If on the other hand we take the approach suggested by the results of behavioral surveys, we will see rape as a larger problem, one enmeshed in intimate relationships and one that is inseparable from norms constructing masculinity, femininity, and heterosexuality. From this perspective the resistance of victims to label their experiences as rape becomes not a methodological glitch, but rather a quite logical outcome shaped by a larger social context of inequality. This approach transforms rape from a technical problem of law enforcement to a political issue, one requiring far deeper and more sweeping social changes that address the social roots of a rape culture. And in fact it is just this kind of feminist social change to which critics are most vocal in their opposition.

Mutual Combat or Wife Battering?
The Debate over Domestic Violence Statistics

A different kind of controversy about victimization data has arisen about feminist claims about the prevalence and consequences of domestic violence. Activists have framed domestic violence as a women's issue, a problem stemming from patriarchal social relations and inequality in heterosexual marriage and intimate relationships. Correspondingly, they have advocated solutions such as battered women's shelters that are targeted to address women's (and their children's) needs. Yet this stance has always been controversial. From the onset of activism about this issue, which began in earnest in the 1970s, there have been critics who have suggested that feminist concerns are overblown and that men, too, are commonly victims of domestic violence. This debate has crystallized recently around the notion of "mutual combat." Mutual combat is the idea that men and women share responsibility for domestic violence and is a rejection of the claim that this is a women's issue.

This concept arose from research employing an instrument (the Conflict Tactics Scale) (Straus 1979) that directs respondents to count instances of their own use of a wide spectrum of physically aggressive techniques against their partners during marital and relationship conflicts. Specifically, the instrument asks respondents the following: "I'm going to read some things that you and your spouse might do when you have an argument. I would like you to tell me how many times in the last 12 months you _____." Response categories and rates of violence reported from the 1985 administration of the survey appear in table 4.4.[17]

It is immediately apparent why this study generated so much controversy. The statistics in this table demonstrate that men are more likely to be victims of relationship violence overall and more likely to experience the most serious forms of violence. Reports of this research created immediate shock waves and calls for attention to the problems of male victims of domestic violence. Remarking on these findings, an op-ed in the *Los Angeles Times* editorialized: "Domestic violence is not either the man's fault or the woman's. Both the male and the female are bound in their dance of mu-

Table 4.4. Estimates of Couple Violence Using the CTS, 1985

	Rate per 1,000 Couples	
	Wife Victim	*Husband Victim*
Threw something	28	43
Pushed, grabbed, or shoved	93	89
Slapped	29	41
Kicked, bit, hit with fist	15	24
Hit or tried to hit with something	17	30
Beat up	8	4
Threat with gun or knife	4	6
Used gun or knife	2	2
Overall	113	121
Severe*	30	44

Source: Gelles and Straus 1988.

*This is an index that combines the last three scale items.

tual destructiveness" (Sherven and Sniechowski 1994). Though the original studies using this instrument were conducted in the 1970s and 1980s, the controversy continues to this day. Still other researchers have used instruments such as the CTS with similar results (e.g., Archer 2000), a pattern of findings that has been offered as a fundamental challenge to feminist constructions of marital violence as a problem primarily experienced by women in the patriarchal context of marriage.[18] Calls for attention to the problem of "battered husbands" followed (Steinmetz 1978), an issue that has achieved wide cultural and disciplinary currency. Criminology texts now largely refer to "partner" or "spousal" violence, and only recently I reviewed a criminology textbook in development that *began* the section on violence in marriage by framing the problem as one of mutual combat.

So what can we make of this controversy? Entire volumes have now been written about it (Loseke, Gelles, and Cavanaugh 2004). Some take these findings as evidence of a hidden epidemic of violence against men, one that battered women's activists have been trying to cover up for years. Warren Farrell (1994) asked, for example: "Why do we protest domestic violence against women and not even know about violence against men?" Feminist critics have responded that the data collected come from an instrument— the Conflict Tactics Scale—that is itself fundamentally flawed. Critics point out that the CTS never asks, for example, who used violence first or what the results of the use of violence were. From other studies we know that women are much more likely than men to use violence in self-defense and to be injured by such acts of violence by their male partners. Gelles and Straus's own data (1988) show that the rate of serious injuries for wives is six times higher than for husbands, and studies of emergency room visits tell us that women are 84 percent of those who seek treatment for violence perpetrated by an intimate (Rand 1997). Violence committed by intimates is much more likely to result in injury for women than violence perpetrated by strangers; the opposite is true for men (Rand 1997; see also Johnson 2008; Warner 2010). Women victims of intimate violence report that they feel more seriously threatened by it than men do, are less likely to be able to effectively defend themselves, experience more depression as a result, and have fewer resources to help them leave violent relationships (Nazroo 1995; Miller 2005; for a review, see Gelles and Loseke 1993). One thing we know for certain—regardless of Straus and Gelles's counts of who threatens whom most frequently with guns or knives—women are much more likely to die at the hands of their intimate partners than are men.

On balance, the evidence suggests that even if the numbers reported by Straus and Gelles are accurate (and there is debate over this issue as well), the experience of intimate violence is not the same for women and men. It is shaped by a preexisting gendered context, the intimate heterosexual relationship, in which men generally possess more physical and economic power than women. Violence arises from and undoubtedly has the effect of reproducing that inequality.[19] One researcher (Johnson 1995, 2008) has recently reframed this debate by arguing that there are essentially two kinds of domestic violence. The first, which he calls "common couple violence," arises out of arguments between couples and often involves both parties in the use of minor physical force (e.g., a husband may shove his wife, who in turn might throw an object at him). This happens relatively rarely, he suggests, and does not typically involve injury, but may be the precisely the kind of violence the CTS captures and that underlies the notion of "mutual combat." "Patriarchal terrorism," on the other hand, arises out of "patriarchal traditions of men's right to control 'their' women. It is a form of terroristic control of wives by their husbands that involves the systematic use of not only violence, but economic subordination, threats, isolation and other control tactics" (Johnson 1995, 284; see also Stark 2007). In short, it is precisely the kind of violence that battered women's advocates have argued that women disproportionately experience, violence that is rooted in gendered inequalities in heterosexual relationships. The CTS may be particularly poorly adapted to capturing this kind of violence. Hence Johnson (2008) argues that both sides may be (at least to some degree) right, but nuance of this kind has often been lost in claims that women in marriages are now "just as violent as men."

These controversies over rape and domestic violence reveal that crime statistics are never simply objective, apolitical descriptions of reality. The passion with which the two sides have mobilized around these issues indicates that these are far more than methodological debates between experts. Both rape and domestic violence touch a cultural nerve. Viewing rape as rare, and as a crime that happens mostly among strangers, suggests a law enforcement solution, or perhaps the training of women in self-defense. Similarly, viewing domestic violence as a problem experienced by intimate partners rather than disproportionately by women seems to evoke solutions like counseling to solve the problems and conflicts that inevitably arise in any intimate relationship. These become essentially neutral technical issues, and addressing them poses no fundamental challenge to existing structures of gender inequality. Viewing rape and domestic violence through a gendered lens, however, transforms them from apparently technical issues to political problems, whose solutions lie in changing the very structures of inequality between men and women in culture as a whole. Even advocates of this latter view realize that making such changes is a daunting task and one that will generate (and has generated) considerable resistance. In the next section of this chapter, I offer a way of thinking about victimization as a cultural issue and begin to examine the practical changes that might follow.

ENGENDERING VICTIMIZATION

I shift in the final part of this chapter from discussing measures of victimization to thinking about explanations for it. As victimization itself is gendered, so must any good theory of victimization take gender into account.
Yet this has rarely been the case. Theories of victimization in criminology
are a somewhat recent development (compared with theories of offending)
and their very existence is controversial. To offer a theory of victimization—
to explain what a person did to become a victim—seems in some ways to
justify the crime committed against her/him. There is thus no comparable
body of victimization theory to match that directed to accounting for criminal offending.

The most commonly used theory of victimization in current criminology
is one on which I have drawn on throughout this book, though not explicitly. The "routine activities" approach (Cohen and Felson 1979; Felson
1994) suggests that people become victims because their everyday actions
expose them to potential offenders. People who spend time in bars with
gang members, or who go to parties where alcohol and weapons are present, or who walk on dangerous streets late at night are engaging in routine
activities that place them at higher risk of victimization than those who
avoid such places. If people in such situations come together with motivated offenders, victimization is likely to result. This seems logical enough
and probably goes some distance toward explaining the vast majority of
personal crimes, which are committed between male strangers or acquaintances. The bar fight or the street robbery certainly fit the assumptions of
the perspective well.

The theory runs into difficulty when one considers women's victimization, however. Though it may in fact account for the woman whose purse
is stolen on a dangerous street late at night, or the relatively rare rape
victim attacked by a stranger outside a bar, it is less well suited to helping
us understand the victimization that disproportionately affects women,
victimization that is more personal and more likely to involve sexual offenses. If a woman is raped on a date with a man, for example, does it
make sense to argue that this routine activity was the cause? Heterosexual
dating is certainly a context in which women are exposed to potential—and
motivated—offenders. If a wife is battered by her husband, is marriage the
routine activity at fault? While one might conceivably be able to avoid dangerous bars or streets, it seems unlikely that heterosexual women would be
similarly able to avoid marriage and dating. The theory thus gives us little
insight into the kinds of victimization women in particular experience.

An older theory of criminal victimization is that of "victim precipitation"
(Wolfgang 1958). The concept describes a scenario in which the victim
himself (or herself) does something to participate in the process of their

own victimization. As I note above, the most common application of this notion has been in the scenario of victim precipitated homicide, which describes a situation in which a war of words is escalated by both sides until it ends in violence and ultimately in death. The law has in fact long recognized that many homicides (and assaults) occur in precisely this way. Depending on the jurisdiction, a homicide offender who commits his crime in the heat of an argument with someone he knows might be charged with second- or third-degree murder, or perhaps even manslaughter. Though we can agree that no one deserves to be murdered in a bar fight or in an argument with a friend, we can certainly understand how such a crime might involve a two-way interaction between the participants.

The situation becomes far more complex when we apply this theory to the victimization that women disproportionately experience. Consider the example of "victim precipitated" rape. In one of the first works on rape by a mainstream criminologist, Menachem Amir's *Patterns in Forcible Rape* (1971), the author argues that many rapes are in fact brought on by their victims. He defines victim precipitated rape as

> those rape situations in which the victim actually, or so it was deemed, agreed to sexual relations but retracted before the actual act or did not react strongly enough when the suggestion was made by the offender(s). The term applies also to risky situations marred with sexuality, especially when she uses what could be interpreted as indecency of language and gestures, or constitutes what could be taken as an invitation to sexual relations. (1971, 266)

Using this definition, Amir defines 19 percent of all of the rapes he studied as victim precipitated.

Critics (e.g., Brownmiller 1975) immediately pointed out that Amir's definition takes the perspective of the rapist. His use of phrases like "or so it was deemed," "could be interpreted as," and "could be taken as an invitation to sexual relations," puts the law firmly on the side of what the rapist, rather than the victim, intended. Essentially, if an offender believes that a woman is somehow immodest (e.g., she uses "indecency of language") or interested in sex, his responsibility for his actions is diminished. There are several problems with the notion of victim precipitated rape. First, from a legal standpoint, all laws regulating sexual assault in the United States today focus responsibility on the victim's consent rather than the offender's perception, seemingly invalidating the notion in a legal sense. We do know, however, that the prosecution of rape cases is sometimes a very different matter. Juries and the observing culture often employ rationalizations about victims' conduct that seemingly absolve offenders of responsibility (Martin 2005; Taslitz 1999). In one Florida rape case in which a victim was abducted from a parking lot, forced into a car, and raped at knifepoint, a jury nonetheless acquitted the offender. The victim had been wearing a tank top and a short skirt, and jurors in the case concluded that this invalidated any evidence of a crime. "She asked for it," said one juror, Roy Diamond. Another juror, Dean Medeiros, said, "We felt she was up to no good the way she was dressed" (Associated Press Wire 1989). These attitudes are far from dated or atypical, as recent high-profile sexual assault cases have demonstrated. Certainly the notion of victim precipitated rape has wide cultural currency.[20]

Its status as criminological theory is another matter. In simple terms, applying the classic definition of victim precipitation to rape is illogical. If, as criminologists agree, a victim precipitated homicide involves escalating levels of threat, then the concept becomes nonsensical. Rapists are not threatened by their victims—the vagina is not a weapon deployed by the victim that evokes the use of a more powerful weapon by the offender in his defense. At best, the notion of victim precipitated rape is less a criminological theory than a barometer of cultural stereotypes about rape victims and sexualized interactions between men and women. All in all, criminological theory has not done a particularly good job at theorizing or understanding gendered victimization.

This does not mean, however, that one must reject theory entirely or look for the cause of violence against women within the psyches of deviant men themselves. Victimization, like almost all social phenomena, is patterned and systematic. It happens to some groups more than others. It is shaped by inequalities of race, gender, and class, and it is not randomly distributed across social contexts. Next, I offer a sociological approach that builds on these facts to understand women's victimization.

A Contextual Theory of Violence against Women

Thirty years ago, anthropologist Peggy Reeves Sanday (1981) published a study in which she set out to determine those characteristics of societies that make them "rape prone." She analyzed information about ninety-five tribal and band societies and found that 18 percent had very high rates of sexual violence against women—and hence could be defined as rape prone— while 47 percent had relatively low rates and could thus be categorized as "rape free." Sanday was interested in what made one kind of society different from another. She found that these cultures differed from one another in a variety of ways that concern the status of women. Rape-prone societies, according to Sanday, are those in which there are high levels of inequality between men and women, in which men (or groups of men) control economic resources and occupy the highest levels of politics, religion, and culture. Violence in these societies is an accepted and legitimate means of solving conflicts, and sex for men is an active, aggressive demonstration of masculinity. Rape-free societies, on the other hand, exhibit far more political and economic equality between women, and there is sharing, or at least complementarity, in the most important positions of power. Violence in these societies is an illegitimate and rarely used method of solving conflicts. A simplified version of Sanday's typology appears in table 4.5.

Sanday's work, intended to differentiate between societies, provides a useful tool for understanding rape within societies as well. Though we sometimes think of rape as a crime that could happen anywhere, to any woman, we know that rape—like every other crime—is not randomly distributed. Just as we can think of some societies as rape prone, so too are some social contexts more conducive to sexual violence than others. Understanding what makes them so may tell us a lot about the cultural and situational causes of violence against women.

I opened this chapter with three such contexts—the military, the fraternity, and the men's athletic team. These three settings, taken together, produce literally hundreds of cases of sexual assault every year. Many of these

Table 4.5. Characteristics of Rape-Prone and Rape-Free Societies

	Rape Free	*Rape Prone*
Religion	Worship a mother goddess or both male and female gods, or are animistic	Worship a single male god or a hierarchy led by a male god or gods
	Women take a major role in religious rituals	Women play few important roles in religious rituals
Politics	Women hold political power equal with/comparable to men	Women play few important political roles
		Power held by homosocial (all male) groups
Economics	Men and women control equal economic resources	High levels of economic inequality between men and women
	Society is relatively economically secure	Society is economically insecure
	Emphasis on living in harmony with the environment	Environment as something to be conquered
		A rigid, gender-based division of labor
Social norms	Violence not viewed as a legitimate method of solving conflicts	Use of violence to solve conflicts routine and legitimate
	Fertility among most valued traits	Sex for men viewed in achievement terms, as proof or masculinity, or as punishment for women
		Separation of the sexes is the rule

are crimes committed by individuals—like the rapes of dozens of women cadets at the Air Force Academy (Schemo 2003; see also United States Department of Defense 2010)—but a disproportionately high number are gang rapes, like the fraternity party assault that opens this chapter or the mass rape of an intellectually disabled teenager by members of a high-school baseball team described in the book *Our Guys* (Lefkowitz 1998). Taking Sanday as a model, I suggest that there are certain characteristics of these settings that make them rape prone.

Before proceeding, however, I want to be very clear that I do not believe that rape occurs only in these settings or that every male soldier, fraternity member, or athlete is a rapist waiting for an opportunity.[21] As a sociologist, I am actually not centrally interested in what an individual rapist thinks or in his seemingly idiosyncratic motive for engaging in rape. What I ask the reader to do is to put aside the prevailing cultural obsession with individual psychology and instead focus on social context. Extensive social psychological research demonstrates that social situations affect people, often to the extent that what they believe are their own individual personalities and desires are secondary (for a review, see Howard and Hollander 1997). In his famous mock prison experiment, Philip Zimbardo (Haney, Banks, and Zimbardo 1973) demonstrated that ordinary male college students, randomly assigned to the roles of prisoner or guard, become over a few days so totally enmeshed in those roles that their own personalities disappeared—they *became* prisoners or guards.[22] The context of the prison defined the role, and the role essentially became the person. This research and other studies like it (e.g., Milgram 1963; Rosenhan 1973) tell us that social situations affect our behavior, and as such they deserve analysis in their own right. And indeed, understanding *social* behavior is what sociology is about.

So if one is willing to accept two premises—one, that social contexts shape individual behavior, sometimes so profoundly that individual actors are literally taken out of themselves, and two, that the contexts I have described are "rape prone," then the next question is—what do these contexts have in common that might make them rape prone? A number of sociological studies provide pieces of the answer. First, all of these settings place a high value on the cultivation of a particular, and narrowly defined, masculinity that prioritizes physical strength and aggression, dominance over women, and—as Sanday posits—an emphasis on heterosexual conquest as proof that one is a real man. The military has long been about "turning boys into men," and male athletic teams and many fraternities also cultivate an aggressive, dominating masculinity. In describing their ideal pledges, fraternity members interviewed by Martin and Hummer (1989) pointed to athleticism, physical strength, and an ability to "hold one's liquor" and "relate socially to women." Conversely, men who were perceived as "wimpy," "geeks," or "nerds" were rarely accepted as pledges (see also

Yeung, Stombler, and Wharton 2006). It is no coincidence that all of these settings place a high value on brotherhood and bonds between men, bonds that are often built on the devaluation of women. Even if individual men in these contexts do not wish to comply, the pressures to do so can often be difficult to resist. One American soldier accused in a 2006 murder case in Iraq said that he went along because a fellow soldier told him to "stop being a pussy" (British Broadcasting Corporation 2006).[23] For those who do conform, the rewards, at least from male peers, can be equally great.

Second, all of these settings are completely or at least mostly sex segregated and have historically been built on the exclusion of women. This is self-evident in the case of fraternities and men's sports teams, but the military has resisted the full integration of women as well. Men who graduated from the Air Force Academy before women were allowed to enroll sometimes sport hats with the initials "LCWB," an acronym that stands for "Last Class Without Bitches" (Janofsky and Schemo 2003). Women cadets who complain have simply been told to deal with it. The fact that these settings are sex segregated heightens the boundaries between masculinity and femininity and makes it far easier for men to objectify women. This pattern has a long tradition in the military, where portraits of shapely women have adorned fighter planes and bombs from their first invention to the present. In wartime, objectification of women is often extreme, as the quotation that opens this chapter attests. A woman who is a "gook" or a "dink" loses her humanity, and rape can easily become "standard operating procedure."[24] Objectification in other settings is perhaps less extreme, but no less persistent. The "jocks" responsible for the gang rape studied by Lefkowitz (1998) commonly viewed pornography together, a finding that has been documented among fraternity men as well (DeKeseredy and Schwartz 1998; Sanday 1990). And a recent study on a college campus (Bleecker and Murnen 2005) found that fraternity men displayed more sexually explicit images of women in their rooms and also exhibited higher levels of agreement than nonfraternity men with statements such as "being roughed up is sexually stimulating to women."

Third, women in all of these settings serve as formal or informal auxiliaries who support men's activities. In the military, women served in explicitly constituted auxiliaries from World War II through the end of the Vietnam War (though these have now been disbanded). In sports, most obviously, women serve as cheerleaders at men's athletic events, and they serve men's athletic programs in other ways. In the wake of rape charges connected to the University of Colorado's football recruiting practices, we learned that many colleges utilize undergraduate women as liaisons (often called "hostesses") for football recruits. At the University of Texas, these are the "Texas Angels." Mississippi State University has the "Bulldog Belles." Critics of this practice argue that women are being used as "bait" to attract the best recruits: "It's seeing women as part of the prize . . . one of the perks a university has to offer, in addition to the best stadium, the best chances for getting on television, the best strength-and-conditioning coaches. Women are just a part of that package of what assets a school has to offer" (Jacobson 2004). Similarly, many fraternities (including some on my own campus) have "Little Sister" organizations, whose members' duties, according to one little sister, include: "go[ing] to all of the intramural games to cheer the brothers on, support[ing] and encourag[ing] the pledges, and . . . support[ing] the brothers in all they do" (quoted in Martin and Hummer 1989, 467–68, see also Stombler 1994). There is evidence that members explicitly attract pledges with promises of access to women. As one fraternity member put it: "We always tell the guys that you get sex all the time. . . . After I became a Greek, I found out that I could be with females at will" (quoted in Martin and Hummer 1989, 468).

Of course, these settings have a number of other characteristics in common. They are composed of young men, a group that we already know is disproportionately likely to engage in a wide variety of criminal behaviors, and these young men are often relatively unsupervised. On most campuses, for example, fraternity houses (at least for those whose members are mostly white) are off campus, and indeed this is part of the appeal, for many, of pledging a fraternity. The "jocks" responsible for the rape of an intellectually disabled teenager in Glen Ridge, New Jersey, were responsible for dozens of acts of unchecked mayhem, in one case completely demolishing the house of a female classmate whose parents were out of town. Men in these settings also often share a sense of privilege and entitlement, for example, as sports heroes, or as the big men on campus (Kimmel 2008). These contexts are conducive to a host of other risky behaviors, like excessive alcohol consumption and elaborate and often dangerous hazing rituals (common in all three settings). And in all of these instances, such behavior is often excused with a sort of "boys will be boys" logic.

But I want to suggest something different. Following Sanday's lead, I suggest that, instead of focusing on the motives of individual men in these settings, we instead look at the settings themselves. In much the same way that students in Zimbardo's prison study *became* prisoners or guards, we can argue that soldiers, athletes, and fraternity members are shaped by the social and institutional contexts of their organizations. If the norms, practices, and structures of these organizations are rape prone, then it makes sense that rape would be more likely among their members. Men may resist these norms, and many do, but the pressure to accede is considerable and undeniable.

Some caveats seem in order. As I said at the outset, I am not suggesting that every member of such an organization is a rapist, or even a potential rapist. I am arguing, however, that rape is more likely in these settings than in others that do not share their characteristics, and just as importantly, it is unlikely to be taken seriously when it does occur. I do not mean to suggest that individual rapists should be excused because of the influence of social structure on their behavior. But it is often easier to change structures than people, and changes in the structures in which we live our lives often alter the way we view the world. Changing individuals, though important, will matter little unless we can change social structures as well.

What would such changes look like? Glen Ridge, New Jersey, the home of the sexual assault described in *Our Guys*, took on this question in the aftermath of the attack and the events that followed. One community member described the changes:

> No longer are athletic trophies the first thing you see as you enter the High School. Now the Honor Roll is prominent. Of the 60 high school seniors 15 have National Merit commendation and 5 are finalists, a new type of competition. Students must do community service to graduate. Many new people have moved in who have brought diversity and a liberal awareness. A Human Relations Committee has worked to create a communications network, to establish an advisory link with the local government, to assist law enforcement and to organize public events to promote understanding, respect and concern for all people. Glen Ridge has come a long way.

There are other implications of a contextual approach. Campuses might, as many already have, move fraternity houses on campus, or establish and enforce alcohol-free policies. Women's auxiliaries, like "hostess" programs for male athletes, might be abolished. The options range from extreme to trivial, but the key in each case is to change a context that is conducive to violence against women.

VICTIMIZATION ENGENDERED

Victimization is powerfully gendered, and the experience of victimization occurs at the intersection of class, race, and gender. Though laws presumably protect the lives and property of all of us, the poor are most likely to fall victim to violent crime and to lose the little property they have. African Americans, particularly young African American men, are dying on our streets in what can only be called an epidemic of violence. For the most part, their killers are other young men, who kill their acquaintances in victim-precipitated incidents that often boil down to contests over masculinity and respect. Women's victimization is less common, but more personal—they are killed, assaulted, and even robbed by men they know, often those closest to them. Again, poor women and those who are members of subordinated racial groups bear the brunt of the violence.

The persistent and extremely contentious battles over the extent and meaning of women's victimization in particular tell us that even statistics themselves emerge from and are interpreted in a gendered political context. For those who want to minimize the importance of gender inequality, a woman who does not define her assault explicitly as rape, and who does not report it to the police has not actually been raped, and domestic violence is a problem of mutual combat in which wives are just as violent as husbands. Such conceptions leave essentially untouched the structures that create and sustain violence against women.

Theories of victimization can themselves play a role in depoliticizing and rationalizing violence, whether they argue from a gender-neutral perspective or one in which victims themselves seemingly entice their rapists or batterers to harm them. I have argued very strongly that any theory that does not take gender into account can do little to help us understand what is unquestionably a fundamentally gendered process. The roots of violence are, as Sanday suggests, to be found in social practices and in culture itself. And if culture is both the origin of and sustainer of violence, then only cultural changes offer lasting solutions.

5

Gender and Work in the Criminal Justice System

Perry Mason is the fictional TV lawyer that Americans would most prefer to have in their corner in a legal dispute, according to a survey by FindLaw, the leading legal Web site. When asked, "Who would you rather have defending you in court?" the results were: Perry Mason (38 percent), Ben Matlock (29 percent), Bobby Donnell (*The Practice*—16 percent), Ally McBeal (9 percent). While men and women age 34 and under preferred Ben Matlock over Perry Mason (32 percent vs. 24 percent), Perry Mason was the solid choice for older respondents. When asked why they chose Perry Mason, people provided explanations such as, "he seems honest," and "would be most likely to win my case." "People seemed to lean towards experience and perceived track record, at least in selecting an imaginary TV lawyer," said Stacy Stern, vice president of FindLaw. (Findlaw 2001)

Police work used to be like a laborer's job . . . the only requirement was that you had to be tough. Now, that's not what we're looking for. . . . [The job] is all about knowing how to talk to people. We screen for drug use, criminal background, but we don't do much screening for people who can get along with other people. . . . A good cop knows how to defuse the situation by talking it out. (quoted in Egan 1991, A14)

It's real funny, they're real protective of me. I have one lieutenant, he said, "I'm never going to put you anywhere where I think you're going to be hurt." Okay, and he would never say that to a guy. "I'll never assign you where I think you'll be in danger." And, I think that's so sweet! I think it's so sexist, but I mean, I appreciate it! (woman correctional officer, quoted in Britton 2003, 175)

To this point, this book has examined differences in the treatment of men and women *by* the law and the criminal justice system. This chapter looks at the work of women and men *in* this system. For most of the time since Europeans in the United States established their own laws, courts, and prisons, women have lacked access to formal positions working in these institutions. Though the numbers of women who served as attorneys, police officers, and prison officers fluctuated slightly (from zero to a high of about 2 percent) over the decades, it was not until the 1970s that their numbers began to grow significantly. Women are now 47 percent of law school graduates (American Bar Association 2010), 12 percent of sworn police officers (Federal Bureau of Investigation 2010), and 24 percent of correctional officers (author calculation, Bureau of Justice Statistics 2009). But as the quotations that open this chapter indicate, ideas about gender continue to shape these occupations. The ideal lawyer, according to most, is Ben Matlock or Perry Mason (or, for the more literary, perhaps even Atticus Finch). Even though ideas about what it takes to enforce the law have changed to some degree over the past few decades—a good cop is a better talker than fighter—stereotypes about the need for tough and protective masculinity continue to limit and shape women's access to and performance of jobs as police and correctional officers in prisons.

In this chapter, I turn a gender lens on work in the criminal justice system, focusing in particular on these three occupations. I begin by sketching a general picture of women's work in the paid labor force, and of the large and persistent wage gap between men and women. Then I offer a theoretical framework for thinking about gender in work organizations, and finally I turn to case studies of women's work as attorneys, police, and correctional officers.

WOMEN, WORK, AND THE WAGE GAP—A STATISTICAL SNAPSHOT

The twentieth century saw a number of major transformations in the labor force participation (LFP) of men and women. In 1900, 54 percent of men and 20 percent of women worked for wages; as of 2009, 72 percent of men and 59 percent of women did so. The percentage of men in the labor force increased by only about 20 points during the past century or so, mostly due to the continuing movement of the population away from agriculture and into waged labor. Women's LFP increased far more dramatically; by 2009 almost two out of three women worked outside the home for wages, 74 percent of them full-time (86 percent of men work full-time). In the early part of the century, women who worked almost always did so out of dire economic necessity. They were single, often with no other means of support, or they were married women whose wages were necessary for survival in poor families. It is partly for this reason that white women's labor force participation has historically lagged behind that of African American women—white married women have had access to the higher wages earned by white men.

Two groups have driven the increase in women's LFP since the 1960s. The first is composed of married women. As figure 5.1 indicates, married women are now more likely than at any time in American history to be employed in the paid labor force. Their numbers have doubled since 1960. More than 60 percent of all married women work for pay, and the bread-winner-husband/homemaker-wife configuration now makes up only 20 percent of all American families. And as the LFP of women has increased, so, too, has that of mothers. As of 2007, 62 percent of married women with children under the age of six were in the paid labor force—as well as 58 percent of women with children under the age of one (United States Census Bureau 2009).

A number of forces have combined to create these changes. The first and most obvious is financial. For most families, women's work is necessary simply to maintain a decent standard of living. The cost of daily life and of items such as housing and health care has risen so quickly that the vast majority of couples simply cannot afford to live on one salary. Similarly,

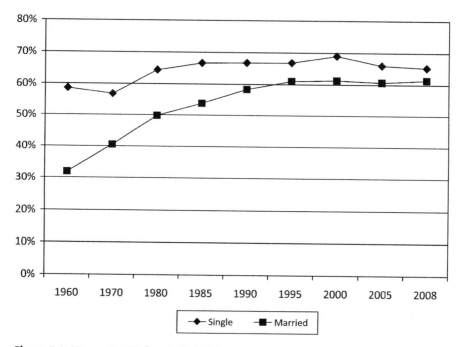

Figure 5.1. Women's LFP, by Marital Status

Source: United States Census Bureau 2009.

rising age at first marriage and divorce rates of around 50 percent mean that women now expect to support themselves for substantial periods of their lives. And far from feeling "forced" into the labor market, many women—particularly those in in higher-status occupations—now say they find equal or greater satisfaction at work than at home (Hochschild 1997) and that work has become a defining part of their identities.

At the same time, ideas about women and work have shifted. We often hear that while society used to think it was improper for women, or for mothers, to work, we now see it as acceptable. Indeed many women were barred from occupations because of notions about their proper role. In a decision barring women from legal practice, a Wisconsin Supreme Court wrote in 1875:

> The law of nature destines and qualifies the female sex for the bearing and nurture of children. . . . The peculiar qualities of womanhood, its gentle graces, its quick sensibility, its tender susceptibility, its purity, its delicacy, its emotional impulses, its subordination of hard reason to sympathetic feeling, are surely not qualifications for forensic strife. (*In the Matter of the Motion to Admit Ms. Lavinia Goodell to the Bar of this Court* [39 Wis. 232, 1875])

The court in this case relied on the separate spheres notion of femininity common in the nineteenth century, an ideology that saw women as suited, by nature, for the roles of making a home and raising children in the domestic arena. Men's nature, on the other hand, fitted them for the rational, impersonal, and combative environment of the public sphere.[1] Though the ideas about women expressed by the court retain a certain currency, most people would now dismiss as ridiculous the notion that women should be restricted to the private sphere. Times do indeed appear to have changed.

The problem with this simple story of progress is that it is not true for all groups of women. Black women's experience of labor in the United States began with slavery, and certainly no slaveholder considered them too delicate to engage in heavy labor or worried that their children would be neglected while they toiled in the fields. Some have argued that the brutal quasi-equality imposed by slavery, combined with disproportionately high rates of poverty among African American families since then, made black women's paid work normative. Certainly their paid labor force participation rates have historically been higher than those of white women (though they are now equivalent). Similarly, poor women of every racial group, married or not, mothers or not, have always engaged in paid labor to support themselves and their families. The ideology that women, or mothers, should not work for pay is based on a foundation of race and class inequality. Those women who cannot conform to this ideology—who have had to work to support their families—have often faced the stigma of being labeled as bad or neglectful. Hence this has been a notion most easily indulged by the white middle class, and it is the white middle class that has recently lost this privilege.

Given these differences, it is perhaps more accurate to say that ideas about women and work have been shaped by women's—particularly white middle-class women's—growing labor force participation. Most young women of every race and class now expect to work for pay, and for the middle class, the days of the "Mrs." college degree have faded almost completely into memory. The reality is that most women do work in the paid labor force, even mothers of small children. As some commentators have noted, the time has passed for asking whether it is a good idea for married women, or for mothers of young children, to work outside the home. We must now confront the question of how all of those who care for children (or parents, or only themselves) can best balance the responsibility of work and family, and what the responsibility of business, government, and society is in helping workers find that balance.

But while equal work may be becoming the norm for American workers, equal pay is not. A woman working full-time, year-round (FTYR) in America in 2009 made about seventy-six cents for every dollar a man working FTYR made (United States Census Bureau 2010a). The good news (perhaps) is that this gap has declined by twelve cents in the fifty-four years since 1955, when a woman working FTYR made only sixty-four cents— though this is a rate of increase of about 0.2 cents per year. At least two factors have helped to narrow the gap. One is the rising level of human capital held by women. Human capital is the term economists use to refer to the set of assets the individual brings to the employer. On this score women have caught up to men quickly. Women are more likely than men to graduate from high school, and are now even more likely to receive bachelor's degrees. As women have spent more time in the paid labor force, they have also acquired more years of work experience. Another factor contributing to narrowing the gap has been a decline in men's wages. Many high-paying jobs historically dominated by men—such as factory labor—have been lost or moved out of the country over the past thirty years; a similar trend is now overtaking the ranks of middle management as well.

The bad news is that the wage gap has recently stabilized, fluctuating only slightly up and down since 1995. The gap also persists even when one controls levels of human capital, e.g., when one compares similarly educated men and women. Table 5.1 presents the most recent data on median incomes among all FTYR workers and by race and education.

In 2009, a woman working FTYR made a median income of $37,234. The median is a statistical value that represents the center of a distribution of numbers—here it means that 50 percent of women working FTYR made less than $37,234, while 50 percent made more. A man working FTYR, on the other hand, received a median income of $49,164. This means that

Table 5.1.   Median Income of FTYR Workers, 2009

	Male ($)	Female ($)	Gap (%)
All	49,164	37,234	76
White	52,469	40,265	77
Black	39,362	32,470	82
Hispanic	31,638	27,883	88
< 9 years education	24,419	18,904	77
HS graduate	40,458	30,289	75
Some college	49,078	35,645	73
BA/BS	66,748	48,688	73
MA/MS	82,328	63,232	77
PhD	102,616	77,851	76
Professional	136,757	84,648	62

Source: United States Census Bureau 2010a.

for every dollar a man received, a woman worker made about seventy-six cents. Race and education affect the wage gap; the disparity among black and Hispanic men and women is smaller than that for whites, but their incomes are correspondingly lower. Black men working FTYR made only seventy-five cents for every dollar made by their white male counterparts; Hispanic men, sixty cents (compared to white men, black women made sixty-two cents, Hispanic women, fifty-three cents). Black men's incomes are slightly lower than white women's; Hispanic men make considerably less. There are gaps at every level of education. A male college graduate with a bachelor's degree, for example, makes $26,000 more than a male high-school graduate—a return on his college education of more than $6,500 per year (assuming a four-year bachelor's degree). A female college graduate earns only about $18,000 more than a female high-school graduate (a return on her education of about $4,600 per year), but only $8,000 per year more than a male high-school graduate.[2] For 2009, the gap is highest among those with professional degrees—women earn only 62 percent of what men earn with the same educational credential.

Debate about the causes of the wage gap has been long and heated. The traditional economic argument, that the gap is due to differing levels of human capital between groups of workers, has become increasingly difficult to sustain as those disparities have lessened. The most obvious reason that men and women earn different salaries is that they are in different jobs. Women are disproportionately found in the service sector, in occupations such as clerical work, nursing, or elementary- and middle-school teaching, and retail. Men dominate in technical fields such as engineering and technology, in many of the professions, in highly paid blue-collar construction trades, and in the transportation and trucking industry. The fact that male-dominated occupations pay more than female-dominated ones accounts for a large portion of the wage gap.

Some economists and other social scientists do not view this as problematic, seeing this kind of occupational segregation entirely as the outcome of men's and women's individual preferences (e.g., Hakim 1998). Others see it as the product of social forces that work together to sustain inequality. The demands of balancing work and family mean that women, more than men, make occupational choices that allow them the flexibility to care for children, and increasingly, for parents. Men are freer to make choices about career, and their higher wages often mean that families are uprooted to follow men's (but not women's) career paths. Employers also play a very important role, making choices about hiring and promotion in accord with their preconceptions about race and gender and about the "ideal" nurse, or attorney, or police officer.

All of this means that while patterns of occupational sex segregation help to explain the wage gap, they are not entirely the result of (mythical) asocial preferences. Segregation is produced by, and at the same time reproduces, the social patterns that create and sustain gender inequality. Even if one were to grant that segregation were the result of preferences, questions would remain. We know, for example, that truck mechanics make more than elementary-school teachers. Yet on the grounds of human capital alone—teachers must have a college degree, and in some states a master's degree—this difference seems illogical. Moreover, large-scale studies that statistically control for the characteristics of workers and the skills required by jobs (among a host of other indicators) consistently find a gap that cannot be explained by those factors alone (see, for example, England 2005).

There are also wage gaps even between workers in the same jobs. Women attorneys, for example, make seventy-five cents for every dollar made by men, women police officers, eighty-three cents, and women correctional officers, eighty-six cents. The gap in many other occupations is much larger—women physicians, for example, make only sixty-four cents for every dollar made by men (Bureau of Labor Statistics 2010). The problem of explaining the wage gap is complicated even further when one examines the results for men and women who cross over into occupations dominated by the opposite sex. In male-dominated occupations, equally qualified women tend to earn less and advance more slowly than their male counterparts. In female-dominated jobs, the opposite is true. Men in jobs such as nursing, teaching, and librarianship earn more and advance more quickly than do equally qualified women. In fact, this pattern is so evident and well established that it has been called the "glass escalator" effect (Williams 1992).[3]

So, while women's labor force participation has been converging with men's fairly quickly over the past century or so, the wages women receive for their work have increased considerably less rapidly. The wage gap appears to have leveled off at about a twenty-five-cent advantage for men, and white men in particular earn more than every other race/sex group of full-time, year-round workers. Patterns of occupational segregation are persistent and reflect notions about the kinds of work for which men and women are suited—as well as the value of that labor. All of this is true across the labor force, as well as in the three occupations that are the focus of this chapter. Before moving to look at them in depth, I offer a theoretical framework for thinking about patterns of sex segregation across the labor force and patterns of inequality within organizations and occupations themselves.

ENGENDERING OCCUPATIONS AND ORGANIZATIONS

Attempts to solve the twin puzzles of occupational sex segregation and the wage gap have come from a number of angles. Some, as I note above, have ascribed these inequalities to the individual choices of workers. Others point to discrimination by employers and the exclusionary efforts of co-workers from dominant groups. A piece of the solution lies in both of these explanations, though academics differ about how much weight to give to each perspective. To some degree, the problem with both is that they assign causality at an individual or, at best, a group level, ascribing differences to the effects of the personal choices of workers or viewing discrimination as something that motivated people or groups do in organizations to maintain their own privilege. It is a fundamental assumption of sociology, however, that all actions, as well as all institutions, exist within a social structural and cultural context. To a sociologist, it makes little sense to speak of "choices" in an asocial way. A woman may *choose* to be a nurse, but she does so in a context in which the occupation itself has been designated as appropriate for women (in fact it was designed by the founders of the profession with women's supposedly inherent nurturing and submissiveness in mind), and in which women dominate among those with whom she will likely work. She must also have the resources to obtain the education necessary to become a nurse, and, until the desegregation of hospitals and nursing programs in the wake of civil rights laws, her chances of becoming employed would have been much greater had she been white. This does not imply that she does not exercise choice, just that all choices occur in a socially bounded context in which gender, race, and class play key roles.

This means that any explanation of occupational segregation or the wage gap must take into account the social context in which these patterns appear. The theory of gendered organizations, a perspective that first appeared in the sociological literature in the 1990s (Acker 1990; see Britton 2000b; Britton and Logan 2008 for reviews) argues that organizations and occupations are themselves gendered (and racialized and classed and sexualized) social contexts whose influence must be considered if we are to understand the inequalities we find within them. Rather than seeing gender only as something that workers bring with them to their jobs, the theory of gendered organizations argues that gender is already there, forming the substance and culture and everyday routines of work environments.

Gendered Cultures

There are three levels at which we can speak of organizations and occupations as gendered. The first is culture. Most people draw on gendered images and symbols when they think of particular jobs. Nursing is an obvious example. Though much of the job is highly technical and specialized, the images attached to the work are those of nurturing and caretaking—skills that are associated with women. Sociologists speak of nursing as an occupation that has been gender typed as feminine (or feminized)—at the level of cultural ideas, it requires qualities that are supposedly inherently women's. Firefighting, one of the most male-dominated of all occupations, is conversely masculinized. Some of the most enduring images to come from national disasters are those of male firefighters, soot on their faces, carrying children, running into burning buildings, or climbing over the rubble of destruction. Firefighting has long been associated with supposedly inherent masculine characteristics—bravery, heroism, physical strength. One firefighting supervisor describes his ideal recruit this way: "What we're really looking for is a man with a big 'S' on his chest" (Skuratowicz 1996).[4] In fact, the association of firefighting with masculinity is so complete that when a woman firefighter tried to draw attention to the heroism of her women colleagues in working alongside men at the World Trade Center on September 11, 2001, she received death threats.[5]

Images of occupations are similarly bound to notions of race and class. The heroic firefighter in the public imagination is not just a man, but a white man. African American men have also faced a long history of discrimination in their attempts to integrate firefighting and currently make up only 7.5 percent of all of those in the occupation. This is in part tied to the fact that, particularly in large cities, firefighters have been drawn primarily from the networks among white ethnic groups (Yoder and Aniakudo 1997). In a similar way, the iconic image of the nurse is that of a white woman. Harvey Wingfield (2009) has documented the challenges that black men face in working as nurses. This man's experience captures the influence of racialized images of the occupation:

> Being a Black male nurse, the hardest thing is the racism. . . . I see it in the attitudes of colleagues, and some patients. [Once] I came in, and introduced myself to [a white woman] patient. I come in in my white uniform—I said good evening, my name's Chris, and I'm going to be your nurse. She says to me, "Are you from housekeeping?" (quoted in Harvey Wingfield 2009, 18–19)

Chris's experience suggests that patients draw on notions of who a nurse is supposed to be. In the mind of this woman—as in that of many patients—a nurse is a white woman. Black men in a hospital, on the other hand, must work in housekeeping, an occupation that is equally racialized.

There are literally thousands of occupations that are gender typed as masculine or feminine. Though such definitions can shift over time (e.g., clerical work shifted from a masculine gender-typed occupation to a feminized one after the invention of the typewriter and back to a more neutral one with the advent of computers), they have real and enduring effects in reproducing occupational sex segregation and fueling the wage gap. These images shape the choices of potential workers—young boys, for example, may face a host of questions from those around them if they express an interesting in nursing, and studies of men in nursing show that they often have to defend their masculinity (Williams 1995). Because heterosexuality and dominant forms of masculinity are so closely tied, men in female-dominated occupations face questions about their sexuality as well (Williams 1995; Harvey Wingfield 2009). Similarly, women in many male-dominated occupations must contend with images (such as those of the firefighter) that make women in the job seem to be contradictions in terms. These ideas also shape employment and promotion practices within organizations.

Gendered Structures

The second level of analysis of the gendered character of organizations and occupations is structural. Here I mean organizational policies and practices that presume and reproduce gender inequality. These may take the form of explicit exclusionary rules, such as those that historically barred women from many male-dominated occupations (and also excluded men from some female-dominated jobs). Most such formal barriers fell with the passage of Title VII of the Civil Rights Act of 1964 and the Equal Employment Opportunity Act of 1972. More commonly, this happens through organizational policies and practices that appear to be gender neutral but that nonetheless presume and reproduce inequality. A simple example would be the requirement, common in the federal prisons I studied (Britton 2003), that correctional officers who are promoted must transfer to another prison. While there are sound organizational reasons for this (e.g., a desire for administrators to have experience in a variety of prison settings), in practice such a policy means that women are less likely to seek promotion than are men. Research tells us that couples are more likely to change residences to advance a husband's career rather than a wife's (Bielby and Bielby 1992), and the persistent wage gap between men and women further ensures that this pattern will generally make logical financial sense.

Still other gender-neutral organizational practices reinforce gender in-equality. For example, in many firms, rules about hiring and promotion are based on unspoken understandings about the kinds of workers who are appropriate for jobs, or those who would make good supervisors or administrators. I once heard a senior colleague at my own institution, for example, say that he would "just know" when a given candidate was ready for promotion to full professor, and encouraged his junior colleagues to seek out his approval before advancing their own cases for promotion. The problem with such unspoken rules is that they create a pattern that Rosabeth Moss Kanter (1993) called homosocial reproduction. Those who are in power—and in many organizations, this is a small group of wealthy white men—identify those most like themselves as the best candidates for hiring and promotion. Hence the race, gender, and class of those in power changes little over time. In contrast, research strongly suggests (Reskin and McBrier 2000) that organizations in which hiring and promotion processes are clearly specified and transparent have greater gender and racial diversity among workers at all levels. Clear, uniform rules allow workers to evaluate their own cases for promotion and encourage evaluation based on clearly defined criteria, rather than personality or norms. Such rules also provide legal recourse for workers who are not successful. While such policies do not guarantee diversity, they facilitate attainment of this goal.

The informal logics guiding practices at work also entrench inequality in organizational structures. In one of the men's prisons I studied, for example, officers were supposed to be assigned posts without regard to their sex (though women were not allowed to conduct strip searches or super-vise men in the showers). Even so, supervisors tended to assign women tasks they thought were appropriate for them, such as clerical work. When I asked a woman officer about why supervisors assigned clerical tasks to women but not to men, she simply shrugged and concluded, "I guess that's what they think our role is." An African American male nurse interviewed by Harvey Wingfield (2009) offers another such example of job tasks asso-ciated with notions of appropriateness based on race and gender:

> The perception of [black men] is that we're there for—we're there because of our strength and that type of thing, not because of our knowledge. You're basi-cally, you're there whenever patients fall on the floor, to go pick patients up and those types of things. You're not there because of your nursing knowledge.

In both of these cases, ideas about race and gender became part of unspo-ken organizational logics, which in turn shape practices. The implications of this are relatively obvious—no one gets promoted in a prison based on their ability to type, just as no nurse advances based on his ability to bench press a heavy patient.

Gendered Agency

The final level of analysis of the gendered character of organizations is that of agency. Here the focus is on workers themselves and the interactions between them. Interactions between workers on the job, or between workers and clients or customers may act to reinforce inequalities by race, class, or gender. In the 1970s and 1980s, pioneer women firefighters in the New York City fire department faced death threats, protests by the wives of their co-workers, and physical violence, and many reported finding their safety equipment sabotaged. In this case, harassment is organized and its intent obvious. Just as insidious, and far more common, is the less organized, seemingly lighthearted harassment that nonetheless serves to reinforce inequality. One highly successful woman manager tells the story of a male co-worker who commented to her at a party: "You know, sometimes I wonder if we took up a collection and got you laid more often if you would still work until nine o'clock at night" (quoted in Sheppard 1989, 155). Here her presumably threatened colleague draws on a host of stereotypes about successful women to reestablish his dominance, if only momentarily, and put this woman in her more appropriate place. Interactions such as this— whether blatant or covert—have the unmistakable effect of reinforcing race and gender hierarchies at work.

Perhaps paradoxically, men may also reinforce their dominance at work by attempting to shield or protect women. This was the case for the woman correctional officer whose quotation opens this chapter. Her supervisor will not assign her anywhere he thinks would be unsafe, and her response to this captures the double bind such women often find themselves in—she thinks he is "sexist," but she "appreciates it" nonetheless. This experience is common for women in male-dominated occupations. One woman marine describes a similar experience:

> Sometimes on the job the men make you the center of attention by wanting to help you. A lot of times I've had to fight with the guys because of things I wanted to do by myself. You try not to be rude . . . but I think they do that because we're women. (quoted in Williams 1989, 80)

Again her story captures the impossible situation women face in dealing with such efforts to "help." If they accept, they appear less capable (and hence confirm that they do not belong), but if they resist, they risk being called "rude" or worse. Either way they cannot help but reinforce gender inequality.[6]

Finally, women and men themselves draw on their identities as workers to help reinforce their sense of themselves as gendered in particular ways. Sometimes this is simple. A man in firefighting, for example, can find a very good fit between his work and his image of himself as masculine. Though the increasing (but still tiny) proportion of women in the occupation has begun to challenge notions that only real men can do the work, most men probably find little difficulty in connecting their masculine identities to their work as firefighters. By the same token, women in elementary-school teaching are able to connect their sense of themselves as feminine to their work with little difficulty. Teaching small children seems a logical extension of women's supposed innate superior ability to nurture.

Men and women who cross over into occupations dominated by members of the opposite sex face a greater challenge in this regard. More than any other sociologist, Christine Williams (1989, 1995) has drawn attention to the identity strategies employed by such workers. Men who move into female-dominated jobs may choose specialties within those fields that are more likely to draw on purportedly masculine traits. Men in nursing can specialize in emergency care or serve as flight nurses. This man worked as a librarian:

> After automation became part of the profession, more and more men are coming. I think that men are looking for more prestigious careers, and automation has given that to the profession. Not just organizing books, but applying technology in the process. (Williams 1995, 126)

This man rejects what he implicitly sees as the menial, feminized aspect of the work, "organizing books," in favor of more masculinized technological skills. In a similar vein, Williams quotes a woman marine drill sergeant: "One thing I liked about the Marine Corps is that it's the only service that requires you to wear make-up during training. . . . I like that because it kind of symbolizes that they really want you to be feminine" (1989, 75; see also Herbert 2000). While not all workers reinforce the extremes of gender in doing such identity work, their efforts play a key role in sustaining gender inequalities at work.

With its emphasis on multiple levels of gendering in organizations and occupations, the gendered organizations framework can help us to understand both the wide and persistent wage gap between women and men workers and the occupational segregation that is its most important cause. Cultural constructions of occupations as masculine and feminine and as appropriate for workers of particular races and classes, help to sort workers into occupations by shaping both workers' choices and the preferences of their employers. These notions also help to determine the worth of particular kinds of labor, ensuring, for example, that truck drivers make more than elementary-school teachers. Practices in organizations, such as rules governing transfers or racialized and gendered assumptions shaping assignments, combine to keep all women (and minority men) at the lowest ranks in male-dominated occupations, while having the paradoxical effect of allowing some men to advance in occupations dominated by women.

Interactions between workers may help to maintain boundaries of exclusion in male-dominated occupations at all income levels, while the identity work in which workers engage—when it conforms to normative notions about gender—helps make occupational segregation and wage inequality seem natural and appropriate. Drawing on this multilevel framework, I now move to a discussion of work in law, policing, and the prison.

GENDER AT WORK IN LAW, POLICING, AND PRISONS

Women work in the criminal justice system in a wide variety of occupations. They serve as probation and parole officers, judges, victims' services coordinators, FBI agents, attorneys, police officers, and correctional officers. I have chosen here to focus on these last three occupations as a way of providing a snapshot of women's experiences working in the system. Table 5.2 provides a statistical snapshot of the three occupations—the proportions of women, African Americans, and Hispanics working in each (data are not available from these sources on workers by sex *and* race), the median weekly wage, and the wage gap. Women are least likely to work in policing, followed by correctional work and law. The numbers of women in all three occupations is at or near historically high levels—women are now about a third of practicing attorneys and a quarter of correctional officers. By comparison, the increase has been slower in policing, where women are still only 16 percent of the force. But even in policing, this is a dramatic increase from forty years ago—in 1972, men were 96 percent of attorneys, 97 percent of police, and 95 percent of correctional officers.

In terms of the racial distribution of workers in these occupations, African Americans are most heavily represented in correctional work; Hispanics are about equally likely to work in policing and in corrections. Wages are highest for attorneys and lowest for correctional officers—and not coincidentally, law is the most white-dominated of the three occupations, and correctional work is the least. The wage gap is largest in law, a situation that derives partly from the facts that the wages are simply higher (which allows

Table 5.2. Statistical Snapshot of Three Occupations, 2009

	Lawyers (%)	Police (%)	Correctional Officers (%)
Women	32	16	27
Black	5	14	22
Hispanic	3	13	13
Median weekly wage (all workers)	$1,757	$951	$688
Wage gap	0.75	0.83	0.86

Source: United States Census Bureau 2009; Bureau of Labor Statistics 2010.

more room for variation) and that policing and corrections are public-sector occupations (for the most part) and wage gaps tend to be smaller in the government sector, where standardized rules governing hiring and promotion help to reduce the influence of discrimination.

In the sections to follow I fill in the details of this broad snapshot, examining the gendering of each of these occupations and the intersections of race, class, gender, and sexuality in shaping the experiences of workers.

From Perry Mason to Rambo: Engendering Law

As the first quotation that opens this chapter indicates, in the public imagination, the practice of law is a gendered enterprise. The first lawyer most baby boomers probably ever saw was Perry Mason, who solved murders weekly with a final climactic confession by the perpetrator on the witness stand. For others, perhaps the iconic lawyer is the folksy (but wily) Ben Matlock, and for those still younger perhaps it is Jack McCoy of *Law & Order*. We have moved beyond the days when the only role for women was legal secretary—though this was the first job after graduating from law school for future Supreme Court Justices Sandra Day O'Connor and Ruth Bader Ginsberg—but the practice of law is still a man's world in many ways.

Table 5.3 tracks law school enrollments and the rise in the number of women and people of color awarded law degrees over time. Title IX was especially instrumental in increasing access to law schools, many of which had been explicitly sex segregated before 1972 (and many more of which had been implicitly sex segregated). Indeed the largest jump in women's law school enrollments came between 1970 and 1975, when classes went from less than 10 percent women to almost a quarter. Women are now

Table 5.3. Law School Enrollment and Degrees

		Percent of Enrollment				Awarded JD or LLB	
Year	Total	Women	African American	Hispanic	Asian/ Pacific Islander	Women	Minorities
1965	55,510	4					
1970	78,018	9					
1975	111,047	23	5	2	1		
1980	119,501	34	5	2	1	33	
1985	118,700	40	5	3	2	39	9
1990	127,261	43	6	4	3	43	12
1995	129,397	44	8	5	6	44	18
2000	125,173	48	7	6	7	48	20
2005	140,298	47	7	6	8	48	22
2008	142,922	47	7	6	8	47	22

Source: American Bar Association 2010, multiple tables.

almost half of those who receive law degrees. It is also worth noting that the sheer number of attorneys has increased dramatically in the past forty years—there are more than three times as many students receiving law degrees now as in the 1960s (Guinier, Fine, and Balin 1997).

Minority enrollments have been much slower to increase, though the rise has been especially sharp for Asians/Pacific Islanders. Even so, African Americans, Hispanics, and Asians still make up only about 22 percent of law school enrollments, and minorities (a broader category) receive only 22 percent of all law degrees.

Though women were about a third of practicing attorneys in 2009, they have faced a persistent glass ceiling in the profession. Women are only 19 percent of partners in law firms but make up 46 percent of associates. Partners are owners who share in the profits of their firms, whereas associates are generally salaried and given a fixed amount of time after which they must either be offered a partnership or be terminated. A large proportion of lawyers work as in-house counsels for major companies, and these positions can be especially lucrative. Yet in 2009, women were only 15 percent of general counsels in Fortune 500 companies, 15.2 percent of general counsels in Fortune 501–1000 companies. Nineteen percent of all law school deans are women, and women currently occupy (a historically unprecedented) three of nine seats on the United States Supreme Court. As of 2009, women lawyers earned about 80 percent of the salaries of their male counterparts (American Bar Association Commission on Women in the Profession 2010).[7]

Gendering Law in Culture

I have already alluded to many of the ways that the occupation of attorney is gendered at the level of culture. The iconic lawyer in the public imagination is masculine. While there have been some positive, realistic depictions of women lawyers, arguably the most prominent such character was Ally McBeal (1997–2002), a woman whose recurring hallucinations of dancing babies (inspired by her ticking biological clock) were not calculated to inspire confidence in prospective clients. Like popular culture depictions of any occupation, those of lawyers are exaggerated and often completely inaccurate. The legal specialty most likely to be depicted on television is criminal litigation (i.e., the prosecution or defense of a criminal case in a courtroom), an area in which the majority of lawyers do not specialize. Indeed, most legal work is done in corporations or governments and involves tasks like the drafting or approval of policy documents or advice on tax or investment strategies—admittedly not the most gripping legal scenarios.[8]

Even so, stereotypes based on ideas about litigators play a role in shaping women's experiences as lawyers. Jennifer Pierce (1995) interviewed a male attorney who described his women counterparts in this way:

> Let me put it this way: I think Clarence Darrow once said women are too nice to be lawyers. I think he was right. It's not that I don't think women are bright or competent—they just don't have that *killer* instinct. (1995, 26)

Regardless of the setting, lawyers are required to be ruthless defenders of their clients, an ability, according to this account, that women simply do not possess.

Cultural constructions of any occupation create ideas about what workers are appropriate for particular jobs—in a very real sense, about who "looks the part." In professional jobs, women of any race are less likely to fit these constructions than are white men, and race and class combine to shape the influence of gender. A Chicana lawyer interviewed by García-López (2008, 600) describes the discrimination she faces from co-workers and colleagues: "Well, I think that if you come packaged in a way that people are used to seeing and perceiving as having knowledge . . . looking like the typical professional, you don't have as much problems. Look at me, I don't fit that." As this woman's experience demonstrates, the notion of the "professional" is far from gender or race neutral. As her experience indicates, while white women may have made some small amount of progress in this regard, women of color must overcome more extreme barriers to be accepted as legitimate.

Gendered Structures in the Practice of Law

There are a number of ways that the legal profession is gendered at the level of structure. One can see this simply by examining stratification by specialty. Men and women are not equally distributed—women are more likely than men to hold jobs in government and are about four times more likely to work as public defenders. Conversely, men outnumber women in private practice (usually in large firms) and private industry. Simply put, men hold the most lucrative, most prestigious jobs in law. Scholars who have studied law have offered a number of reasons for this distribution. Lawyers who hold government jobs generally have regular, or at least predictable, hours, a fact that might make them more attractive to women with family responsibilities. There is also no requirement to "make rain" (acquire new clients), an obligation common in large firms and one that requires significant time cultivating contacts outside of standard work hours. And government employers generally utilize standardized, transparent recruitment and promotion criteria, a fact that has also eased women's entry into these positions. It perhaps goes without saying that this is the sector of the law with the lowest salaries and most restricted advancement prospects.

The highest salaries are found in private business, generally in large law firms that often employ hundreds of attorneys. It is here that performance pressures are highest and young associates are expected to work extraordinarily long hours. The structure of this kind of legal career requires someone with few family commitments, or the presence of a spouse who handles these responsibilities. Private firms are also those most likely to rely on hiring and promotion practices that are unspoken parts of company culture, of the way things have always been done. Such practices can have negative effects on women, as the landmark case of *Price Waterhouse v. Hopkins* (490 U.S. 228, 1989) demonstrated.

Ann Hopkins worked as an associate for the giant accounting firm Price Waterhouse. As in most private firms, at Price Waterhouse, attorneys were hired as associates and after a certain period of time (often five years) are either promoted to partner, a status which allows them to share in the ownership and profits of the firm, or are fired. At the time of the consideration of her promotion, Hopkins had worked at the firm for five years and had brought in a $25 million government contract. Seven of the firm's 662 partners were women. Of the thirty-two partners (all men) who voted on her case, thirteen recommended that she be promoted, the remainder either had no opinion or voted to reject or delay her candidacy. The promotion was put on hold, and eventually denied. Hopkins filed suit, citing Title VII's protection against sex discrimination in employment.

During the trials that followed, it became very clear that gender had been an unspoken, but powerful, criterion for denying Hopkins's promotion. Letters in her promotion file indicated that one partner described her as "macho," another suggested that she "overcompensated for being a woman," and a third advised her to take "a course at charm school." To improve her chances for partnership, one partner advised that she should "walk more femininely, talk more femininely, dress more femininely, wear make-up, have her hair styled, and wear jewelry" (618 F. Supp., at 1117). Still another had repeatedly commented that he could not consider any woman seriously as a partnership candidate and believed that women were not even capable of functioning as senior managers. Though all of the lower courts ruled in Hopkins's favor, the Supreme Court disagreed, remanding the case back to the lower courts for a decision about whether Hopkins would have been denied partnership regardless of her gender.

Though we do not usually get this kind of window into promotion decisions, *Hopkins* provides powerful proof that ideas about gender matter greatly in blocking women's access to the highest levels of power. The logic employed by the partners in this case clearly indicates processes of homosocial reproduction, in which—in lieu of clear and transparent standards—

those with power are free to select those most like them for advancement. Hopkins's prior performance and her $25 million government contract were not enough to cancel the influence of her gender (though her race was presumably one advantage). This explains the presence of just seven women partners among 662, and the lack of objectively applied criteria helps ensure that, no matter how well women perform, the race and gender of those who reach the top will match that of those already there. This case also provides some insight into the ongoing persistent segregation of women into the lowest-paying sectors of the legal profession—the barriers blocking integration remain highest in the most lucrative areas of the law.

Law and Gendered Agency

The practice of law is also gendered at the level of agency. A study of women in litigation, one of the most male dominated legal specialties, found considerable resistance by men to the presence of women attorneys. One woman related such an experience:

> I'd been with the firm for about eight months working with James (a partner) when Jerry (another partner) came up to me and asked me to type something. I looked surprised and said, "I'm an attorney, not a secretary." Even worse, I knew he knew me. He laughed and said with a conspiratorial wink, "Oh, yeah, but don't all women know how to type?" I was furious. (Pierce 1995, 108)

This woman's experience exemplifies a process Rosabeth Moss Kanter (1993) calls boundary heightening. This happens (in this case) when men in an occupation relegate women as a group to an inferior position while at the same time emphasizing the superiority of men as a group—as in "don't all women know how to type?"[9]

Attorneys themselves also engage in the identity work that allows them to align their work with notions of themselves as masculine or feminine. In her study of litigation, Pierce (1995) finds that men in this specialty draw on readily available cultural stereotypes to interpret themselves as masculine. Pierce demonstrates that many view themselves in almost "Rambo"-like terms, as warriors who single-mindedly destroy their enemies without concern for the effects their actions will have on the lives of the people involved. Successful litigators brag about the size and amount of their "wins" and describe good courtroom performance in terms of having "seduced" the jury, or, more chillingly, having "raped" a witness. Attorneys who lose cases are "weak" or "impotent" or "hav[e] no balls" (Pierce 1995).

In this environment, women litigators must make constrained choices between accommodation and resistance. To be successful, they often decide to take on, to the extent possible, the attributes of their successful male colleagues. Doing so requires a complicated negotiation of gender, however, as in this woman's case:

> I've fought so hard to be recognized as a lawyer—not a woman lawyer. I actually used to be flattered when people told me I think like a man. . . . To be a lawyer, somewhere along the way, I made a decision that it meant acting like a man. To do that I squeezed the female part of me into a box, put on the lid, and tucked it away. (quoted in Pierce 1995, 134)

Though this woman frames lawyer as a gender-neutral category, in fact her experience reveals how deeply it is masculinized. Indeed, to be an attorney she believes she must learn to "think like a man" and put away "the female part" of her. As Ann Hopkins's case perhaps demonstrates, this strategy has considerable risks as well—women who play the role too convincingly risk being consigned for a term in charm school. Pierce found some women litigators among those she studied who chose to resist this role, but they usually did so at the cost of success, at least as the term was defined by their male counterparts and senior partners in their firms.

Identity work can have positive effects at the individual level, of course. Women may desire to work as public defenders because of their sense that the system is unjust and imprisons the innocent. And many women attorneys speak of being drawn to a career in law because it provides them with tools to address gender-based injustice, such as violence against women (Epstein 1993; Pierce 1995; Siemsen 2004). But of course gender is not the only important component of identity. Race/ethnicity and class are also key elements of who we are and how we experience the world. It thus makes sense that we connect these aspects of identity to our work as well. This Chicana attorney interview by García-López (2008) makes this connection explicitly:

> Growing up on the border you see a lot of discrimination against the Mexican-American community—a lot of injustice; you see a lot of trampling of people's rights and so I was inspired to do social justice work. (García-López 2008, 604–605)

In this instance, this woman's experiences of racial and ethnic injustice shape her sense of herself and of her work. It is worth noting, however, that the areas to which women are purportedly drawn by their gendered interests and socialization—public defense, violence against women, social justice—are among the least lucrative in legal practice.

Gender in Policing: From Crime Fighters to Kinder, Gentler Cops?

As the second quotation that opens this chapter indicates, definitions of the occupation of policing are currently contested. Once a job reserved for working-class white men and seemingly requiring little more than brute force, today's officers are increasingly required to mediate, to engage with citizens, to defuse conflict by "talking it out." This might seem to give women an advantage in the occupation, and indeed there are now more women in policing than ever before. But as we shall see, conflict over law enforcement strategies and the desired qualities of law enforcers themselves has been ongoing for more than a century.

Table 5.4 tracks trends in the occupation over time.[10] As of 1972, the year that the protections of Title VII of the Civil Rights Act were extended to public-sector employees, women made up about 3 percent of all sworn officers. As the table indicates, women's progress in the occupation has been slow, increasing by only about 13 percentage points (from 3 to 16) over a span of thirty years. After 1972, the number of African American officers, in particular, rose due to an increase in the number of African American men in the occupation. Similarly, the number of Hispanic officers (again, primarily men) has risen rapidly. Though such men have faced—and continue to face—considerable racial discrimination at work, some have argued that African American men in particular have found it easier to integrate policing because they are more likely to conform to the ideal type of physical strength, size, and street smarts that have traditionally defined the occupation (Rabe-Hemp 2009; Texeira 2002, 526). The presence of women of any racial group, on the other hand, presents a considerable challenge to the notion that policing is properly men's domain.

Like law (and almost all occupations), policing is internally stratified. Women are concentrated in the lowest-status positions, including those as officers who are not sworn (i.e., are not allowed to carry firearms). According to the latest comprehensive data available, collected by the National Center for Women in Policing (2002a), women are 14.2 percent of those

Table 5.4. Historical Trends in Policing, Selected Years

Year	Women (%)	Black (%)	Hispanic (%)
1972	3	8	
1979	6	10	
1980	6	8	
1983	6	10	4
1987	11	15	5
1991	10	11	7
1994	13	14	6
1997	12	13	9
2000	12	13	10
2003	12	13	11
2009	16	14	13

Source: United States Census Bureau, Statistical Abstract (multiple years).

working as city/municipal officers, 13.9 percent of sheriff/county officers, and 5.9 percent of state police. The proportion of women varies widely across agencies, however. For example, women made up almost 32 percent of city officers in Madison, Wisconsin, but only 2 percent of state police in Oklahoma (in all states, women are least likely to serve as state police officers). Women's access to supervisory positions is limited; while they are 13.5 percent of line staff, they make up only 9.6 percent of supervisors and 7.3 percent of those in top command positions. Fifty-six percent of police agencies in the United States have no women at all in top command positions. Women of color in particular are found in the lowest levels of the occupation—though they accounted for 5 percent of sworn officers in 2001, they made up only 3 percent of those in supervisory positions and were 1.6 percent of those in top command posts.

The Gender of Policing in Culture

For most of the twentieth century, the prevailing cultural image of the police officer was that of the crime fighter, the fierce soldier in the war against crime. As historians of the occupation have shown, this model arose during the 1930s and was partly a result of the efforts of J. Edgar Hoover's FBI to portray his "G-Men" as tough, fearless defenders of the public. It was also a response to challenges, during the late nineteenth century, by a movement that argued for the hiring of policewomen. The policewomen's movement, which grew out of other women's reform efforts of this period, argued that women possessed unique skills that equipped them to work with women, young girls, and families to prevent crime. This "social work" model of policing emphasized prevention, rather than arrest, and community relations, rather than law enforcement. Within this limited sphere, the movement had some success. Major cities across the United States hired policewomen, with some establishing separate women's police stations. Alice Stebbins Wells was the first woman hired by a major city, reporting to work in Los Angeles in 1913 (for a more complete history, see Appier 1992, 1998; Martin and Jurik 2006; Miller 1999; Schulz 1995). By the early 1930s, however, the policewomen's movement lost momentum in the face of increasing resistance, and the succeeding years were marked by the rise of a crime-fighting model in which men, and the brute force supposedly inherent to masculinity, gained ascendance. From this time through the early 1970s women's roles in policing were severely limited and involved tasks such as dispatching, serving as "meter maids," questioning children, and supervising women in jails. Largely as a result of legal pressure, departments began to hire women of all races and racial minority men during the 1970s.

The most enduring images of police officers are those that draw on the masculine crime-fighting model. Images of women police in popular culture remain somewhat rare, and where women do appear, they are not generally main characters. A recent study of 291 police action films from 1967 to 2006 (King 2008) found that women were the central characters in only 24 such movies, while men were the stars in 267. Only five films starred black women, with three of these having been produced during the "blaxploitation" era of the 1970s. The study also found that women were portrayed in predictably gendered ways—women cops were more likely to be rookies (in a proportion that remained constant over the period), more likely to be featured in stories in which they discovered, often too late, that their husbands or boyfriends were murderers, far less likely to use physical violence, and much more commonly involved in stories that involved a love story with a male character (though they quite often wound up arresting or killing their new lovers). These story lines depict women as peripheral to policing, uninvolved in violent crime fighting, and as characters with a central sexual or romantic motive. Culturally, the mainstream of policing remains a masculine preserve.

Gendered Structures in Policing

Policing is also gendered at the level of structure. Though explicit bans on the hiring of women are now a thing of the past, policies and practices continue to play a role in gendering the occupation. One of the most straightforward examples lies in the common hiring preference accorded to military veterans. Most government jobs, policing included, give preference in hiring to those with military backgrounds. While this seems facially neutral, in fact it advantages men, who are about 86 percent of active duty military personnel. Gendered logics also structure the physical tests required by many police departments. Physical abilities testing has been a contentious issue in the fight to integrate many male-dominated occupations, among them policing and firefighting. In general, courts have ruled that occupational tests of this kind must measure skills that are clearly and functionally related to abilities actually required on the job. The question then becomes whether certain abilities are job-related. For example, most physical abilities tests place a priority on upper body strength, an area in which many men outperform women. Critics have argued, however, that brute force should actually be a last resort for officers, who are in fact trained *not* to engage suspects if at all possible, or to do so only with assistance from other officers. One man, who is an administrator of a police training academy, notes, "The idea that a woman must do the same number of push-ups as a man is hocus-pocus, but it's been bred into many officers, including the women" (quoted in National Center for Women in Policing 2003). Conversely, skills in which many excel, like endurance, agility, and particularly the ability to defuse conflict, are not part of the testing, as the second quotation that opens this chapter indicates. Gendered logics are also embedded in evaluation procedures and advancement criteria that give more weight to measures like number of arrests made (rather than crimes prevented) and "control of conflict through physical skill." One study of police evaluations found that male supervisors consistently rated male applicants for promotion higher on every required skill—with the exception of report writing (National Center for Women in Policing 2003).

Women officers continue to face resistance to their presence in many departments. In fact, eight of the ten departments in the United States with the highest proportions of women officers have increased their hiring of women only after court-ordered consent decrees that required them to do so (National Center for Women in Policing 2003). Even once hired, assignment practices in departments sometimes slot women into lower-status, gender-typed assignments that hark back to their days as policewomen.

For example, some have argued that women officers are—by nature—better at handling domestic violence and sexual assault cases. There is in fact some evidence that supports this argument. The Christopher Commission report, produced by a committee charged with investigating the Los Angeles Police Department (LAPD) in the aftermath of the Rodney King riots in 1992, contains some frightening and explicit transcripts of mobile display unit conversations between male LAPD patrol officers called to handle domestic violence cases. In one transmission, one officer typed to another, "'Domestic' female, huh? . . . Well, just slap that silly broad senseless." And in yet another: "U won't believe this . . . that female called again said susp[ect] returned. . . . I'll check it out, then I'm going to stick my baton in her" (quoted in Willwerth and Prudhomme 1991). Male police officers themselves are involved in domestic violence at high rates—some studies suggests that more than 40 percent of the wives of police officers have been victims of abuse by their husbands (Johnson 1991; Neidig, Russell, and Seng 1992; see also Teichroeb and Davidow 2003 for an account of the problem in one city).

Given this, it seems that women might in fact be better suited to handle such calls. But these assignments are a double-edged sword for women officers. Though they may draw on women's skills at handling conflict, they are also among the lowest status of all cases. Women officers often get slotted into handling "women's" issues and thus find it difficult to advance. It is also the case that the mere fact that an officer is a woman is not enough to guarantee that she will handle such calls any more sensitively than her male counterparts. Women are far from immune from the effects of a masculinist police culture that evaluates the claims of women victims with suspicion (Martin 2005). All of this is to say that while women have been touted as "kinder, gentler" officers, the real key to transforming the everyday practices of policing lies in changing the structure of the occupation itself.

Gendered Agency in Policing

The masculinist culture of policing means that for most men, not much work is required to bring their identities as masculine into line with their jobs. Whether they represent the extreme conveyed in popular culture or the more realistic model of policing characteristic of their everyday routine, police officers are ultimately protectors, a role that fits well with conventional ideas about masculinity (Kurtz 2008; Rabe-Hemp 2009).

Ideas about appropriate masculinity are always tied up with heterosexuality, however. Being a man, particularly in an environment like a police station, means being a heterosexual man. Though some big city police departments now specifically recruit gay and lesbian officers, the underlying culture of policing has changed little. Miller, Forest, and Jurik (2003) interviewed a sample of gay and lesbian officers about their work experience. Not surprisingly, they found that most remained closeted, as these two men did:

> On the surface, it appears that most of my colleagues are either married or think that they are a gift to women. Most of that (straight) pressure is very uncomfortable because if I don't join in I would be viewed with suspicion. (2003, 366)

> As you well know, everyone wants to be accepted and if making fun of gay people gets you accepted, then you make fun of them. (2003, 366)

As their experiences indicate, hiding their orientation was not without costs and required a considerable amount of "playing straight" to fit into the prevailing heterosexual, masculinist culture. Lesbian officers in this study who were "out" on the job reported some discrimination based on their sexual orientation. But the more common theme among them was the resistance by men to the presence of any woman, straight or gay, and a sense that women had to work twice as hard as men to prove themselves (Miller, Forest, and Jurik 2003, 367; see also Hassell and Brandl 2009).

For women, the day-to-day culture of policing is a highly masculinist enterprise that can be difficult to navigate. An especially egregious case of organized resistance against women officers came to light in the Christopher Commission report, which revealed the existence of a clandestine informal organization, called "Men Against Women," in the LAPD. Male officers in the organization opposed women working as officers, and vowed to do what they could to resist their presence and make their working lives difficult, up to and including refusing to provide backup when called upon. Perhaps its most infamous member, Mark Fuhrman (who was also a lead detective on the O. J. Simpson case) put it this way: "Women don't make good cops because you've got to be able to shoot people, beat people beyond recognition. Women just don't pack those qualities."

Of course it was policing of just this kind that led to the videotaped beating of Rodney King, and ultimately to the riots themselves. Though most resistance is not so extreme or organized, studies of women police officers reveal rates of sexual harassment from co-workers and supervisors in the range of 42 to 68 percent of all women surveyed (City of Los Angeles Commission on the Status of Women 1992; Hassell and Brandl 2009; Janus et al. 1988; Texeira 2002). In one small study of African American officers (Texeira 2002), the twenty-seven women who reported harassment related 114 separate instances.[11]

For some women, however, the fact that models of policing are now returning to a more citizen-oriented, preventive, community-oriented style may actually create an opportunity to align themselves more closely with their work. Women officers perceive that they are better at defusing conflict than men, and there is some evidence to bear this out (Miller 1999; Rabe-Hemp 2009). We know, for example, that women officers are rarely involved in brutality or misconduct cases. Of $66.3 million paid by the city of Los Angeles to settle excessive use of force cases between 1990 and 1999, 95.8 percent was paid out due to male officers' misconduct (National Center for Women and Policing 2002b). And women themselves are often attracted to community policing models that create more opportunities for interactions with citizens and the ability to shape communities in positive ways (Miller 1999). As in the case of dealing with victims, however, there is a danger in presuming that women officers, *simply because they are women*, will be more attracted to community policing or more proficient at it than are men.

Prisons as Gendered Organizations

As the final quotation that opens this chapter demonstrates, prisons immediately call to mind the possibility of violence. When most people imagine what prisons are like, they envision almost constant battles between warring inmates and between inmates and guards. In terms of its position in society, however, the prison presents an interesting paradox. It may be the single most significant social institution of which most people have no direct experience. Very few have ever visited a prison, and though our incarceration rate is now the highest in our history—and in the world— a relatively small part of the total U.S. population has ever spent time in prison. Hence for most people, their images of life in prison—which are invariably images of life in men's prisons—exist largely in the form of the nightmarish images they see on television and in movies.

If these depictions were accurate, prison would be a very dangerous place for anyone to work. At the very least, it would require strong men, willing and able to use violence to defend themselves. Yet as table 5.2 indicates, women are now about a quarter of those who work as correctional officers. Data from a survey of prisons themselves (Bureau of Justice Statistics 2009) tells us that women are 55 percent of those serving as officers in women's prisons and 22 percent of officers working in men's prisons. Ninety-six percent of all men who work as correctional officers serve in men's prisons, as do 84 percent of women. Women now work at all levels of the system—local, state, and federal.

Table 5.5 provides historical data on the employment of officers by race and sex. Perhaps the most striking thing about this table is the increase in the total number of officers during this period—up over 3,000 percent. The period of most rapid increase corresponds with the explosion in the U.S. prison population in the wake of the war on drugs and the prison-building boom that followed.[12] As in policing, the number of women in the occupation began to increase dramatically in the 1970s, largely as a result of litigation that eventually allowed women to work in men's prisons. And also parallel to policing, the number of African American officers has increased more rapidly than the number of women, which indicates a faster rise in the number of African American men working in the occupation. Though such men have faced considerable racism from their co-workers and supervisors (Owen 1988), the masculine culture in men's prisons has been more open to the entry of African American men than to women of any race.

Table 5.5. Correctional Workforce by Sex, Race, and Ethnicity, Selected Years, 1870–2009

Year	Total	Female (%)	Black (%)	Hispanic (%)
1870	13,252	0.1		
1880	38,153	0.2		
1890	78,263	0.4		
1900	103,590	0.8		
1910	78,268	0.1		
1920	115,553	0.3		
1930	159,964	0.6		
1940	219,437	1.1		
1950	237,203	2.2	4.6	
1960	242,229	2.9	5.8	
1970	318,611	5.1	13.5	
1977	490,000	10.2	18.0	
1980	548,000	12.4	16.8	
1985	722,000	20.9	20.2	6.6
1990	184,667	18.9	23.5	6.4
1995	278,000	17.8	28.2	6.4
2000	315,000	23.5	24.9	8.7
2005	373,000	22.5	25.9	6.9
2009	435,000	26.9	22.0	12.9

Source: United States Census Bureau, multiple sources (see Britton 2003 for more information).

Prisons as Gendered through Culture

Because so few people have direct experience of the prison, cultural images of the institution and work within it play a greater role in shaping perceptions of the prison than they do perceptions of law and policing (and this is true even for those who will eventually work there). Depictions of the prison in popular culture are deeply gendered in ways that place a violent, animalistic masculinity center stage. Of the 748 "prison" films or television series catalogued in the Internet Movie Database (www.imdb.com) by 2002, 657 focused on men's prisons. Movies about prisons began to be made early in the film era, for example, *Penitentiary* (1938), and remain popular into the present. The image presented in these films is almost uniformly chaotic and violent. The 1947 film *Brute Force* is a B-movie vehicle that starred Burt Lancaster, who appears bare-chested and holding a rifle on the promotional movie card produced to be displayed in theaters. The tag line on that card is: *"Raw! Rough! Ruthless! Caged men, cut off from their women by a wall of stone and steel . . . !"* Though this seems—at least in retrospect—more than a little over the top, it captures the conventions of the genre even now. The year 2000 saw the release of a film called *Animal Factory*, starring Willem Dafoe, a low-grossing affair promoted with the line: *"On the Inside the Rules are Brutal and the Stakes are High."* Films set in women's prisons are not as common, but those that have been made tell a very different story. The majority, particularly among those made after the 1960s, take the form of soft-core porn films, with titles like *Chained Heat* (1983), *Reform School Girls* (1986), and *She Devils in Chains* (1976). In simple terms, men's prison films are about violence, and women's prison films are about sex.

Though these images are made for the sake of entertainment, they matter in shaping the way people think about the prison. In my study of seventy-two men and women officers who worked in men's and women's prisons (Britton 2003), I found that those who became officers felt the effects of those images but also found them to be exaggerated. This man's experience is typical: "You know, when you come into the prison system, you know you see all these movies and stuff and you think, that's prison life, but it's not. It's not as rough, anyway, at least where I've worked. It's a lot better than what's portrayed on the movies" (quoted in Britton 2003, 91). Indeed few officers would survive if prisons in the real world were like those depicted on the screen. Officers quickly come to realize that the bulk of almost any prison's inmates are nonviolent offenders and that the heart of the job involves a routine that varies little from day to day. Even so, notions like this about the prison gave some officer recruits pause about their choice to enter the occupation. And it is reasonable to expect that such images, with their depictions of relentless violence and the exercise of brute force, would be more likely to dissuade women recruits than men. Indeed, many of the women I interviewed said they had been "scared to death" before they began work. But they, too, soon discovered that their fears were overstated. As one woman who worked in a men's prison put it: "I [used to be] a teacher in a day-care center. And it's basically the same except for the kids are a lot bigger" (quoted in Britton 2003, 87).

Gendered Structures in Prison

Prisons are gendered at the level of structure in myriad ways—not least of which is their physical, architectural forms. Men's and women's prisons are the products of different historical projects and have been designed at various moments in time in accord with ideas about how men and women should best be rehabilitated and/or confined. Hence most men's prisons fit the stereotypical model of imposing structures, cellblocks, and yards; many women's prisons, in contrast, designed on a reformatory model, feel a bit like campuses (albeit with fences and razor-ribbon wire), with large open areas and smaller, individual housing units (once called "cottages") (though this is changing; see Kruttschnitt and Gartner 2005). Gendered labor market structures outside the prison mean that men and women come to prison work from very different backgrounds; in my study, the most common category of previous experience for men was the military; for women, it was service and clerical occupations. I focus here, however, on the gendered logics that guide assignment practices in prisons.

As the experience of the woman officer whose story opens this chapter demonstrates, assignments in prison are often based on gendered notions about the skills and abilities of men and women officers. This woman was white, and like other white women I interviewed, she believed that her supervisors, who were mostly white men, tried to protect her from violence. The same was not true for the black women I interviewed, though they, too, observed that their assignments often involved what supervisors saw as gender-appropriate tasks. This African American male officer observed: "Most women here, they have a position where they can possibly type if needed, or work in a control [room] where they're answering the phones, or work beside the supervisors, like the lieutenant or whatever, while the male officers have to work [cell]blocks more" (quoted in Britton 2003, 173). This was particularly the case in the state system I studied. In the federal system more bureaucratized policies made it less likely that supervisors could assign officers in line with their ideas about gender-appropriate tasks. The implication for women's advancement opportunities is clear—the ability to answer phones is not a key component in any officer's annual evaluation; the ability to deal with violence is central.

In women's prisons, ideas about gender produced a very different result for male officers. The assignments of men in women's prisons often draw on supervisors' beliefs that men are more able to handle violence. This woman related a recent incident in the prison where she works:

> They always want the males in there. [During a recent incident] there were two men that were holding [the inmate] down, a woman was holding her legs, and the lieutenant looked at me, and she said: "I need another male, where is there another male? Where is there another male?" So they sent another officer to go relieve that male officer in the dorm, and he came and took over for the woman that was involved. (quoted in Britton 2003, 184)

Men and women officers were ambivalent about this. Some men saw dealing with violence as a way to do gender in a female-dominated environment—to emphasize their sense of themselves as masculine. Others were less enthusiastic. Similarly, some women agreed that men were simply better at handling violence, while others resented the discrimination that they believed prevented them from doing their jobs. Regardless of how officers felt, the outcome of the application of gender in these two cases is very different. Women are disadvantaged by practices that restrict their assignments in men's prisons, whereas men benefit from such gendered logics in women's institutions. Prisons can presumably survive without clerical help, but not without enforcers.

Gendered Agency in Prison

Like cultural images of prisons and the structures within them, interactions in prisons are shaped by gender, race, and class. African American officers I interviewed related stories of discrimination from co-workers and supervisors, as in this woman's case:

> When you hear a supervisor call an inmate, "that nigger," and you're standing right there, what is that telling you? If he'll say that about him, even though he's an inmate, he'll say that about you too. They'll justify them saying nigger because they are inmates, but that is no justification. Not for saying that word, not around me. I get offended. Or, "that wetback," you know. To me, those are all signs that you are racist in your own way. Kind of undercover, that's what we call it. I'd rather for you to be upfront with me, and say, "Hey, I don't like you because you're Black." I don't like anyone grinning in my face, and then go back and say, "I really don't like that nigger." *Britton: And you think there's a lot of that undercover . . . ?* Yeah, there is. (quoted in Britton 2003, 201)

This woman's comment captures the everyday racism that is the subtext of daily life in prisons, where the officer corps is usually made up mostly of whites, often from surrounding rural areas, and supervises an inmate population that is disproportionately black and Hispanic. African American and Hispanic officers must find strategies that allow them to establish themselves among their white co-workers, while at the same time appearing in some ways to be visible representatives of the controlled, rather than the controllers. For African American women who work, as this woman does, in men's prisons, stereotypes about gender and race often intersect in ways that make the challenges with which they must deal very different from those faced by white women.

Though other interactions in prisons—between officers and supervisors, officers themselves, and officers and inmates—are fundamentally shaped by gender, race, and class, I focus in this final section on the way officers do the identity work required to think of themselves as masculine or feminine as they do their jobs. As I have already suggested, for men, work as a correctional officer in either a men's or a women's prison aligns well with notions about culturally appropriate masculinity. This white male officer makes this point nicely: "I tell [the inmates], I say, I like my job. They say why? Cause I'm keeping you off the street. Keeping my family safe from people like you" (quoted in Britton 2003, 16). Certainly not all officers held such an uncomplicated negative view of inmates,[13] but many men did frame themselves as protectors in this way. For women, particularly those who worked in men's prisons, this was a bit more difficult. Some women, like the women attorneys in Pierce's (1995) study, adopted the male model. Others on the opposite end of the spectrum emphasized qualities they believed were unique to women. This white woman discusses her approach: "I do like [my job]. The way I see it, every man has had a woman in his life as a role model, mother, or an aunt, or a grandmother, telling him what to do at some point in his life. And they will do what you ask them as long you don't step on their ego too much (quoted in Britton 2003, 224). Not all women drew on images of motherhood. For others, the fact that they were women meant they were more able to communicate, to defuse conflict before it started (a sentiment very much like that expressed by women police officers). Most women fell somewhere in between the extremes of masculine and feminine models. No matter what strategy they chose, however, the outcomes of identity work for men and women were very different. In the already masculinized structure of the prison, choosing to emphasize gender difference benefited men, but it almost invariably disadvantaged women.

GENDERING WORK IN THE SYSTEM

Women are more likely to be employed in the paid labor force now than ever before, but progress in closing the wage gap between men and women has recently slowed and shows every sign of having stopped completely (England 2010). Academics largely agree that the major cause of the wage gap is occupational sex segregation—the fact that men and women work in different jobs and that jobs dominated by women pay less. The three occupations on which I focus in this chapter, law, policing, and prison work, allow us to sidestep the question of occupational sex segregation for a moment and focus on men's and women's experiences as workers in the same jobs. Even in this somewhat controlled comparison, there are differences of gender, and race, and class.

The number of women in all three occupations is now higher than at any point in history, as is the number of African Americans and Hispanics. Even so, none of these occupations has reached parity, and policing has been particularly slow to change. In this chapter, I offer a model—the theory of gendered organizations—that highlights the role of gender as a characteristic of organizations and occupations rather than of workers themselves. Comprehending the ways gender shapes the cultural understanding of these occupations, the practices and policies that govern them, and the lives of workers within them, underscores the complicated reasons for persistent inequalities and begins to suggest avenues for change.

Men, and particularly white men, are the iconic attorneys in the public imagination. Their favorite fictional attorneys exhibit a "killer instinct" that, according to many of their male counterparts, women simply do not possess. Women in policing—of whatever race or sexual orientation—are disadvantaged by evaluation criteria that prioritize brute strength over endurance or the ability to defuse conflict. In prisons, African American and Hispanic officers must contend with an everyday racism that stems from the actions of a system that fills those institutions disproportionately with inmates of color.

If inequalities are in fact lodged in organizations at each of these levels, then the task of producing change becomes correspondingly more difficult. Training women to behave more like men will not work, as those women who have tried this strategy have inevitably found. Nor will implementing policies that mandate fairness be enough unless those who enact such policies are held accountable for their transparent administration. Cultural ideals and the stories we tell may be the most recalcitrant barriers of all, often shifting decades after transformations in institutions and everyday lives. Though the framework I offer here complicates our understanding, it also confirms that solutions targeting only one aspect of inequality, or one cause, will never solve entrenched problems of race, class, and gender.

6

Conclusion

In this book, I have turned a gender lens on criminology. I have shown that our understanding of criminal offending, the criminal justice system, victimization, and occupations in the system are fundamentally incomplete without an appreciation of the roles of gender, race, class, and sexuality in forming, shaping, and reproducing all of these social institutions and processes. Criminology's practitioners have historically been resistant to adopting this perspective. This is an interesting paradox—few disciplines study phenomena that are as sex differentiated as crime. Surely it is significant that 93 percent of those in prison are men, or that men are three times more likely to be arrested than are women. Yet it has not been until the past thirty years that gender (or even sex) has consistently appeared on the criminological research agenda. Even today, it is not uncommon for criminologists to publish research based on samples of boys or men without mentioning this fact. Criminology texts rarely consider gender, the few that do often relegate it to a chapter on feminist criminology. I hope to have demonstrated here that gender, race, class, and sexuality cannot just be added in—they are indispensable to any understanding of crime, victimization, and the social institutions dedicated to controlling crime.

In the time line that opens this book, I listed twelve high-profile school shootings of the past two decades. Contrary to media framing of these events, the shootings were not caused by "youth" out of control. A gender lens on these shootings draws attention to the fact that all of these shooters were boys, and correspondingly, to the social construction of masculinity in our culture. Gender is fundamental, not incidental, to understanding these events. I suspect that objections to my argument may come from two quarters. The first objection might be that not *all* boys take guns to school and open fire on their classmates; in fact, most do not. This is fortunately true. However, this does not mean that masculinity and violence of this kind are not associated. In the social sciences, and in sociology in particular, we look for patterns and associations. We rarely find one-to-one causality—and indeed this would be extremely unusual in an arena as complicated as human social behavior. Not every man need go to prison for criminologists to look at the prison population and observe a link between masculinity and violence. The same is true for school shootings. Second, the fact that a handful of girls have been perpetrators does not undermine this general association. In fact, as Miller (1998, 2002b; Miller and White 2004) has illustrated in her studies of men and women street robbers and gang members, these offenses might be gendered differently.

As I demonstrate in chapter 1, defining crime, the presumptive subject matter of criminology, is far from straightforward. The most common definition is the legalistic one. A crime is an act that violates the law. For enforcers on the street, or prosecutors, or most of the rest of us who get our exposure to the criminal justice system through cop shows or the occasional televised trial, the key question is—"Did they do it?" not "How is 'it' defined?" Framing the issue in this way obscures two important things. First, it ignores the fact that the creation of "law" is a social process. The criminal code was not inscribed on stone tablets and handed down from a mountaintop. While there is undoubtedly consensus among human beings that murder should be illegal, not all taking of human lives counts as murder. The state kills (in those jurisdictions with the death penalty), soldiers kill, police officers kill, and corporations kill. Reiman and Leighton (2009) argue that corporations annually account for far more loss of human life than conventional street-level homicide offenders. The criminal code counts none of these instances of taking life as murder. Even in the case of an offense seemingly so incontestable as murder, social distinctions have been made between the criminal versus the noncriminal taking of life. There is a much larger body of offenses about which there is far more considerable debate—drug crimes, for example—whose offenders now fill our prisons and together account for more arrests than all violent crimes combined.

Second, taking the legalistic definition for granted obscures the inequalities that are both built into and perpetuated by the process of defining acts as criminal. Though the savings and loan collapse of the 1980s and the outright fraud that caused it resulted in the loss of more money than street criminals could dream of stealing, none of those implicated were charged with common, garden variety theft (75 percent of cases were never prosecuted at all), and those convicted served an average of two years. Ultimately U.S. taxpayers paid an estimated $256 billion to bail out this system. All of this underscores the fact that in most instances, acts that would be considered criminal if committed by individuals are not treated as crimes if committed by corporations or by governments (which are, after all, made up of individuals, mostly white, wealthy men at the upper levels), and in all cases suite crime is not treated as harshly as street crime.

Race, gender, class, and sexuality have explicitly been encoded in law. From the "one drop" rule that legally established race—and with it, the privileges that attached to being white—to statutes that prohibited interracial marriage or regulated the age of consent for boys and girls, the law has played a historical role in maintaining social inequalities and enforcing the dominant group's contemporary notion of moral propriety. Until 2003, states could and did criminalize sexual behavior between consenting adults of the same sex; remaining civil and administrative rules that make distinctions on the basis of sexual orientation continue the process of enforcing inequalities even into the present.

Criminal offending is a deeply gendered enterprise, as I demonstrate in chapter 2. According to official statistics and unofficial self-reports, crime is very much a sex-segregated arena. The differences lie not so much in what kinds of crimes men and women commit, but in their frequency. Drug crimes account for 9 percent and 13 percent of women's and men's arrests, respectively, but this works out to about 242,000 arrests for women versus more than one million for men. As an understanding of the construction of gender leads us to expect, men dominate among serious violent criminals, and the highest proportions of women are arrested for nonviolent property offenses. This is a well-established pattern that has been consistent over many years.

Though criminology has developed a large body of theory to account for crime, gender has rarely been a key concept in its theoretical models. None of the classic paradigms—strain theory, social disorganization, differential association, social control—considered gender. Theorists instead wrote about generic criminals who just happened to be men. The notion of masculinity has been reintroduced (though often in a marginal way) through studies of men who victimize women, and to a much lesser extent, in reconceptualizing key theories or creating theory that takes gender into account (Messerschmidt 1993; for a more extensive review, see Belknap 2007). The study of femininity has taken an even stranger route into criminology, but feminist criminologists are now exploring how gender shapes the contexts in which crime is committed and its motivations, risks, and rewards. As the legitimate labor market is gendered and shaped by inequalities of race, class, gender, and sexuality, so, too, is the criminal labor market. Men specialize in violent offenses and control the trade in lucrative illegal goods. Women, on the other hand, specialize in sex work and find niches in the service sector of the criminal marketplace. The ways men and women commit crime are shaped by gendered inequalities, and men and women do gender by doing crime.

The criminal justice system—the complex of laws and enforcement agencies dedicated to defining, controlling, and punishing crime—is also gendered, as I show in chapter 3. To call an institution gendered, as I do in this book, means that gender forms a part of its structure. More specifically, gendered assumptions are built into the content of law and the assumptions and practices of enforcement agencies. In a similar fashion, the system is classed, racialized, and sexualized.

One of the most common stereotypes about the practices of criminal justice systems in fact explicitly invokes gender—the notion of chivalry theory. As I show in chapter 3, however, this idea—that women are treated more leniently by a system that perceives them as too delicate to bear harsh punishment—is at best an oversimplification and at worst an outright falsehood. African American women do not benefit from chivalry and, along with African American men, have historically borne the worst excesses of the criminal justice system's brutalities. In the leasing camps of the post–Civil War South, for example, black women not only worked alongside black men but faced sexual exploitation at the hands of their white guards (Oshinsky 1997). As recently as March 2000, a federal government report found that African American women U.S. citizens were nine times more likely than white women citizens to be searched with x-ray machines by U.S. Customs (now TSA) officials at airports for drugs and contraband (General Accounting Office 2000). This same study also found black, Asian, and Hispanic women twice as likely to be strip-searched as men from these racial/ethnic groups. It is worth noting in this context that although far more likely to be searched, African American women were less than half as likely to actually be *carrying* contraband. These data (like the traffic stop data I reviewed in chapter 3) also fail to show chivalry exercised on behalf of white women—among citizens, white men and women were about equally likely to be subjected to x-ray or strip searches. The evidence I have reviewed in this book tells us that chivalry does not apply to all women. In fact, some women—particularly those who violate gendered norms—may be subject to stronger condemnation and punishment than are men who commit the same crimes. The stigma faced by mothers who kill their children is a particularly good example.

In chapter 4, I turn a gender lens on crime victimization. Here again the stereotypes are infused with gendered meanings. I often find that students—and even some of my colleagues with no background in criminology—believe that women's levels of victimization are far higher than are men's. Popular culture portrayals of crime suggest that women are far more likely to be victims of violent crimes than victimization statistics suggest— though again this effect holds most strongly for white women (Eschholz, Mallard, and Flynn 2004). On any given episode of *CSI* or other popular crime drama, one is likely to find the camera lingering on a (supposedly) dead woman's body, often arranged or clothed suggestively. The idea that women are more likely to be victimized than are men also resonates with notions about feminine weakness and masculine invulnerability. The data reveal, however, that men are more likely than women to be victims of violent crimes, most often in altercations with other men with whom they are acquainted. This parallels patterns of masculine socialization in American culture. Boys and young men, more so than girls, carry and use weapons and dominate the world of the streets. Victimization rates for young black men in particular are extremely high, so high in fact that some have labeled such violence of epidemic proportions. White women, on the other hand, are less often victims than any other race/sex group, while black women's risks of victimization from violence—particularly homicide—are actually higher than those faced by white men. The complexity of these statistics indicates that not only is victimization (like offending) gendered, but it is also racialized. While in a general sense it is true that men are more likely to be victimized than women, some women are more likely to be victimized than are some men.

Victimization statistics such as those collected as part of the UCR and NCVS tell only part of the story, however. Women's victimization is far more personal than men's. Homicide statistics (which are the most reliable of all crime numbers; dead bodies are difficult to conceal and easy to count) show that women are most likely to be killed by someone they know—a husband or boyfriend, most commonly. It is far harder to track assaults, particularly between intimates. Yet surveys of sexual assault victims consistently demonstrate that women are far more likely to be sexually assaulted by men they know than by strangers. Within marriage or other intimate relationships women are more likely to be assaulted—and suffer more serious injuries and negative long-term effects of violence—than are men. The controversies over rape statistics and the debate around the "mutual combat" hypothesis are evidence of the fact that even these consistently well-documented patterns are far from an article of faith in the "culture wars" raging around gender.

In chapter 4 I offer a contextual model for thinking about victimization. Here I draw on the strengths of the sociological perspective and the knowledge that violence is not generally a random event. Some contexts are, demonstrably, more risky, more "rape prone" than others. The roots of this violence lie in organizations and situations that foster and accentuate inequalities between men and women and that encourage violence or at least ensure that it will be ignored or minimized when it does occur (for an application of this model to neighborhood contexts, see Miller 2008). The problem with such a model is that we live in an individualist culture—recognizing that some situations are more risky than others seems to require that we blame individual victims for putting themselves at risk and absolve offenders of blame. As I hope is clear by now, this is not the path I advocate. Certainly offenders should be held responsible for their behaviors, and victims should never be blamed for their own victimization.

Instead, I hope that by recognizing that problems such as sexual assault have structural roots, we might begin to pursue structural solutions. As I note in chapter 4, after the rape of an intellectually disabled girl in Glen Ridge, New Jersey, by members of a high-school baseball team, some members of the community came to understand the structural roots of the problem as well as their own community's willingness to disbelieve the victim and defend the perpetrators. Community members held a summit meeting and acted to change the culture and structure of the town and the community, establishing community service programs and replacing the "win at all costs" ethic of men's athletics in favor of a priority on academic achievement. Most rape prevention programs reflect our culture's individualist bias. Risk reduction campaigns on my own campus often take the form of self-defense classes for women or "safe ride home" services. Changes of the kind introduced in Glen Ridge, in contrast, will likely have longer-term effects, because they attempt to change culture and structure. Creating school environments in which the "boys will be boys" mentality that so often comes with big-time men's athletics (and even the small-time high-school variety) is minimized, and environments in which students are connected to their communities, and in which those communities become more diverse and more respectful of difference, is likely to do far more to decrease violence than any "safe ride" program ever could. But large-scale change requires a commitment that most communities, at least those untouched by a horror on the scale of the Glen Ridge rape, are unlikely to muster.

Finally, in chapter 5, I discuss work in the criminal justice system itself. In most regards, these systems are quintessentially masculinized organizations. Litigators must have the "killer instinct" to manipulate juries; police are tough, aggressive crime fighters, and prison officers must be willing to "bang heads" to enforce discipline. Though, as usual, these images are more the stuff of Hollywood imagery than reality, this does not alter the fact that these three occupations, and the organizations in which they are performed, are gendered. At the level of structure, workloads in large private firms based on norms about the ideal worker mean that women are underrepresented in this sector of law and more likely than men to be found in government law and public defense work. In cultural terms, policing is still very much a masculinized occupation, as even a casual perusal of prime-time television cop dramas will demonstrate. Women also face departmental cultures that are often still the preserve of white, heterosexual men and in which they have to work twice as hard to prove themselves. In prison work, the identity strategies of women and men officers must contend with ideas about gender in the prison and beyond the walls—men who work in men's prisons find it easy to see themselves as protectors, while women sometimes emphasize what they see as their greater abilities to defuse violence and conflict. As I note in chapter 5, the implications of these strategies are very different—while one may be recognized for subduing a violent inmate or stopping a fight, it is more difficult to climb the ladder of promotion by emphasizing people skills, particularly when the people in question are inmates.

What I hope to have demonstrated is that the understandings of offending, victimization, and the criminal justice system provided by mainstream criminology and criminal justice studies are incomplete. Though criminologists know well that violence is rarely random, they have generally failed to consider it within the contexts of inequalities of gender, race, class, and sexuality (class has received the most attention of these, gender and sexuality the least). While any criminology textbook will tell you that men are about ten times more likely than are women to be arrested for homicide, few provide any discussion of what masculinity might have to do with this fact. What I have tried to demonstrate here is that our picture of the realities of crime is far richer, more nuanced, and more complete when viewed through a gender lens. I close with one final example to underline this point.

ENGENDERING CRIME: A FINAL NOTE

On February 12, 2008, fifteen-year-old Lawrence [Larry] King was sitting in a computer lab in Oxnard, Calif.'s E. O. Green Junior High School. . . . At 8:30 a.m., a half hour into class, Brandon [McInerney, age fourteen] quietly stood up. Then, without anyone's noticing, he removed a handgun that he had somehow sneaked to school, aimed it at Larry's head, and fired a single shot. [A teacher], who was across the room looking at another student's work, spun around. "Brandon, what the hell are you doing!" she screamed. Brandon fired at Larry a second time, tossed the gun on the ground and calmly walked through the classroom door. Police arrested him within seven minutes, a few blocks from school. Larry was rushed to the hospital, where he died two days later of brain injuries. (Setoodeh 2008)

Like the incidents that open this book, this is another in a long line of school shootings, another instance of a "kid" with a gun, a "kid" out of control. Happening as it did just two days before a mass shooting at Northern Illinois University, in which another young man, Steven Kazmierczak, killed eight people, it might have gotten lost in the media shuffle. Yet several key facts about the case immediately drew attention—Lawrence King had told teachers he was gay, and he sometimes wore makeup and women's clothing to school. By most accounts he had been taunted and bullied for many years. According to his classmates, a day or two before he was killed he had—as part of a game he was playing with some girls who were asking boys they liked to be their Valentines—approached Brandon during a playground basketball game and asked him to be his Valentine. That same day Brandon threatened to kill Lawrence, but no one who heard the threat apparently took it seriously. On February 12 Brandon carried out that threat. He now faces a sentence of fifty-one years to life in prison (Cathcart 2008; Setoodeh 2008).

On the face of it, this homicide looks like most of those that make up the UCR statistics. It is a homicide in which the victim and the perpetrator are both men (albeit very young men) who knew each other, and it involves a handgun. But these sparse facts tell us almost nothing of value about the death of Lawrence King. This crime was embedded in norms of masculinity and heterosexuality that are especially toxic in high school and middle school (Pascoe 2007), where any deviation from enthusiastic heterosexual masculinity is likely to lead to taunts of "fag," as they did in King's case. McInerney's defense is likely to allege that he was himself sexually harassed by King (indeed, this suggestion has already been made); certainly classmate accounts suggest he was embarrassed in front of his male peers. It is worth noting, perhaps, that such a defense would seem almost ridiculous if the shooter had been a girl asked to be the Valentine of a boy in whom she was not interested. This should tell us something very important about the gendered norms underlying heterosexuality—norms that frame boys as natural pursuers and girls as naturally pursued. In perhaps a final bizarre twist in this case, King's parents sued the school district, not for failing to protect their son from bullying, but for allowing him to dress in women's clothing and makeup at school. Had he not been allowed to dress like a girl, the suit alleges, he would never have been shot. The school was hence negligent in failing to enforce a gender-appropriate dress code (Wilson 2008).

King's murder is a hate crime. By definition, such crimes are motivated by bias on the basis of race, religion, sexual orientation, gender, or other categories of difference. It is easy, in this case, to argue that gender and sexual orientation matter. What I have tried to demonstrate in this book is that gender, sexuality, race, and class shape all aspects of crime and what we can know about crime, victimization, and the criminal justice system. Without a lens that allows us to see the intersections of these patterns of power and inequality, our understanding is necessarily incomplete. Lacking this clarity of vision, so too will it be impossible to comprehend the real dimensions of the harm caused by crime, the damage to lives changed and taken away, and ultimately to forge real and lasting solutions to the problems crime causes in our communities.

Notes

CHAPTER 1: A GENDER LENS ON CRIMINOLOGY

1. For many years, the FBI published data on arrests only for whites, blacks, and "others." Recently, data have begun to appear for "American Indian or Alaska Natives" and "Asian and Pacific Islanders." There are no statistics available on arrests of Hispanics, who are probably found predominantly in the "white" category.

2. The FBI reports data on national origin bias in two categories, anti-Hispanic and "other" national origin bias. Though the number of incidents in the former category remained essentially stable from 2000 to 2001 (at around 500), those in the latter increased by more than 400 percent, from 354 to 1,501. Given the events of September 11, 2001, it is reasonable to assume that much of the increase is due to crimes motivated by anti-Arab prejudice.

3. My discussion of definitions of crime owes much to Beirne and Messerschmidt (2000).

4. Edwin Sutherland, the first American criminologist to draw attention to what he labeled "white collar crime," was also critical of the strictly legalistic definition, though he proposed a narrower alternative, to include both criminal and regulatory law (Beirne and Messerschmidt 2000).

5. Several outlets monitor corporate crime. Two such sources on the Internet are Multinational Monitor (http://multinationalmonitor.org) and the Corporate Crime Reporter (http://corporatecrimereporter.com).

6. I have drawn extensively here from David Oshinsky's (1997) history of Mississippi's Parchman prison farm and the systems of incarceration that preceded it. For other discussions of convict leasing in the South, see Mancini (1996) and Walker (1988). I discuss this material in more detail in chapter 2 of my book *At Work in the Iron Cage* (Britton 2003).

7. Other important early sex discrimination cases include *Reed v. Reed* (404 U.S. 71, 1971) and *Frontiero v. Richardson* (411 U.S. 677, 1973).

8. In 1996, a version of ENDA came within one vote of passage in the Senate and was never voted on in the House of Representatives. In 2007, ENDA (H.R. 3685) passed by a vote of 235–184 in the House. It awaits action in the Senate.

9. Such cases are common, though most do not garner the same media attention. The Human Rights Campaign estimates that approximately one out of every thousand homicides in the United States is an anti-transgender hate-based crime. In 2009, that fraction equates to fifteen murders of transgender individuals (Human Rights Campaign, undated).

10. As of 2009, the federal government may exercise jurisdiction over crimes based on a victim's actual or perceived race, color, religion, national origin, gender, sexual orientation, gender identity, or disability. These powers were granted to the Department of Justice by the Matthew Shepard and James Byrd, Jr., Hate Crimes Prevention Act, signed into law by President Barack Obama on October 28, 2009. The act was named in honor of two victims of notorious hate crimes. Matthew Shepard was a young gay man who was the victim of a bias-motivated murder in Wyoming in 1998. James Byrd, Jr., was an African American man who was the victim of a racially motivated murder committed by three white men in Jasper, Texas, in 1998.

11. How legislators came to equate common sexual practices between consenting adults and bestiality is a mystery. It is interesting, however, that many commentators opposed to gay marriage have framed it the first step down a slippery slope at the bottom of which humans will be able to marry their pets. During the 2008 presidential campaign, candidate Mike Huckabee said: "I don't think that's a radical view to say we're going to affirm marriage. I think the radical view is to say that we're going to change the definition of marriage so that it can mean two men, two women, a man and three women, a man and a child, a man and animal. Again, once we change the definition, the door is open to change it again" (quoted in Waldman and Gilgoff 2008). The association persists.

12. On the whole, jobs that are associated with femininity (like nursing or secretarial work) pay less than those associated with masculinity (like truck driving or corporate management). However, men in both kinds of jobs advance more quickly, disproportionately hold positions of authority, and earn more than their female counterparts; for example, on the whole, men in nursing do better than their equally qualified and experienced women counterparts. The same is true for truck drivers and managers (Williams 1992, 1995).

CHAPTER 2: GENDER AND CRIMINAL OFFENDING

1. The probability of arrest for all index offenses is 22 percent. The rate varies widely by offense, however, from a high of 67 percent for homicide to a low of 12.5 percent for burglary and 12.4 percent for motor vehicle theft.

2. For one discussion of the complicated context in which women use violence in film, see Spelman and Minow (1992).

3. Joanne Belknap (2007) and others have described women in criminology as "invisible" given the discipline's historic lack of attention to women as either offenders or victim. Though I agree with this claim, I mean to offer a broader critique. Criminologists have paid far less attention to *gender* than they have even to women

(though neither omission is positive). Studies of the intersections between masculinities and crime are extremely rare, and even in the growing genre of work on women and crime, gender is still sometimes not a central focus.

4. Others built on and extended Cohen's work during this period and specifically focused on the subcultures of working-class boys. See, for example, Cloward and Ohlin (1960) and Miller (1958).

5. It is worth mentioning that women are rarely participants in high-level white-collar crimes; if nothing else, they lack access to the positions that would allow them to engage in such activities. Though women's arrest rates have converged with men's from crimes like embezzlement and fraud, these are usually low-level violations. Women predominate among those arrested for embezzling small amounts of money (often from cash registers) and in the ranks of those arrested for committing welfare fraud or writing bad checks. Arrest rates for embezzlement present an interesting paradox. Small embezzlers are much more commonly arrested than those who steal large amounts, a fact that tips the balance in women's "favor." There is also reason to believe that companies are more likely to criminally prosecute those who embezzle small amounts versus those whose crimes involve millions of dollars. CEOs of publicly held companies are loath to endure the publicity that comes with the exposure of major embezzlement—quiet terminations and restitution arrangements are probably much more common.

CHAPTER 3: GENDER AND THE CRIMINAL JUSTICE SYSTEM

1. Many have objected to the term *criminal justice system*, arguing that it is by definition loaded and pointing out that the system often does little to mete out "justice" in any real sense. Such critics (Belknap 2007) instead offer terms such as *crime processing system* as more accurate and neutral substitutes. I have followed the convention of using the term *criminal justice system*. As I hope is obvious, I, too, am skeptical of the system's ability to provide justice.

2. Only one of these legal precedents, that established in *Plessy v. Ferguson*, has been overturned. Decisions in the other two cases, allowing the internment of citizens and the sterilization of the mentally ill, technically remain the law of the land.

3. As of May 2010 the Kansas statute on sodomy (21-3505) still criminalizes only same-sex sodomy. For all practical purposes, the statute has been invalidated by the Supreme Court decision in *Lawrence v. Texas* (539 U.S. 558, 2003).

4. The focus of this section is on criminal law, where statutes that distinguish between classes of people on the basis of statuses like race and sex are now relatively rare. Many such distinctions remain in civil law, however, with most states' bans on marriage for gay men and lesbians a key case in point.

5. All of the minimums discussed in this chapter assume either a first offense or a minimal prior offense history (0 or 1 "criminal history points"). Only 50 percent of drug offenders sentenced in 2009 were classified at level 1 or below. Sentences for those with a more serious offense history can be dramatically higher. Minimum five-year sentences correspond to level 26 in the federal sentencing guidelines; minimum ten-year sentences correspond to level 32. The 2009 guidelines table

can be found here—the drug quantity table begins on page 149: http://www.ussc.gov/2009guid/GL2009.pdf (United States Sentencing Commission 2009).

6. Until 2007, this disparity was one hundred to one. Possession of five grams of crack cocaine produced the same five-year sentence as possession of five kilograms of powder cocaine.

7. According to the 2010 National Drug Threat Assessment (National Drug Intelligence Center 2010), the average level of purity of street-level methamphetamine is approximately 68 percent. Translating this into the amounts required for mandatory minimums, the street dealer or user would have to possess about 7.5 grams (0.25 ounces) to receive a five-year minimum sentence, about seventy-five grams (2.5 ounces) to receive a ten-year minimum sentence.

8. The relatively large number of Hispanics prosecuted for powder cocaine offenses undoubtedly has something to do with their roles as couriers and drug "mules." About 30 percent of all prosecutions (the largest single category) for powder cocaine target those who transport the drug, usually from Latin America. Crack, conversely, is a homemade product, formulated from powder cocaine already in the country. The overwhelming majority of federal crack cocaine prosecutions (67 percent) are against street-level dealers (United States Sentencing Commission 2002).

9. Percentages of methamphetamine users were calculated using population estimates and data from an NSDUH report on methamphetamine use (Substance Abuse and Mental Health Services Administration 2005). These are rough estimates but should capture broad differences in proportions of users.

10. It is worth noting again that whites are the majority of crack cocaine users. African Americans, at 38 percent of users, are nonetheless *overrepresented*; African Americans are a higher percentage of crack users than of the total population. Whites are conversely underrepresented.

11. A number of organizations are involved in the fight against mandatory minimums. See, for example, the Sentencing Project (www.sentencingproject.org), the Drug Policy Alliance (www.drugpolicy.org), and Families Against Mandatory Minimums (www.famm.org).

12. In fact, the courts are beginning to examine this evidence more critically. The South Carolina Supreme Court recently overturned the conviction of Regina McKnight, who had been convicted of homicide by child abuse because the lower courts held that her cocaine use had caused her stillbirth. A number of organizations are working on issues related to pregnant women and the criminal justice system; see, for example, National Advocates for Pregnant Women (www.advocatesforpregnantwomen.org).

13. Women are similarly disadvantaged by civil forfeiture laws, under which the government may seize jointly held property involved in or obtained through criminal enterprises (Massey, Miller, and Wilhelmi 1998).

14. A recent study (Moore and Padavic 2010) demonstrates that disparities exist across categories of juvenile offenders as well—though not in any linear way. In their study of the cases of girls in Florida, they find that—up to a certain threshold of offense severity and prior record—black girls receive harsher sentences than either white or Hispanic girls. As offending severity and seriousness of prior record increases, decisions become harsher for white girls than for black girls. They argue that this is due to the intersections of race, gender, and judicial stereotypes. In the

minds of judges and prosecutors, white girls who commit serious offenses and who have long criminal histories may violate racialized gender expectations more severely than black girls who share these same characteristics.

15. These are prisoners held on sentences of more than one year. Most serve time in state and federal prisons, but some may be held in local jails under some circumstances. Though the terms are often used interchangeably, prisons and jails are not the same thing. With some exceptions, those in prison have been convicted of felony crimes and are serving sentences of one year or more. Jail inmates, on the other hand, have generally been convicted of misdemeanors that carry sentences of less than one year. As I note in chapter 1, many people in jail have not been convicted of any crime; they are awaiting trial and have been denied bail or are unable to post a bond to secure their release pending trial.

16. The "three strikes" law, first passed in Washington in 1993 and more famously adopted by California one year later, prescribes a life sentence after a third felony conviction (in California's version of the law the felonies need not be violent offenses). The "hard forty" law is a variation on this theme, imposing a forty-year sentence without parole for some recidivists and for crimes the courts or the legislature deem particularly heinous. Though "persistent felon" laws of this kind have been common in our legal history (with some in the early part of the century legislating mandatory sterilization for eugenic purposes), the new laws tie the hands of the judiciary to an unprecedented degree. Modern judges have little discretion in the imposition of these sentences; if an offender meets the criteria, the sentence must generally be imposed.

17. Some women in prison do report sexual abuse by girlfriends—in the 2004 survey of state prison inmates, this represented 139 total incidents, or 0.4 percent of all sexual abuse reported. Boyfriends and spouses, on the other hand, accounted for about a quarter of all incidents of sexual abuse reported by women. The remainder was accounted for by parents, relatives, friends or acquaintances, or "others." Women are also more likely than men to report physical abuse by intimates. Though peculiarities in the questionnaire design of the 2004 survey of state prison inmates (in particular, the items regarding the perpetrators of physical abuse) make this calculation difficult, I estimate that about 40 percent of women state prison inmates report physical abuse by a spouse, ex-spouse, boyfriend, or girlfriend (though again, the latter is very rare), while only 1 percent of men report physical abuse by these adult intimates. This estimate is broadly similar to other published comparative data on the physical abuse of adult men and women in prison (e.g., Morton and Snell 1994; Harlow 1999) but should nonetheless be treated with caution.

CHAPTER 4: GENDER AND CRIME VICTIMIZATION

1. I compiled accounts of this case from several Web sources. These include Colavecchio 1999; Hanford 1999; Reid 2001.

2. Response rates for the NCVS been historically been very high; in 2008, 90.4 percent of eligible households in the sample responded, as did 86.2 percent of eligible individuals.

3. Reporting varies by type of crime. Those offenses most likely to be reported to police are not, as one might expect, the most serious violent crimes. They are in fact property offenses, like motor vehicle theft, for which one might expect some financial recovery from an insurance company.

4. Most tables in this chapter report victimization data from the NCVS conducted in 2007; this is the last year for which detailed statistical tables are now available. Where possible, I have used more recent data; see table 4.3, for example.

5. Burglary is counted as a "household" crime, hence individual-level data for sex and race are not reported by the NCVS.

6. DeKeseredy and Schwartz (2009) dispute this general pattern in the case of domestic violence.

7. The Bureau of Justice Statistics discontinued production of this table in 2005. In that year, violent victimization rates in urban areas were 29.8 (per 1,000 population twelve or older), suburban, 18.6, and rural, 16.4 (Bureau of Justice Statistics undated).

8. Some criminologists have pointed out that the rich may be less likely to be burglarized because they are more likely to engage in guardianship of their property; for example, they buy burglar alarms or hire security services. These undoubtedly serve as a deterrent. Extreme patterns of racial and class segregation in American communities also mean that an impoverished burglar would have to be willing to travel and to operate in a neighborhood in which he or she would certainly be visible and out of place. Both of these facts probably contribute to the higher property victimization rates of the poor.

9. Author calculation using Census Bureau population estimates for 2009 and FBI homicide data for the same year. Detailed information on homicide victimization and offending trends over time may be found in Fox and Zawitz (2010).

10. Though this account certainly fits with prevailing stereotypes about the dangerous classes, it tends to ignore the fact that acts of white collar and corporate crime, which by most accounts claim more victims than conventional crimes like robbery and homicide (Reiman 2006), are disproportionately committed by men with access to money, status, and other legitimate resources. It is hence more accurate to say that regardless of the type of offense, men are overwhelmingly more likely to victimize others than women.

11. The NCVS is not better than the UCR in some objective sense, however. The UCR provides valuable data on the activities of police agencies and collects data on a very wide variety of offense and offender circumstances. The NCVS is a victim survey and can thus provide important information on crime from the victim's point of view. Whether one relies on one data source or the other largely depends on the question one is asking about crime.

12. I dislike the phrase *domestic violence*; it minimizes the experience of assault by an intimate by separating that experience from the realm of violence in a general sense. In its gender neutrality, it also encourages a false perception that men's and women's experiences are somehow symmetrical and identical (though some argue that they are). For want of a better term however, I will use the phrase *domestic violence* throughout this work.

13. I discuss many of these same ideas in Britton 2000a; some of this discussion is taken from that work.

14. The title of this section is taken from an important early feminist work on rape, funded by the Ms. Foundation (Warshaw 1994).

15. The National Violence against Women Survey estimated the prevalence of marital rape at 7.7 percent for women and 0.3 percent for men (Tjaden and Thoennes 2000, 2006).

16. Even fewer marital rapes are prosecuted. There is widespread resistance to viewing any sexual activity between married couples as rape, and this resistance extends to the legal system. In dismissing a charge of marital rape, Australian Supreme Court Justice Derek Bollen asserted: "There is, of course, nothing wrong with a husband, faced with his wife's initial refusal to engage in intercourse, in attempting, in an acceptable way, to persuade her to change her mind, and that may involve a measure of rougher than usual handling" (cited in Milliken 1993).

17. The authors reported very similar results from their 1975 administration of the same survey. See Gelles and Straus (1988).

18. Claims of symmetry have recently become very common in research on dating violence (e.g., Carney, Buttell, and Dutton 2006; Romans et al. 2007; Straus 2007; Whitaker et al. 2007). See Reed et al. (2010) for a critique.

19. This framing of the issue undoubtedly raises questions for some readers about violence in gay and lesbian relationships. Some studies on this topic do exist, but many draw on reports of clinical populations (i.e., men and women in therapy), and few attempt generalizable estimates of the overall prevalence of same-sex relationship violence. Given the state of the data, the accuracy of any such estimate seems highly questionable. Hence I do not speculate about this issue.

20. For similar accounts of the treatment of battered women by the criminal justice system, see Gillespie (1990) and Miller (2005).

21. The federal government has commissioned many studies of sexual violence against women in the military and in military service academies. For recent examples, see Defense Task Force on Sexual Assault in the Military Services (2009), General Accounting Office (2008), and United States Department of Defense (2010).

22. For more information on the Stanford Prison Experiment, see the website maintained by Philip Zimbardo: http://www.prisonexp.org. The prisoner abuse scandal at Abu Ghraib in Iraq demonstrates the power of this study's findings in a new era (see, e.g., Hersh 2004).

23. The desire to avoid being seen as unmasculine also often fosters an aversion to seeking psychological counseling, which likely leads to higher rates of post-traumatic stress and even suicide. A soldier captured on a leaked video carrying wounded children after a firefight in Iraq said in an interview: "After the incident, we went back to the FOB [forward operating base] and that's when I was in my room. I had blood all down the front of me from the children. I was trying to wash it off in my room. I was pretty distraught over the whole situation with the children. So I went to a sergeant and asked to see [the mental health person], because I was having a hard time dealing with it. I was called a pussy and that I needed to suck it up and a lot of other horrible things. I was also told that there would be repercussions if I was to go to mental health" (Zetter 2010).

24. Mass rapes are common during wartime; they are a weapon of war as well as a consequence of the chaos that follows in its wake. Over a four-day period during the summer of 2010, Rwandan rebel fighters gang raped nearly two hundred

women and some baby boys in the Democratic Republic of Congo. The attacks happened within miles of a United Nations base. The United Nations estimates that more than eight thousand women were gang raped during fighting in the Congo in 2009—by both soldiers and civilian men (British Broadcasting Corporation 2010).

CHAPTER 5: GENDER AND WORK IN THE CRIMINAL JUSTICE SYSTEM

1. The Supreme Court had established this precedent two years earlier, in *Bradwell v. The State* (83 U.S. 130, 1872). Myra Bradwell, a married woman, had applied to be admitted to the state bar in Illinois. The court held that she was not entitled to this right. In a concurring opinion, Justice Douglas wrote: "The civil law, as well as nature herself, has always recognized a wide difference in the respective spheres and destinies of man and woman. Man is, or should be, woman's protector and defender. The natural and proper timidity and delicacy which belongs to the female sex evidently unfits it for many of the occupations of civil life. The Constitution of the family organization, which is founded in the divine ordinance as well as in the nature of things, indicates the domestic sphere as that which properly belongs to the domain and functions of womanhood. The harmony, not to say identity, of interest and views which belong, or should belong, to the family institution is repugnant to the idea of a woman adopting a distinct and independent career from that of her husband."

2. Some of my women students, upon learning of the greater value men get from their college education, have suggested that their tuition be 25 percent higher. I find it extremely doubtful that this idea will catch on, but it is an interesting way to impose equity.

3. As opposed to the "glass ceiling" that blocks women's advancement into high-status, high-paying positions. Williams uses the term *glass escalator* to symbolize the ease of men's movement upward, but also to illustrate the fact that many of her respondents advanced whether they wanted to or not. There is increasing evidence, however, that the glass escalator effect may not apply to all men equally. More on this below, and see also Harvey Wingfield (2009).

4. Though presumably not in tights.

5. Pioneer woman New York City firefighter Brenda Berkman, in the documentary *Taking the Heat* (2005). For more information, see the companion website for the film: http://www.pbs.org independentlens/takingtheheat/film.html.

6. While it is of course theoretically possible that women in female-dominated occupations could band together to exclude men, research indicates just the opposite. Women in jobs such as nursing, social work, elementary-school teaching, and other such occupations have tended to welcome the presence of men. Leaders in many of these fields have in fact advocated recruiting men to raise the status of the occupations (Williams 1995).

7. I report two different figures for the wage gap between men and women attorneys in this chapter—75 cents and 80 cents. The former is based on Bureau of Labor Statistics data, the latter on a survey conducted by the American Bar Association. The Bureau of Labor Statistics figure is based on larger sample of workers and

so is likely more reliable. In either case, there is a substantial gap between men and women with essentially the same educational credential and working in the same occupation.

8. There are a surprising (to me at least) number of websites dedicated to tracking attorneys and judges on television. For just two examples, see the University of Texas law school's "Law and Popular Culture" collection: http://tarlton.law.utexas .edu/lpop/index.html, and this site on women attorneys on television, maintained by a Louisiana State University law professor: http://faculty.law.lsu.edu/ccorcos/ lawhum/womenlawyerstvseries.htm.

9. Kanter thought this process was gender-neutral—that is, she believed any dominant group in an occupation or organization would seek to heighten boundaries against outsiders who threatened them. As I have noted, however, this does not appear to be the case in female-dominated jobs and organizations.

10. Some of the fluctuations in this table occur because census categories change over time. For police officers in 1972, 1979, and 1987, the category is "police and detectives." For 1983 and 1994 through 2000, the category is "police and detectives, public service," and in 2003 and 2009 the category is "police and sheriff's patrol officers."

11. In line with the contextual analysis of violence against women I offered in chapter 4, it is worth noting that policing organizations share many of the same characteristics of fraternities, the military, and men's athletics teams—they are historically sex-segregated organizations in which aggressive masculinity has been valued, oversight has sometimes been minimal, and women have historically served in auxiliary roles. For a detailed study of sexual assaults committed by police officers, see Human Rights Watch (1998).

12. Census categories for correctional officers have varied quite significantly over the years covered by this table. From 1870 to 1900, the category was "guards, watchmen, and doorkeepers, detectives, firemen, policemen, probation and truant officers, marshals and constables, experienced labor force," from 1910 to 1930, "guards, watchmen, and doorkeepers, experienced labor force," from 1940 to 1960, "guards, watchmen, and doorkeepers, employed labor force," in 1970, "guards and watchmen," from 1980 to 1985, "guards," from 1990 to 2000, "correctional institution officers"—a far narrower category, hence the lower totals, and in 2005 and 2009, "bailiffs, correctional officers, and jailers."

13. For African American and Hispanic officers I interviewed, both men and women, views of inmates were complicated by the fact that their own race in many ways identified them with the inmates they supervised. Though I cannot generalize from my sample of seventy-two officers, I can say that an orientation toward rehabilitating inmates was somewhat more common among African American and Hispanic officers in my sample than among whites, but also more likely to be espoused among those with more education (who were in all racial categories, of course). This Hispanic man is typical of many of those in this group:

> Britton: For you, what's the most enjoyable aspect of your job? I would probably say, help make a difference in a person. I actually had that experience, former inmates have come back to me, "Man, you really helped me out, and I'll never forget you," and stuff like that. I even had an inmate that, he left to another institution, and he got me by surprise, he gave me a hug, and I was like "Oh my god!" [laughs] His intention was like, saying

thank you to me, but I was kinda, he did catch me off guard a little bit. (quoted in Britton 2003, 209)

Quantitative studies with much larger samples generally bear out this association between race, education, and a rehabilitation orientation among correctional officers (e.g., see Britton 1997; Crouch and Alpert 1982; Van Voorhis et al. 1991; and Whitehead and Lindquist 1989).

References

Acker, Joan. 1990. Hierarchies, jobs, bodies: A theory of gendered organizations. *Gender & Society* 4: 139–58.

———. 1992. Gendering organizational theory. In *Gendering organizational analysis*, ed. Albert J. Mills and Peta Tancred, 248–60. Twin Oaks, CA: Sage.

Adler, Freda. 1975. *Sisters in crime: The rise of the new female criminal.* New York: McGraw Hill.

Allard, Patricia. 2002. Life sentences: Denying welfare benefits to women convicted of drug offenses. Sentencing Project. http://www.sentencingproject.org/doc/pub lications/women_lifesentences.pdf (retrieved October 12, 2005).

American Bar Association. 2010. Commission on women in the profession. http://www.abanet.org/women/womenstatistics.html (accessed June 9, 2010).

American Psychological Association. 1999. Warning signs. American Psychological Association. http://helping.apa.org/warningsigns (accessed August 23 2003).

Amir, Menachem. 1971. *Patterns in forcible rape.* Chicago: University of Chicago Press.

Anderson, Elijah. 1992. *Streetwise: Race, class, and change in an urban community.* Chicago: University of Chicago Press.

———. 2000. *Code of the streets: Decency, violence, and the moral life of the inner city.* London, New York: W. W. Norton.

Anderson, Kristen L., and Debra Umberson. 2001. Gendering violence: Masculinity and power in men's accounts of domestic violence. *Gender & Society* 15: 358–80.

Appier, Janis. 1992. Preventative justice: The campaign for women police, 1910–1940. *Women and Criminal Justice* 4: 3–36.

———. 1998. Policing women: The sexual politics of law enforcement and the LAPD. Philadelphia: Temple University Press.

Archer, John. 2000. Sex differences in aggression between heterosexual partners: A meta-analytic review. *Psychological Bulletin* 126: 651–80.

Associated Press Wire. 1989. Defendant acquitted of rape; "she asked for it," juror says. *New York Times*, October 7. http://www.nytimes.com/1989/10/07/us/defendant-acquitted-of-rape-she-asked-for-it-juror-says.html (accessed November 10, 2000).

Bachman, Ronet, and Linda E. Saltzman. 1995. Violence against women: Estimates from the redesigned National Crime Victimization Survey. Bureau of Justice Statistics. http://bjs.ojp.usdoj.gov/index.cfm?ty=pbdetail&iid=805 (retrieved March 22, 2001).

Baker, Al. 2010. New York minorities more likely to be frisked. *New York Times*, May 12. http://www.nytimes.com/2010/05/13/nyregion/13frisk.html (accessed June 18, 2010).

Beckett, Katherine, Kris Nyrop, Lori Pfingst, and Melissa Bowen. 2005. Drug use, drug possession arrests, and the question of race: Lessons from Seattle. *Social Problems* 52: 419–41.

Beirne, Piers, and James Messerschmidt. 2000. *Criminology*. 3rd ed. Boulder, CO: Westview.

Belknap, Joanne. 2007. *The invisible woman: Gender, crime, and justice*. 3rd ed. Belmont, CA: Thomson/Wadsworth.

Bernstein, Elizabeth. 2007. *Temporarily yours: Intimacy, authenticity, and the commerce of sex*. Chicago: University of Chicago Press.

Bielby, William T., and Denis D. Bielby. 1992. I will follow him: Family ties, gender-role beliefs, and reluctance to relocate for a better job. *American Journal of Sociology* 97: 1241–67.

Bissinger, H. G. 1995. Lone star hate: On the trail of Texas's brutal gay killings. *Vanity Fair*, February.

Bleecker, Timothy E., and Sarah K. Murnen. 2005. Fraternity membership, the display of sexually degrading sexual images of women, and rape myth acceptance. *Sex Roles* 53: 487–93.

Brecht, Mary Lynn, Ann O'Brien, Christina von Maryhauser, and M. Douglas Anglin. 2004. Methamphetamine use: Behaviors and gender differences. *Addictive Behaviors* 29: 89–106.

Brezina, Timothy, Robert Agnew, Francis T. Cullen, and John Paul Wright. 2004. The code of the streets: A quantitative assessment of Elijah Anderson's subculture of violence thesis and its contribution to youth violence research. *Youth Violence and Juvenile Justice* 2: 303–28.

British Broadcasting Corporation. 2006. US medic jailed over Iraq murder. *British Broadcasting Corporation*, October 7. http://news.bbc.co.uk/2/hi/middle_east/5415216.stm (retrieved June 18, 2006).

———. 2010. UN investigates claims of mass rape by DR Congo rebels. August 24. http://www.bbc.co.uk/news/world-africa-11079135 (retrieved August 31, 2010).

Britton, Dana M. 1997. Perceptions of the work environment among correctional officers: Do race and sex matter? *Criminology* 35: 85–105.

———. 1999. Cat fights and gang fights: Preference for work in a male-dominated organization. *Sociological Quarterly* 40(3): 455–74.

———. 2000a. Feminism in criminology: Engendering the outlaw. *Annals of the American Academy of Political and Social Science* 571: 57–76.

———. 2000b. The epistemology of the gendered organization. *Gender & Society* 14(3): 418–35.

———. 2003. *At work in the iron cage: The prison as gendered organization.* New York: New York University Press.

Britton, Dana M., and Laura Logan. 2008. Gendered organizations: Progress and prospects. *Sociological Compass* 2: 107–21.

Brown, Amy L., and Maria Testa. 2007. Social influences on judgments of rape victims: The role of the negative and positive social reactions of others. *Sex Roles* 58: 490–500.

Browning, Sandra Lee, Francis T. Cullen, Liqun Cao, Renee Kopache, and Thomas J. Stevenson. 1994. Race and getting hassled by the police: A research note. *Police Studies* 17: 1–11.

Brownmiller, Susan. 1975. *Against our will: Men, women, and rape.* New York: Simon & Schuster.

Bureau of Justice Statistics, United States Department of Justice. Undated. Victim-ization rates for persons 12 and over, by type of crime and locality of residence of victims, 2005. http://bjs.ojp.usdoj.gov/content/pub/pdf/cvus/previous/cvus52 .pdf (retrieved June 18, 2010).

———. 2007. Survey of inmates in state and federal correctional facilities, 2004 [Computer file]. ICPSR04572-v1. Ann Arbor, MI: Inter-university Consor-tium for Political and Social Research [producer and distributor], 2007-02-28. doi:10.3886/ICPSR04572.

———. 2008. Police-public contact survey, 2005 [United States] [Computer file]. ICPSR20020-v2. Washington, DC: U.S. Dept. of Justice, Bureau of Justice Sta-tistics [producer]. Ann Arbor, MI: Inter-university Consortium for Political and Social Research [distributor], 2008-05-06. doi:10.3886/ICPSR20020.

———. 2009. Census of state and federal adult correctional facilities, 2005 [Computer file]. ICPSR24642-v1. Ann Arbor, MI: Inter-university Consortium for Political and Social Research [distributor], 2009-04-03. doi:10.3886/ ICPSR24642.

Bureau of Labor Statistics, United States Department of Labor. 2010. *Highlights of women's earnings in 2009.* Washington, DC, June. http://www.bls.gov/cps/cps wom2009.pdf (retrieved August 2, 2010).

Butler, Anne. 1997. *Gendered justice in the American West: Women prisoners in men's penitentiaries.* Urbana: University of Illinois Press.

Cain, Maureen. 1990. Towards trans-gression: New directions in feminist criminol-ogy. *International Journal of the Sociology of Law* 18: 1–18.

Campbell, Jacquelyn C. 1992. If I can't have you no one can: Power and control in homicide of female partners. In *Femicide: The politics of woman killing,* ed. Jill Radford and Diana H. Russell, 99–113. New York: Twayne.

Carney, Michelle, Fred Buttell, and Don Dutton. 2006. Women who perpetrate intimate partner violence: A review of the literature with recommendations for treatment. *Aggression and Violent Behavior* 12: 108–15.

Carr, Nicole T., Kenneth Hudson, Roma S. Hanks, and Andrea N. Hunt. 2008. Gen-der effects along the juvenile justice system: Evidence of a gendered organization. *Feminist Criminology* 3: 25–43.

Casselman, Ben. 2010. Gulf rig owner had rising tally of accidents. *Wall Street Journal*, May 1. http://online.wsj.com/article/NA_WSJ_PUB:SB1000142405274870 43078045752344471807539054.html (retrieved August 5, 2010).

Cathcart, Rebecca. 2008. Boy's killing, labeled a hate crime, stuns a town. *New York Times*, February 28. http://www.nytimes.com/2008/02/23/us/23oxnard.html (retrieved June 18, 2010).

CBS News. 2010. Blowout: The Deepwater Horizon disaster. http://www.cbsnews .com/stories/2010/05/16/60minutes/main6490197.shtml (retrieved August 6, 2010).

Chauncey, George. 1985. Christian brotherhood or sexual perversion—Homosexual identities and the construction of sexual boundaries in the World-War-I era. *Journal of Social History* 19: 189–211.

Chesney-Lind, Meda, and Katherine Irwin. 2008. *Beyond bad girls: Gender, violence and hype.* New York: Routledge.

Chesney-Lind, Meda, and Nikki Jones. 2010. *Fighting for girls: New perspectives on gender and violence.* Albany: State University of New York Press.

Chilton, Roland, and Susan K. Datesman. 1987. Gender, race, and crime: An analysis of urban arrest trends, 1960–1980. *Gender & Society* 1: 152–71.

City of Los Angeles Commission on the Status of Women. 1992. Report of the City of Los Angeles 1992 sexual harassment survey. Los Angeles: Commission on the Status of Women.

Cloward, Richard, and Lloyd Ohlin. 1960. *Delinquency and opportunity: The culture of the gang.* New York: Free Press.

Cobbina, Jennifer E., Jody Miller, and Rod Brunson. 2008. Gender, neighborhood danger, and risk avoidance strategies among urban African American youth. *Criminology* 46: 501–38.

Cohen, Albert Kircidel. 1955. *Delinquent boys: The culture of the gang.* New York: Free Press.

Cohen, Lawrence, and Marcus Felson. 1979. Social change and crime rate trends: A routine activity approach. *American Sociological Review* 44: 588–608.

Colavecchio, Shannon. 1999. Delta Chi stripper to serve six-month probation. *Independent Florida Alligator*, July 29. http://www.alligator.org/edit/issues/99 -sumr/990729/b03king29.htm (retrieved Feburary 10, 2005).

Colvin, Mark. 1997. *Penitentiaries, reformatories, and chain gangs: Social theory and the history of punishment in nineteenth-century America.* New York: St. Martin's.

———. 2000. *Penitentiaries, reformatories, and chain gangs: Social theory and the history of punishment in nineteenth-century America.* New York: St. Martin's.

Connell, Raewyn. 2002. *Gender.* Cambridge: Polity Press.

Crouch, Ben M., and Geoffrey P. Alpert. 1982. Sex and occupational socialization among prison guards: A longitudinal study. *Criminal Justice and Behavior* 9: 159–76.

Daly, Kathleen, and Rebecca Bordt. 1995. Sex effects and sentencing: An analysis of the statistical literature. *Justice Quarterly* 12: 141–75.

Daly, Kathleen, and Meda Chesney-Lind. 1988. Feminism and criminology. *Justice Quarterly* 5: 497–538.

Daly, Kathleen, and Lisa Maher. 1998. "Crossroads and intersections: Building from feminist critique." In *Criminology at the crossroads: Feminist readings in crime and justice,* edited by Kathleen Daly and Lisa Maher, 1–21. New York: Oxford University Press.

Daniels, Jessie. 1997. *White lies: Race, class, gender and sexuality in white supremacist discourse.* New York: Routledge.

Danner, Mona, and Dianne Carmondy. 2001. Missing gender in cases of infamous school violence: Investigating research and media explanations. *Justice Quarterly* 18: 87–114.

Davis, F. James. 1991. *Who is black? One nation's definition.* University Park: Pennsylvania State University Press.

Defense Task Force on Sexual Assault in the Military Services. 2009. Annual report. http://www.dtic.mil/dtfsams/docs/11_09docs/DTFSAMS-Rept_Dec09.pdf (retrieved December 16, 2010).

DeKeseredy, Walter S., and Martin D. Schwartz. 1998. *Woman abuse on campus: Results from the Canadian national survey.* Thousand Oaks, CA: Sage.

———. 2009. *Dangerous exits: Escaping abusive relationships in rural America.* New Brunswick: Rutgers University Press.

Dodge, L. Mara. 1999. "One female prisoner is of more trouble than twenty males": Women convicts in Illinois prisons, 1835–1896. *Journal of Social History* 32: 907–30.

Dumm, Thomas L. 1987. *Democracy and punishment: Disciplinary origins of the United States.* Madison: University of Wisconsin Press.

Dworkin, Andrea. 1979. *Pornography: Men possessing women.* New York: Plume.

Egan, Timothy. 1991. New faces, and new roles, for the police. *New York Times,* April 25. http://www.nytimes.com/1991/04/25/us/new-faces-and-new-roles-for-the-police.html (retrieved September 16, 2003).

Ehrenreich, Barbara, and Deirdre English. 1989. *For her own good: 150 years of the experts' advice to women.* New York: Anchor Books.

Engel, Robin Shepard, James J. Sobol, and Robert E. Worden. 2000. Further exploration of the demeanor hypothesis: The interaction effects of suspects' characteristics and demeanor on police behavior. *Justice Quarterly* 17: 235–58.

England, Paula. 2005. Gender inequality in labor markets: The role of motherhood and segregation. *Social Politics: International Studies in Gender, State and Society* 12: 264–88.

———. 2010. The gender revolution: Uneven and stalled. *Gender & Society* 24: 149–66.

Enos, Sandra. 2001. *Mothering from the inside: Parenting in a women's prison.* Albany: State University of New York Press.

Epstein, Cynthia F. 1993. *Women in law.* Champaign: University of Illinois Press.

Erez, Edna, Madeleine Adelman, and Carol Gregory. 2009. Intersections of immigration and domestic violence: Voices of battered immigrant women. *Feminist Criminology* 4: 32–56.

Eschholz, Sarah, Matthew Mallard, and Stacey Flynn. 2004. Images of prime time justice: A content analysis of "NYPD Blue" and "Law & Order." *Journal of Criminal Justice and Popular Culture* 10: 161–80.

Evans, Rhonda D., Craig J. Forsyth, and DeAnn K. Gauthier. 2002. Gendered pathways into and experiences with crack cultures outside of the inner city. *Deviant Behavior* 23: 483–510.

Fagan, Jeffrey, and Garth Davies. 2000. Street stops and broken windows: Terry, race, and disorder in New York City. *Fordham Urban Law Journal* 28: 457.

Families against Mandatory Minimums. Undated. Profiles of injustice: Tammi Bloom. http://www.famm.org/ProfilesofInjustice/FederalProfiles/TammiBloom .aspx (retrieved August 17, 2006).

Farnworth, Margaret, and Raymond H. C. Teske, Jr. 1995. Gender differences in filling court processing: Testing three hypotheses of disparity. *Women and Criminal Justice* 6: 23–44.

Farrell, Amy S. 2003. Effects of gender and family status on downward departures in federal criminal sentences. http://www.ncjrs.gov/pdffiles1/nij/grants/199684 .pdf (retrieved December 16, 2010).

Farrell, Warren. 1994. Spouse abuse: A two-way street. *USA Today,* June 29.

Fausto-Sterling, Anne. 2000. *Sexing the body: Gender politics and the construction of sexuality.* New York: Basic Books.

Federal Bureau of Investigation, United States Department of Justice. 1998. Crime in the United States, 1997. http://www.fbi.gov/ucr/97cius.htm (retrieved February 4, 2010).

———. 2009. Crime in the United States, 2008. http://www2.fbi.gov/ucr/cius2008/ index.html (retrieved February 4, 2010).

———. 2010. Crime in the United States, 2009. http://www2.fbi.gov/ucr/cius2009/ index.html (retrieved December 16, 2010).

Felson, Marcus. 1994. *Crime and everyday life: Insight and implications for society.* Thousand Oaks, CA: Pine Forge Press.

Ferguson, Ann A. 2001. *Bad boys: Public schools in the making of black masculinity.* Ann Arbor: University of Michigan Press.

FindLaw. 2001. Perry Mason, Ben Matlock are our favorite TV lawyers. http:// company.findlaw.com/pr/2001/110801.tvlawyers.html (retrieved September 16, 2003).

Fine, Michelle, Nick Freudenberg, Yassar Payne, Tiffany Perkins, Kersha Smith, and Katya Wanzer. 2003. Anything can happen with police around: Urban youth evaluate strategies of surveillance in public places. *Journal of Social Issues* 59: 141–58.

Finns, Deborah. 2009. Death row USA, summer 2009. NAACP Legal Defense and Educational Fund. http://www.deathpenaltyinfo.org/documents/DRUSASum mer2009.pdf (retrieved August 29, 2010).

Fisher, Bonnie S., Francis T. Cullen, and Michael G. Turner. 2000. The sexual victimization of college women. National Institute of Justice. Bureau of Justice Statistics. http://www.ncjrs.gov/pdffiles1/nij/182369.pdf.

Flavin, Jeanne. 2008. *Our bodies, our crimes: The policing of women's reproduction in America.* New York: New York University Press.

Flavin, Jeanne, and Lynn M. Paltrow. 2010. Punishing pregnant drug-using women: Defying law, medicine and common sense. *Addictive Behaviors* 29: 231–44.

Fox, James Alan, and Marianne W. Zawitz. 2010. Homicide trends in the United States. Bureau of Justice Statistics. http://bjs.ojp.usdoj.gov/content/homicide/ homtrnd.cfm (retrieved June 18, 2010).

Freedman, Estelle B. 1981. *Their sisters' keepers: Women's prison reform in America, 1830–1930.* Ann Arbor: University of Michigan Press.

García-López, Gladys. 2008. "Nunca te toman en cuenta [they never take you into account]": The challenges of inclusion and strategies for success of Chicana attorneys. *Gender & Society* 22: 590–612.

Gelles, Richard J., and Donileen R. Loseke. 1993. *Current controversies on family violence*. Newbury Park, CA: Sage.

Gelles, Richard, and Murray Straus. 1988. *Intimate violence: The definitive study of the causes and consequences of abuse in the American family*. New York: Simon & Schuster.

General Accounting Office. 1997. Defense of marriage act. http://www.gao.gov/archive/1997/og97016.pdf (retrieved November 10, 2000).

———. 2000. U.S. customs service: Better targeting of airline passengers for personal searches could produce better results. http://www.gao.gov/archive/2000/gg00038.pdf (retrieved June 15, 2003).

———. 2008. Military personnel: DOD's and the Coast Guard's sexual assault prevention and response. Programs face implementation and oversight challenges. http://www.gao.gov/products/GAO-08-924 (retrieved June 18, 2010).

Gibbs, Nancy, et al. 1999. The Littleton massacre: . . . In sorrow and disbelief. *Time*, May 3, 1999. http://www.time.com/time/magazine/article/0,9171,990870-5,00.html (accessed August 29, 2010).

Gilbert, Neil. 1997. Advocacy research and social policy. In *Crime and justice: A review of research*, ed. Michael H. Tonry. Chicago: University of Chicago Press.

Gillespie, Cynthia K. 1990. *Justifiable homicide: Battered women, self-defense and the law*. Columbus: Ohio State University Press.

Glaze, Lauren E., and Laura M. Maruschak. 2008. Parents in prison and their minor children. Bureau of Justice Statistics. http://bjs.ojp.usdoj.gov/index.cfm?ty=pbdetail&iid=823 (retrieved April 16, 2010).

Goetting, Ann. 1995. *Homicides in families and other special populations*. New York: Springer.

Griffin, Susan. 1981. *Pornography and silence: Culture's revenge against nature*. New York: Harper & Row.

Guinier, Lani, Michelle Fine, and Jane Balin. 1997. *Becoming gentlemen: Women, law school, and institutional change*. Boston: Beacon Press.

Hakim, Catherine. 1998. Developing a sociology for the twenty-first century: Preference theory. *British Journal of Sociology* 49: 137–43.

Haney, Craig, Curtis Banks, and Philip G. Zimbardo. 1973. Interpersonal dynamics in a simulated prison. *International Journal of Criminology and Penology* 1: 69–97.

Haney, Lynne. 2004. Introduction: Gender, welfare, and states of punishment. *Social Politics: International Studies in Gender, State & Society* 11: 333–67.

Haney-López, Ian. 1996. *White by law: The legal construction of race*. New York: New York University Press.

Hanford, Cindy. 1999. Campus rape ignored . . . Even when there's a videotape. National Organization for Women. http://www.now.org/nnt/fall-99/campus.html (retrieved February 10, 2005).

Harlow, Caroline Wolf. 1999. Prior abuse reported by inmates and probationers. Bureau of Justice Statistics. http://bjs.ojp.usdoj.gov/index.cfm?ty=pbdetail&iid=837 (retrieved April 11, 2002).

Harrison, Paige M., and Allen J. Beck. 2005. Prisoners in 2005. Bureau of Justice Statistics. http://morehousemaleinitiative.com/wp-content/uploads/2008/11/doj-prison-stats2.pdf.

Harvey Wingfield, Adia. 2009. Racializing the glass escalator: Reconsidering men's experiences with women's work. *Gender & Society* 23: 5–26.

Hassell, Kimberly D., and Steven G. Brandl. 2009. An examination of the workplace experiences of police patrol officers: The role of race, sex, and sexual orientation. *Police Quarterly* 12: 408–30.

Hawkins, Darnell Felix. 1995. *Ethnicity, race, and crime: Perspectives across time and place*. Albany: State University of New York Press.

Herbert, Melissa. 2000. *Camouflage isn't only for combat: Gender, sexuality, and women in the military*. New York: New York University Press.

Hersh, Seymour. 2004. Annals of national security: Torture at Abu Ghraib. *New Yorker*, May 10. http://www.newyorker.com/archive/2004/05/10/040510fa_fact (retrieved August 31, 2010).

Hickman, Susan E., and Charlene L. Muehlenhard. 1999. "By the semi-mystical appearance of a condom": How young women and men communicate sexual consent in heterosexual situations. *Journal of Sex Research* 36: 258–72.

Hirsch, Adam J. 1992. *Rise of the penitentiary: Prisons and punishment in early America*. New Haven: Yale University Press.

Hirschel, David, Eve Buzawa, April Pattavina, Don Faggiani, and Melissa Reuland. 2007. Explaining the prevalence, context, and consequences of dual arrest in intimate partner cases. http://www.ncjrs.gov/pdffiles1/nij/grants/218355.pdf.

Hochschild, Arlie R. 1997. *The time bind: When work becomes home and home becomes work*. New York: Henry Holt.

Hockett, Jericho M., Donald A. Saucier, Bethany H. Hoffman, Sara J. Smith, and Adam W. Craig. 2009. Oppression through acceptance?: Predicting rape myth acceptance and attitudes toward rape victims. *Violence against Women* 15: 877–97.

Howard, Judith, and Jocelyn Hollander. 1997. *Gendered situations, gendered selves: A gender lens on social psychology*. Newbury Park, CA: Sage.

Human Rights Campaign. Undated. How do transgender people suffer from discrimination? http://www.hrc.org/issues/1508.htm (retrieved December 16, 2010).

Human Rights Watch. 1998. Shielded from justice: Police brutality and accountability in the United States. http://www.hrw.org/reports98/police/index.htm (retrieved November 5, 2005).

Humphreys, Laud. 1975. *Tearoom trade: Impersonal sex in public places*. Chicago: Aldine.

Hurst, Yolander G., James Frank, and Sandra Lee Browning. 2000. The attitudes of juveniles toward the police: A comparison of black and white youth. *Police Studies: International Review of Police Development* 23: 37–53.

Ignatiev, Noel. 1995. *How the Irish became white*. New York: Routledge.

Jacobson, Jennifer. 2004. Sex and football. *Chronicle of Higher Education*, February 27. http://chronicle.com/article/SexFootball/14954 (retrieved February 24, 2005).

Janofsky, Michael, and Diana Jean Schemo. 2003. Women recount cadet life: Forced sex and fear. *New York Times*, March 16. http://www.nytimes.com/2003/03/16/national/16CADE.html (retrieved April 11, 2005).

Janus, Samuel, Cynthia Janus, Leslie Lord, and Thomas Power. 1988. Women in police work: Annie Oakley or little orphan Annie? *Police Studies* 11: 124–27.

Jenkot, Robert. 2008. "Cooks are like gods": Hierarchies in methamphetamine-groups. *Deviant Behavior* 29: 667–89.

Johnson, L. B. 1991. On the front lines: Police stress and family well-being. Hearing before the Select Committee on Children, Youth, and Families, House of Representatives: 102 Congress First Session May 20 (pp. 32–48). Washington, DC: Government Printing Office.

Johnson, Michael P. 1995. Patriarchal terrorism and common couple violence: Two forms of violence against women. *Journal of Marriage and the Family* 57: 283–94.

———. 2008. *A typology of domestic violence: Intimate terrorism, violent resistance, and situational couple violence.* Boston: Northeastern University Press.

Jones, Nikki. 2009. *Between good and ghetto: African American girls and inner city violence.* New Brunswick NJ: Rutgers University Press.

Jurik, Nancy C., and Peter Gregware. 1992. A method for murder: The study of homicides by women. In *Perspectives on social problems,* ed. Gale Miller and James A. Holstein, 179–201. London: JAI Press.

Kanter, Rosabeth Moss. 1993. *Men and women of the corporation.* 2nd ed. New York: Basic Books.

Katz, Jackson, and Sut Jhally. 1999. The national conversation in the wake of Littleton is missing the mark. *The Boston Globe,* May 2, E1.

Kessler, Suzanne J., and Wendy McKenna. 1978. *Gender: An ethnomethodolgical approach.* New York: Wiley.

Kimmel, Michael. 1999. Manhood and violence: The deadliest equation. Cultivating Peace. http://www.cultivatingpeace.ca/cpmaterials/module1/dwnld/les2-eng/cccples2hand2.pdf (retrieved on August 25, 2003).

———. 2008. *Guyland: The perilous world where boys become men.* New York: Harper Collins.

Kindlon, Dan, and Michael Thompson. 1999. *Raising Cain: Protecting the emotional life of boys.* New York: Random House.

King, Neal. 2008. Gendered womanhood: Gendered depictions in cop action cinema. *Gender & Society* 22: 238–60.

Koons-Witt, Barbara A. 2002. The effect of gender on the decision to incarcerate before and after the introduction of sentencing guidelines. *Criminology* 40: 297–328.

Koss, Mary P. 1988. Stranger and acquaintance rape. *Psychology of Women Quarterly* 12: 1–24.

Koss, Mary P., Christine A. Gidycz, and Nadine Wisniewski. 1987. The scope of rape: Incidence and prevalence of sexual aggression and victimization in a national sample of higher education students. *Journal of Consulting and Clinical Psychology* 55: 162–70.

Kruttschnitt, Candace, and Rosemary Gartner. 2005. *Marking time in the Golden State: Women's imprisonment in California.* New York: Cambridge University Press.

Kurtz, Don L. 2008. Controlled burn: The gendering of stress and burnout in modern policing. *Feminist Criminology* 2: 114–29.

Lauritsen, Janet L., Karen Heimer, and James P. Lynch. 2009. Trends in the gender gap in violent offending: New evidence from the national crime victimization survey. *Criminology* 47: 361–99.

Lefkowitz, Bernard. 1998. *Our Guys.* Berkeley: University of California Press.

Leland, John. 2003. Everything a man can do, decapitation included. *New York Times,* October 19. http://www.nytimes.com/2003/10/19/fashion/19KILL.html (retrieved April 29, 2004).

Locke, Benjamin D., and James R. Mahalik. 2005. Examining masculinity norms, problem drinking, and athletic involvement as predictors of sexual aggression in college men. *Journal of Counseling Psychology* 52: 279–83.

Loke, Tien-Li. 1997. Note: Trapped in domestic violence: The impact of United States immigration laws on battered immigrant women. *Boston University Public Interest Law Journal* 6: 589.

Lombroso, Cesare. 1909. *The female offender.* New York: D. Appleton and Company.

———. 1911. *Crime, its causes and remedies.* Boston: Little, Brown.

Lopez, Vera, Nancy Jurik, and Stacia Gilliard-Matthews. 2009. Gender, sexuality, power and drug acquisition strategies among adolescent girls who use meth. *Feminist Criminology* 4: 226–51.

Loseke, Donileen R., Richard J. Gelles, and Mary M. Cavanaugh. 2004. *Current controversies on family violence.* Thousand Oaks, CA: Sage.

Lundman, Richard J. 1994. Demeanor or crime? The Midwest city police-citizen encounters study. *Criminology* 32: 631–56.

———. 1996. Demeanor and arrest: Additional evidence from unpublished data. *Journal of Research in Crime and Delinquency* 33: 306–23.

———. 1998. City police and drunk driving: Baseline data. *Justice Quarterly* 15: 701–20.

Lundman, Richard J., and Robert L. Kaufman. 2003. Driving while black: Effects of race, ethnicity, and gender on citizen self-reports of traffic stops and police actions. *Criminology* 41: 195–220.

Lusane, Clarence. 1991. *Pipe dream blues: Racism and the war on drugs.* Boston: South End Press.

Maguire, Kathleen, ed. Undated. Sourcebook of criminal justice statistics. http://www.albany.edu/sourcebook/pdf/t6282009.pdf (retrieved December 16, 2010).

Maher, Lisa. 1997. *Sexed work: Gender, race, and resistance in a Brooklyn drug market.* New York: Oxford University Press.

Malamuth, Neil. 1981. Rape proclivity among males. *Journal of Social Issues* 37: 138–57.

Mancini, Matthew. 1996. *One dies, get another: Convict leasing in the American South, 1866–1928.* Columbia: University of South Carolina Press.

Mann, Coramae Richey. 1998. Getting even? Women who kill in domestic encounters. *Justice Quarterly* 5: 33–51.

Mann, Coramae Richey, and Marjorie S. Zatz. 1998. *Images of color, images of crime.* Los Angeles: Roxbury.

Manza, Jeff, and Christopher Uggen. 2006. *Locked out: Felon disenfranchisement and American democracy.* New York: Oxford University Press.

Martin, Patricia Yancey. 2005. *Rape work: Victims, gender, and emotions in organization and community context.* New York: Routledge.

———. 2003. "Said and done" vs. "saying and doing": Gendering practices, practicing gender at work. *Gender & Society* 7: 342–66.

Martin, Patricia Yancey, and Robert A. Hummer. 1989. Fraternities and rape on campus. *Gender & Society* 3: 457–73.

Martin, Susan Ehrlich, and Nancy C. Jurik. 2006. *Doing justice, doing gender: Women in legal and criminal justice occupations.* Thousand Oaks, CA: Sage.

Massey, James, Susan L. Miller, and Anna Wilhemi. 1998. Civil forfeiture of property: The victimization of women as innocent owners and third parties. In *Crime Control and Women: Feminist Implications of Criminal Justice Policy*, 15–31. Thousand Oaks, CA: Sage.

Maston, Cathy. 2010. Criminal victimization in the United States, 2007: Statistical tables. http://bjs.ojp.usdoj.gov/content/pub/pdf/cvus07.pdf (retrieved April 16, 1010).

Mastrofski, Stephen D., Michael D. Reisig, and John D. McCluskey. 2002. *Police disrespect toward the public: An encounter-based analysis. Criminology* 40: 519–52.

McCall, Nathan. 1994. *Makes me wanna holler: A young black man in America.* New York: Vintage.

Merton, Robert K. 1938. Social structure and anomie. *American Sociological Review* 3: 672–82.

Messerschmidt, James W. 1993. *Masculinities and crime: A critique and reconceptualization of theory.* Boston: Rowman & Littlefield.

———. 1995. Managing to kill: Masculinities and the space shuttle *Challenger* explosion. *Masculinities* 3(4): 1–22.

———. 2000. *Nine lives: Adolescent masculinities, the body and violence.* Boulder, CO: Westview.

———. 2002. On gang girls, gender, and structured action theory: A reply to Miller. *Theoretical Criminology* 6: 461–75.

Michael, Robert T., John. H. Gagnon, Edward O. Laumann, and Gina Kolata. 1994. *Sex in America: A definitive survey.* New York: Warner Books.

Milgram, Stanley. 1963. Behavioral study of obedience. *Journal of Abnormal Social Psychology* 67: 371–78.

Miller, Jerome G. 1996. *Search and destroy: African American males in the criminal justice system.* New York: Cambridge University Press.

Miller, Jody. 1998. Up it up: Gender and the accomplishment of street robbery. *Criminology* 36: 37–66.

———. 2002a. Reply to Messerschmidt. *Theoretical Criminology* 6: 477–80.

———. 2002b. The strengths and limits of "doing gender" for understanding street crime. *Theoretical Criminology* 6: 433–60.

———. 2008. *Getting played: African American girls, urban inequality, and gendered violence.* New York: New York University Press.

Miller, Jody, and Norman A. White. 2004. Situational effects of gender inequality on girls' participation in violence. In *Girls' violence? Myths and realities*, ed. Christine Alder and Anne Worrall, 167–90. Albany: SUNY Press.

Miller, Susan L. 1999. *Gender and community policing: Walking the talk.* Boston: Northeastern University Press.

———. 2005. *Victims as offenders: The paradox of women's violence in relationships.* New Brunswick, NJ: Rutgers University Press.

Miller, Susan L., Kay B. Forest, and Nancy C. Jurik. 2003. Diversity in blue: Lesbian and gay police officers in a masculine occupation. *Men and Masculinities* 5: 355–85.

Miller, Walter. 1958. *Delinquent behavior.* Washington: Juvenile Delinquency Project.

Milliken, Robert. 1993. Judge's rape tales infuriate Australian women. *Independent*, January 14. http://www.independent.co.uk/news/world/judges-rape-tales-infuriate-australian-women-1478386.html (retrieved June 18, 2010).

Minton, Todd D., and William J. Sabol. 2009. Jail inmates at midyear 2008—Statistical tables. U.S. Department of Justice. http://bjs.ojp.usdoj.gov/content/pub/pdf/jim08st.pdf (retrieved on June 18, 2010).

Mokhiber, Russell. 2005. Crime without conviction: The rise of deferred and non-prosecution agreements. *Corporate Crime Reporter*, December 28. http://www.corporatecrimereporter.com/deferredreport.htm (retrieved October 4, 2006).

Moore, Lisa D., and Irene Padavic. 2010. Racial and ethnic disparities in girls' sentencing in the juvenile justice system. *Feminist Criminology* 5: 263–85.

Morris, Allison, and Ania Wilczynski. 1995. Rocking the cradle: Mothers who kill their children. In *Moving targets: Women, murder and representation*, ed. Helen Birch, 198–217. Berkeley: University of California Press.

Morton, Danielle C., and Tracy L. Snell. 1994. Women in prison. Bureau of Justice Statistics. http://bjs.ojp.usdoj.gov/index.cfm?ty=pbdetail&iid=569 (retrieved April 11, 2002).

Mufson, Steven. 2007. BP settles propane price-fixing suit. *Washington Post*, October 24. http://www.washingtonpost.com/wp-dyn/content/article/2007/10/23/AR2007102302255.html (retrieved August 5, 2010).

Mustard, David B. 2001. Racial, ethnic, and gender disparities in sentencing: Evidence from the U.S. federal courts. *Journal of Law and Economics* 44: 285–314.

Musto, David F. 1991. Opium, cocaine and marijuana in American history. *Scientific American*, July, 40–47.

Nagel, Ilene, and Barry Johnson. 1994. The role of gender in a structured sentencing system: Equal treatment, policy choices, and the sentencing of female offenders under the United States sentencing guidelines. *Journal of Criminal Law and Criminology* 85: 181–221.

National Center for Women and Policing. 2002a. Equality denied: The status of women in policing: 2001. http://www.womenandpolicing.org/PDF/2002_Status_Report.pdf (retrieved June 10, 2010).

——. 2002b. Men, women, and police excessive force: A tale of two genders: A content analysis of civil liability cases, sustained allegations & citizen complaints. http://www.womenandpolicing.org/PDF/2002_Excessive_Force.pdf.

——. 2003. Hiring and retaining more women: The advantages to law enforcement agencies. http://www.womenandpolicing.org/pdf/NewAdvantagesReport.pdf (retrieved June 10, 2010).

National Drug Intelligence Center, United States Department of Justice. 2010. National drug threat assessment 2010. http://www.justice.gov/ndic/pubs38/38661/index.htm (retrieved June 18, 2010).

Nazroo, James. 1995. Uncovering gender differences in the use of marital violence: The effect of methodology. *Sociology* 29: 475–94.

Neidig, Peter H., Harold E. Russell, and Albert F. Seng. 1992. Interspousal aggression in law enforcement families: A preliminary investigation. *Police Studies* 15: 30–38.

Oshinsky, David M. 1997. *Worse than slavery: Parchman farm and the ordeal of Jim Crow justice*. New York: Free Press Paperbacks.

Osland, Julie A., Marguerite Fitch, and Edmond E. Willis. 1996. Likelihood to rape in college males. *Sex Roles* 35: 171–83.

Owen, Barbara. 1988. *The reproduction of social control: A study of prison workers at San Quentin.* New York: Praeger.

Pascoe, C. J. 2007. *Dude, you're a fag: Masculinity and sexuality in high school.* Berkeley: University of California Press.

Pierce, Jennifer. 1995. *Gender trials: Emotional lives in contemporary law firms.* Berkeley: University of California Press.

Pisciotta, Alexander W. 1994. *Benevolent repression: Social control and the American reformatory-prison movement.* New York: New York University Press.

Ptacek, James. 1990. Why do men batter their wives? In *Feminist perspectives on wife abuse,* ed. Kersti Yllo and Michele Bograd. 133–57. Newbury Park: Sage.

Rabe-Hemp, Cara. 2009. POLICEwomen or policeWOMEN? Doing gender and police work. *Feminist Criminology* 4: 114–29.

Rafter, Nicole Hahn. 1990. *Partial justice: Women, prisons, and social control.* 2nd ed. New Brunswick: Transaction.

Rand, Michael. 1997. Violence-related injuries treated in hospital emergency departments. Bureau of Justice Statistics. http://bjs.ojp.usdoj.gov/content/pub/pdf/VRITHED.PDF (retrieved October 1, 2002).

Rapaport, Elizabeth. 1991. The death penalty and gender discrimination. *Law & Society Review* 25: 369–74.

Reed, Elizabeth, Anita Raj, Elizabeth Miller, and Jay G. Silverman. 2010. Losing the "gender" in gender-based violence: The missteps of research on dating and intimate partner violence. *Violence against Women* 16: 348–54.

Reid, Paul. 2001. Documentary explores UF rape allegation. *Rakontur,* February 12. http://www.rakontur.com/journal/2001/2/12/raw-deal-review-the-palm-beach -post.html (accessed February 5, 2005).

Reiman, Jeffrey H. 2006. *The rich get richer and the poor get prison: Ideology, class, and criminal justice.* 8th ed. Boston: Allyn & Bacon.

Reiman, Jeffrey, and Paul Leighton. 2009. *The rich get richer and the poor get prison: Ideology, class, and criminal justice.* New York: Prentice Hall.

Reskin, Barbara, and Debra McBrier. 2000. Why not ascription? Organizations' employment of male and female managers. *American Sociological Review* 65: 210–33.

Rodriguez, Fernando S., Theodore R. Curry, and Gang Lee. 2006. Gender differences in criminal sentencing: Do effects vary across violent, property, and drug offenses? *Social Science Quarterly* 87: 318–39.

Roiphe, Katie. 1993. Date rape's other victim. *New York Times Magazine,* June 13. http://www.nytimes.com/1993/06/13/magazine/date-rape-s-other-victim.html (accessed November 11, 2005).

Romans, Sarah, Tonia Forte, Marsha M. Cohen, Janice Du Mont, and Ilene Hyman. 2007. Who is most at risk for intimate partner violence? A Canadian population-based study. *Journal of Interpersonal Violence* 22: 1495–1514.

Rosenfeld, Richard. 1997. Changing relationships between men and women: A note on the decline in intimate partner homicide. *Homicide Studies* 1: 72–83.

Rosenhan, David L. 1973. On being sane in insane places. *Science* 179: 250–58.

Russell, Diana E. H. 1982. *Rape in marriage.* New York: Macmillan.

———. 1984. *Sexual exploitation: Rape, child sexual abuse, and workplace harassment.* Beverly Hills, CA: Sage.

Russell-Brown, Katheryn. 1998. *The color of crime: Racial hoaxes, white fear, black protectionism, police harassment, and other macroaggressionisms.* New York: New York University Press.

Sabol, William J., Heather C. West, and Matthew Cooper. 2009. Prisoners in 2008. Bureau of Justice Statistics, U.S. Department of Justice. http://bjs.ojp.usdoj.gov/content/pub/pdf/p08.pdf.

Sachdev, Ameet. 2009. Judge dismisses charges of price fixing against former BP propane traders. *Chicago Tribune,* September 9. http://newsblogs.chicagotribune.com/chicago-law/2009/09/bp-propane-traders-.html (retrieved August 5, 2010).

Sanday, Peggy Reeves. 1981. The socio-cultural context of rape: A cross-cultural study. *Journal of Social Issues* 37: 5–27.

———. 1990. *Fraternity gang rape: Sex, brotherhood, and privilege on campus.* New York: New York University Press.

Scelfo, Julie. June 13, 2005. Bad girls go wild. *Newsweek,* June 13. http://www.newsweek.com/2005/06/12/bad-girls-go-wild.html (retrieved September 23, 2005).

Schemo, Diana Jean. 2003. Rate of rape at academy is put at 12% in survey. *New York Times,* August 29. http://www.nytimes.com/2003/08/29/national/29ACAD.html (retrieved June 18, 2010).

Schilt, Kristen. 2006. Just one of the guys? How transmen make gender visible at work. *Gender & Society* 20: 465–90.

———. 2010. *Just one of the guys? Transgender men and the persistence of gender inequality.* Chicago: University of Chicago Press.

Schneider, Lawrence J., Lisa T. Mori, Paul L. Lambert, and Anna O. Wong. 2009. The role of gender and ethnicity in perceptions of rape and its aftereffects. *Sex Roles* 60: 410–21.

Schrock, Douglas, and Irene Padavic. 2007. Negotiating hegemonic masculinity in a batterer intervention program. *Gender & Society* 21: 625–49.

Schulz, Dorothy Moses. 1995. *From social worker to crimefighter: Women in the United States municipal policing.* Westport, CT: Praeger.

Schwartz, Jennifer, and Bryan D. Rookey. 2008. The narrowing gender gap in arrests: Assessing competing explanations using self-report, traffic fatality, and official data on drunken driving. *Criminology* 46: 637–71.

Schwendinger, Herman, and Julia Schwendinger. 1975. Defenders of order or guardians of human rights? In *Critical Criminology,* ed. Ian Taylor, Paul Walton, and Jock Young, 113–46. London: Routledge & Kegan Paul.

Scully, Diana. 1994. *Understanding sexual violence: A study of convicted rapists.* New York: Routledge.

Scully, Diana, and Joseph Marolla. 1985. "Riding the bull at Gilley's": Convicted rapists describe the rewards of rape. *Social Problems* 32: 251–63.

Senjo, Scott R. 2005. Trafficking in meth: An analysis of the differences between male and female dealers. *Journal of Drug Education* 35: 59–77.

———. 2007. The insidious allure of methamphetamine: Female patterns of purchasing, use, consequences of use and treatment. In *New research on methamphetamine abuse,* ed. Gerald H. Toolaney, 53–68. New York: Nova Science Publishers.

Sentencing Project. 2010. Felony disenfranchisement laws in the United States. March. http://www.sentencingproject.org/doc/publications/fd_bs_fdlawsinus March2010.pdf (retrieved June 18, 2010).

Setoodeh, Ramin. 2008. Young, gay and murdered. *Newsweek*, July 19. http://www .newsweek.com/2008/07/18/young-gay-and-murdered.html (accessed June 18, 2010).

Shaw, Katerina. 2009. Note: Barriers to freedom: Continued failure of U.S. immigration laws to offer equal protection to immigrant battered women. *Cardozo Journal of Law & Gender* 15: 663–89.

Sheppard, Deborah L. 1989. Organizations, power and sexuality: The image and self-image of women managers." In *The sexuality of organization*, ed. Jeff Hearn, Deborah Sheppard, Peta Tancred Sheriff, and Gibson Burrell, 139–57. London: Sage Publications.

Sherven, Judith, and James Sniechowski. 1994. Perspectives on domestic violence. *Los Angeles Times*, June 21. http://articles.latimes.com/1994-06-21/local/me -6497_1_domestic-violence (accessed August 16, 2006).

Siemsen, Cynthia. 2004. *Emotional trials: The moral dilemmas of women criminal defense attorneys*. Boston: Northeastern University Press.

Simon, David R. 2002. *Elite deviance*. 7th ed. Boston: Allyn & Bacon.

Simon, Rita J. 1975. *Women and crime*. Lexington, MA: Lexington Books.

Simpson, Sally S. 1989. Feminist theory, crime, and justice. *Criminology* 27: 605–31.

Simpson, Sally S., and Lori Ellis. 1995. Doing gender: Sorting out the caste and crime conundrum. *Criminology* 33: 47–81.

Skuratowicz, Eva. 1996. Damping down the fires: Male dominance and the second stage of women's integration into the fire service. Paper presented at the annual meetings, American Sociological Association, New York.

Smith, Brad W., and Malcolm D. Holmes. 2003. Community accountability, minority threat, and police brutality: An examination of civil rights criminal complaints. *Criminology* 41: 1035–64.

Snell, Tracy. 2006. Capital punishment, 2005. Bureau of Justice Statistics. http://bjs .ojp.usdoj.gov/content/pub/pdf/cp05.pdf.

Sommers, Christina Hoff. 1995. *Who stole feminism? How women have betrayed women*. New York: Touchstone/Simon & Schuster.

Sommers, Ira, and Deborah Baskin. 1992. Sex, race, age and violent offending. *Violence and Victims* 7: 191–201.

Spelman, Elizabeth V., and Martha Minow. 1992. Outlaw women: An essay on *Thelma & Louise. New England Law Review* 26: 1281.

Spohn, Cassia, and David Holleran. 2000. The imprisonment penalty paid by young, unemployed black and Hispanic male offenders. *Criminology* 38(1): 281–306.

Stark, Evan. 2007. *Coercive control: The entrapment of women in personal life*. Oxford; New York: Oxford University Press.

Steffensmeier, Darrell, and Emilie Allan. 1996. Gender and crime: Toward a gendered theory of female offending. *Annual Review of Sociology* 22: 459–88.

Steffensmeier, Darrell, John H. Kramer, and Cathy Streifel. 1993. Gender and imprisonment decisions. *Criminology* 31: 441–46.

Steffensmeier, Darrell, Jennifer Schwartz, Hua Zhong, and Jeff Ackerman. 2005. An assessment of recent trends in girls' violence using diverse longitudinal sources. Is the gender gap closing? *Criminology* 43: 355–405.

Steffensmeier, Darrell, Jeffery Ulmer, and John Kramer. 1998. The interaction of race, gender, and age in criminal sentencing: The punishment cost of being young, black, and male. *Criminology* 36: 763–97.

Steffensmeier, Darrell, Hua Zhong, Jeff Ackerman, Jennifer Schwartz, and Suzanne Agha. 2006. Gender gap trends for violent crimes, 1980–2003. *Feminist Criminology* 1: 72–98.

Steinmetz, Suzanne. 1978. Battered husband syndrome. *Victimology* 2: 499–509.

Stolzenberg, Lisa, and Stewart J. D'Alessio. 2004. Sex differences in the likelihood of arrest. *Journal of Criminal Justice* 32: 442–54.

Stombler, Mindy. 1994. "Buddies" or "slutties": The collective sexual reputation of fraternity little sisters. *Gender & Society* 8: 297–323.

Straus, Murray A. 1979. Measuring intrafamily conflict and violence: The conflict tactics scales. *Journal of Marriage and the Family* 41: 75–88.

———. 2007. Dominance and symmetry in partner violence by male and female university students in 32 nations. *Children and Youth Services Review* 30: 252–75.

Substance Abuse and Mental Health Services Administration. 2005. Methamphetamine use, abuse, and dependence: 2002, 2003, 2004. Department of Health and Human Services. http://www.oas.samhsa.gov/2k5/meth/meth.htm (retrieved March 1, 2006).

———. 2009. Results from the 2008 National Survey on Drug Use and Health: National findings (detailed tables). Department of Health and Human Services. http://www.oas.samhsa.gov/NSDUH/2K8NSDUH/tabs/toc.htm (retrieved June 18, 2010).

Sutherland, Edwin H. 1947. *Principles of criminology.* 4th ed. Chicago: J. B. Lippincott.

Swatt, Marc L., and Ni "Phil" He. 2006. Exploring the difference between male and female intimate partner homicides: Revisiting the concept of situated transactions. *Homicide Studies* 10: 279–92.

Taslitz, Andrew. 1999. *Rape and the culture of the courtroom.* New York: New York University Press.

Teichroeb, Ruth, and Julie Davidow. 2003. Cops who abuse their wives rarely pay the price. *Seattle Post-Intelligencer,* July 23. http://www.seattlepi.com/local/131879_cops23.html (accessed June 10, 2010).

Terrill, William, and Michael D. Reisig. 2003. Neighborhood context and police force. *Journal of Research in Crime & Delinquency* 40: 291–321.

Texeira, Mary Thierry. 2002. "Who protects and serves me?" A case study of sexual harassment of African American women in one U.S. law enforcement agency. *Gender & Society* 16: 524–45.

Thomas, Pierre, Lisa A. Jones, Jack Cloherty, and Jason Ryan. 2010. BP's dismal safety record. *ABC News,* May 27. http://abcnews.go.com/WN/bps-dismal-safety-record/story?id=10763042 (retrieved August 6, 2010).

Tjaden, Patricia, and Nancy Thoennes. 2000. Full report of the prevalence, incidence, and consequences of intimate partner violence against women: Findings from the national violence against women survey. National Institute of Justice and the Centers for Disease Control and Prevention. http://www.ncjrs.gov/pdffiles1/nij/183781.pdf.

Tjaden, Patricia, and Nancy Thoennes. 2006. Extent, nature, and consequences of rape victimization: Findings from the national violence against women survey. National Institute of Justice. http://www.ncjrs.gov/pdffiles1/nij/210346.pdf.

Truman, Jennifer, and Michael Rand. 2010. Criminal victimization, 2009. http://bjs.ojp.usdoj.gov/content/pub/pdf/cv09.pdf (retrieved December 16, 2010).

United States Census Bureau. 2009. *Statistical abstract of the United States: 2010.* 129th ed. Washington, DC. http://www.census.gov/compendia/statab (retrieved January 28, 2010).

United States Census Bureau. 2010a. Income, poverty and health insurance coverage in the United States: 2009. http://www.census.gov/prod/2010pubs/p60-238.pdf (retrieved December 16, 2010).

———. 2010b. Net worth and asset ownership of households: 2004. http://www.census.gov/hhes/www/wealth/wealth.html (retrieved August 6, 2010).

United States Department of Defense, Sexual Assault Prevention and Response. 2010. Annual report on sexual harassment and violence at the military service academies. http://www.sapr.mil/media/pdf/reports/FINAL_APY_09-10_MSA_Report.pdf (retrieved December 16, 2010).

United States Sentencing Commission. 2002. Annual report. http://www.ussc.gov/ANNRPT/2002/ar02toc.htm (accessed February 3, 2005).

United States Sentencing Commission. 2004. Fifteen years of guidelines sentencing: An assessment of how well the federal criminal justice system is achieving the goals of sentencing reform. http://www.ussc.gov/15_year/15year.htm (accessed June 18, 2010).

United States Sentencing Commission. 2009. United States Sentencing Commission guidelines manual. http://www.ussc.gov/2009guid/GL2009.pdf (retrieved June 18, 2010).

United States Sentencing Commission. 2010. Sourcebook of federal sentencing statistics: 2009. http://www.ussc.gov/ANNRPT/2009/SBTOC09.htm (retrieved June 18, 2010).

Urbina, Ian. 2010. Workers on doomed rig voiced safety concerns. *New York Times,* July 21. http://www.nytimes.com/2010/07/22/us/22transocean.html (retrieved August 5, 2010).

Van Voorhis, Patricia, Francis T. Cullen, Bruce G. Link, and Nancy Travis Wolfe. 1991. The impact of race and gender on correctional officers' orientation to the integrated environment. *Journal of Research in Crime and Delinquency* 28: 472–500.

Visher, Christy A. 1983. Gender, police arrest decisions, and notions of chivalry. *Criminology* 21: 5–28.

Waldman, Steven, and Dan Gilgoff. 2008. Republican presidential candidate Mike Huckabee on God's presence, the debates, and Christianity. Beliefnet, January. http://www.beliefnet.com/News/Politics/2008/01/Mike-Huckabee-The-Lord-Truly-Gave-Me-Wisdom.aspx (retrieved July 21, 2008).

Walker, Donald R. 1988. *Penology for profit: A history of the Texas prison system, 1867–1912.* College Station, TX: Texas A&M University Press.

Warner, Tara D. 2010. Violent acts and injurious consequences: An examination of competing hypotheses about intimate partner violence using agency-based data. *Family Violence* 25: 183–93.

Warshaw, Robin. 1994. *I never called it rape: The Ms. report on recognizing, fighting and surviving date and acquaintance rape.* New York: Harper Collins.

Weiss, Karen G. 2010. Too ashamed to report: Deconstructing the shame of sexual victimization. *Feminist Criminology* 5: 286–310.

Weitzer, Ronald. 1999. Citizens' perceptions of police misconduct: Race and neighborhood context. *Justice Quarterly* 16: 819–46.

West, Candace, and Sarah Fenstermaker. 1995. Doing difference. *Gender & Society* 9: 8–37.

West, Candace, and Don H. Zimmerman. 1987. Doing gender. *Gender & Society* 1: 125–51.

Whitaker, Daniel J., Tadesse Haileyesus, Monica Swahn, and Linda S. Saltzman. 2007. Differences in frequency of violence and reported injury between relationships with reciprocal and nonreciprocal intimate partner violence. *American Journal of Public Health* 97: 941–47.

Whitehead, John T., and Charles A. Lindquist. 1989. Determinants of correctional officers' professional orientation. *Justice Quarterly* 6: 69–87.

Williams, Christine L. 1989. *Gender difference at work: Women and men in nontraditional occupations.* Berkeley: University of California Press.

———. 1992. The glass escalator: Hidden advantages for men in the "female" professions. *Social Problems* 39: 253–67.

———. 1995. *Still a man's world: Men who do "women's work."* Berkeley: University of California Press.

Willwerth, James, and Alex Prudhomme. 1991. Los Angeles: Will Gates give up the fight at last? *Time,* July 22. http://www.time.com/time/magazine/article/0,9171,973444,00.html (accessed June 10, 2010).

Wilson, Kathleen. 2008. Slain student's family files claim against district, county. *Ventura County Star,* August 15. http://www.vcstar.com/news/2008/aug/15/county-schools-face-king-claims (retrieved August 6, 2010).

Wolfgang, Marvin. 1958. *Patterns in criminal homicide.* Philadelphia: University of Pennsylvania Press.

Wooldredge, John D. 1998. Analytical rigor in studies of disparities in criminal case processing. *Journal of Quantitative Criminology* 14: 155–79.

Worden, Robert E., and Robin L. Shepard. 1996. Demeanor, crime and police behavior: A reexamination of police services study data. *Criminology* 34: 83–105.

Wright, Richard T., and Scott H. Decker. 1997. *Armed robbers in action: Stickups and street culture.* Boston: Northeastern University Press.

Yeoman, Barry. 1999. Bad girls. *Psychology Today,* November 1. http://www.psychologytoday.com/articles/199911/bad-girls (retrieved November 10, 2000).

Yeung, King-To, Mindy Stombler, and Renee Wharton. 2006. Making men in gay fraternities: Resisting and reproducing multiple dimensions of hegemonic masculinity. *Gender & Society* 20: 5–31.

Yoder, Janice D., and Patricia Aniakudo. 1997. "Outsider within" the firehouse: Subordination and difference in the social interactions of African American women firefighters. *Gender & Society* 11: 324–41.

Zatz, Majorie S. 2000. *The convergence of race, ethnicity, gender, and class on court decision making: Looking toward the 21st century.* National Institute of Justice. http://www.ncjrs.gov/criminal_justice2000/vol_3/03j.pdf (retrieved September 16, 2002).

Zetter, Kim. 2010. U.S. soldier on 2007 Apache attack: What I saw. *Wired*, April 20. http://www.wired.com/dangerroom/2010/04/2007-iraq-apache-attack-as-seen -from-the-ground (retrieved June 18, 2010).

Index

Frontiero v. Richardson (411 U.S. 677, 1973), 149n7

gangs, 23, 29–30, 36, 100, 142
Gelles, Richard J., 97–98, 155n17
gender as performance/doing gender, 14, 20–21, 23, 37, 41–42, 46–47, 50, 91, 121, 138–139, 143
gender, definitions of, as structure, 12
gendered organizations, 21, 75, 116–122, 140

hate crimes, 4, 13, 15, 39–40, 148, 150n8, 150n10
heroin, 6–7, 48, 58
heterosexuality: bullying and, 39, 42, 105, 148; criminal offending and, 3, 22, 37–40, 43, 46, 48, 50, 55, 87, 89, 104, 148; definitions of, 16; femininity and, 21, 37, 43, 79, 82, 100, 105, 148; instability of, 17, 37–39; legal regulation of, 17, 55; masculinity and, 3, 18, 37–42, 50, 91, 96, 103–105, 118. 133, 146, 148; victimization and, 82, 89, 91, 93, 96–100, 102, 145; work/occupations and, 118, 133, 146. *See also* sexual orientation
heterosexuality as performance/doing heterosexuality, 37–39, 43, 87, 104, 133, 148
homicide, 1–3, 7–8, 10, 13, 15, 24, 26–28, 30–33, 41, 44, 60, 66, 68–69, 85, 87–89, 91, 101–102, 105, 123, 131, 141–142, 145, 147–148, 150n9, 150n1, 152n12, 154n9–10; intimate, 44, 68–69, 88–89, 91; victim precipitated, 85, 88–89, 101–102. *See also* corporate crime; hate crimes

incest, 17, 54
intersectionality, 15–22, 45, 64, 66, 75, 79, 107, 116, 121, 123, 144–145, 148, 152–153n14
intimate partner violence. *See* domestic violence

jails, 56, 81, 130, 153n15, 157n12
job segregation by sex, 115–116, 118, 120–122, 127, 131, 137–138, 140, 143, 156n6, 157n9
Johnson, Michael, 98–99
Jones, Nikki, 29, 66
juvenile delinquency/offending, 1–2, 27, 35–36, 38–39, 54, 66, 106, 107, 130, 143, 145, 147–148, 152–153n14; gender socialization and, 37, 118; social control of, 67, 130
juveniles, victimization of, 84–87, 107, 145, 148

Kimmel, Michael, 2, 106
Korematsu v. United States (323 U.S. 214, 1944), 54
Koss, Mary P., 94–95

labor force participation rates: by marital status, 110–113; by parental status, 111–112; by race, 110–113; by sex, 110–113
larceny-theft, 10–11, 24–32
law: class distinctions and discrimination in, 7–10, 54, 56, 143; gender distinctions and discrimination in, 3, 12, 59–61, 143, 149n7, 151n4; racial/ethnic distinctions and discrimination in, 5, 7, 10–12, 18–19, 53–54, 56–59, 143, 151n3–4; sexual orientation distinctions and discrimination in, 5, 12, 16–18, 55, 49, 143, 150n8, 150n11, 151n4
Lawrence v. Texas (599 U.S. 558, 2003), 55, 151n3
lawyers. *See* attorneys
Lombroso, Cesare, 30, 35, 43, 50

Maher, Lisa, 44, 47, 50, 61
mandatory minimum sentences, 6, 56–59, 61–62, 70–71, 151–152n5, 152n6–8, 152n11, 153n16
manslaughter, 7, 41, 101
marijuana, 6–7, 71